DAUGHTER
OF HEAVEN

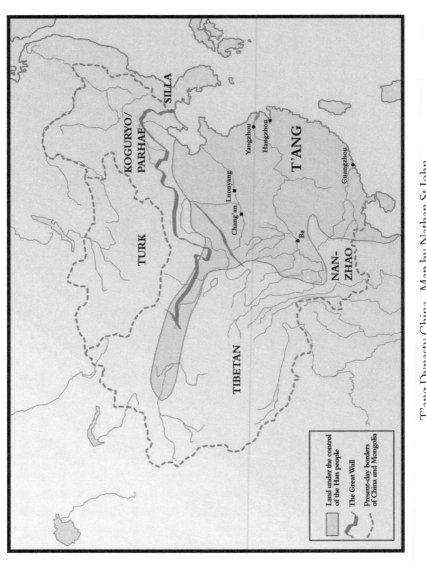

T'ang Dynasty China. Map by Nathan St John.

DAUGHTER
OF HEAVEN

THE TRUE STORY OF THE ONLY WOMAN
TO BECOME EMPEROR OF CHINA

NIGEL CAWTHORNE

ONEWORLD
OXFORD

A Oneworld Book

Published by Oneworld Publications 2007
Copyright © Nigel Cawthorne 2007

ISBN-13:978–1–85168–530–1

Typeset by Jayvee, Trivandrum, India
Cover design by D. R. Ink
Printed and bound by The Maple-Vail Book
Manufacturing Group, Braintree, MA, USA

Oneworld Publications
185 Banbury Road
Oxford OX2 7AR
England
www.oneworld-publications.com

CONTENTS

ACKNOWLEDGEMENTS

I should like to thank Wallace Kwong for all his hard work fact checking and correcting my manuscript. I am greatly indebted to him.

CHAPTER ONE
THE CALL OF HEAVEN

IT WAS THE YEAR 3275 when they came to take her to the imperial harem. She would not have known that she was living in the thirty-third century as computed by learned scholars, any more than she would have known that it was the seventh century – AD 638 to be exact – by the Christian calendar, or that it was the thirty-fifth year of the fifty-fifth cycle as dated from the invention of the calendar by China's legendary Yellow Emperor in the sixty-first year of his reign. For the adolescent Wu Chao, it was simply the year of the dog and the twelfth year of the reign of Chen Kuan as the Chinese calendar begins again at year one with each new Emperor. For the whole of his reign, the Emperor T'ai-tsung used the reign name Chen Kuan, also known as the 'era of good government'.

But she did know that it was a great honour to be picked as an imperial consort, even though she was just thirteen – or fourteen under the Chinese system where children are reckoned to be one when they are born. In China, age was computed from the putative time of conception, which the medieval Chinese believed was ten months before the birth. For the sake of simplicity, this was then rounded up to a year. Wu Chao's selection as a concubine reflected great honour on the whole family, even though it came before the age of 'pinning'. At fifteen, a girl had her hair pinned up on top of her head to show she had become a woman. Wu Chao had been selected as an imperial concubine because she came from an esteemed family. One of her cousins was already one of the Emperor's favourites and had recommended her, and her youthful beauty was so breathtaking that it was talked of hundreds of miles away in China's then capital Ch'ang-an. Now the *nü-shih*, the lady of the court who organized the Emperor's sexual life, came to see the aspirant Wu Chao for herself.

Although being picked as a concubine was a unique experience for Wu Chao, thousands of young women were taken into service in the imperial palace. There is no record of Wu Chao's induction, but in *Secret Sketches of the Han Palace* an anonymous author described a visit that the *nü-shih* Madame Wu and the eunuch Ch'ao made some time earlier to examine the girl Nu Ying, who, like Wu Chao, was the daughter of a general:

> With Ch'ao in the outer room, Madame Wu took Nu Ying into the bedroom. The maids were sent away and the door was locked. Nu Ying's face was lit by the sun. She looked radiant, like snow in the morning sunlight. Her eyes were as clear as a tranquil sea. Her eyebrows were long and shapely. Her white teeth stood out against her tiny red mouth. Madame Wu pulled out Nu Ying's hairpin and her hair cascaded like black satin to the floor.
>
> After feeling the hair, Madame Wu told Nu Ying to take off her underwear. Blushing, the young girl refused. The older woman told her that it was an imperial order and she must obey. Nu Ying began to cry and turned her face to the wall. Then Madame Wu gently undressed her. She carried her naked body into the sunlight. It was smooth. Her skin was creamy and the fragrance of her body filled the air. Her breasts were firm and large enough to fill a cupped hand and her navel was deep enough to carry a pearl half-an-inch in diameter.
>
> Madame Wu was delighted with Nu Ying's slightly raised pubic mound. Then, gently, she parted the young girl's thighs to find her jade gate scarlet like a glowing fire. 'She is a pure and chaste virgin,' cried the older woman.

Virginity was particularly prized in China, but not for the usual reasons of masculine pride as in the West, but for vitality and health. The great master P'êng-Tsu, also known as Peng the Methuselah, explained: 'If a man wants to obtain the greatest benefit from sex, he should find inexperienced women. Making love to virgins will restore his youthful looks.'

'What a pity there are not more virgins about,' he lamented.

In T'ang China, measures were taken to guarantee that a girl was a virgin. Lizards were fed with ten pounds of cinnabar, or mercuric sulphide, then killed and pulverized. The resulting dye was painted on the girl's legs. If it was rubbed off or disturbed, this would show that she had had intercourse.

'The ideal virgin is between fourteen and nineteen,' said P'êng-Tsu, 'though any woman under thirty will do, provided she has not had a child. My late master followed the principles strictly and he lived to the age of three thousand. One can become immortal if one takes herbs at the same time.'

According to P'êng-Tsu, the legendary Yellow Emperor, Huang-ti, had sexual intercourse with twelve hundred women and became immortal. The principal method of attaining longevity, P'êng-Tsu said, was 'to have frequent intercourse with young girls, but emit semen only on rare occasions; this method makes a man's body light and will expel all diseases'. This way the man drank in the female yin energy from the woman, but rarely expended any of his own male yang energy, thereby increasing his *ch'i*, or 'life force'.

The Emperor T'ai-tsung, into whose service Wu Chao was being taken, was much in need of youthful vitality. He was already thirty-eight, a considerable age in medieval China, and he was in low spirits and broken-hearted. He had buried his beloved Empress Went-te just over year before and the imperial records show that he mourned her for a long time. To restore his spirits, he needed all the fresh yin essence that he could get and his *nü-shih* were busy scouring the country for new young virginal consorts for him.

Although no image of Wu Chao at that age exists, we know what Chinese men of that era looked for in a lover. Under the heading 'Women Suited for Coitus', the book *Secret Prescriptions for the Bedchamber* says, 'A man should pick young women whose breasts have not yet developed and who are well covered with flesh. They should have hair fine as silk and small eyes, where separation of the pupil and the white is well defined. Her face and body should be smooth and her speech harmonious. All her joints should be well covered with flesh and her bones should not be large. Either she should have no pubic hair or other bodily hair, or it should be fine and smooth.'

When the renowned beauty Wu Chao was inducted into the Emperor's harem at the age of thirteen, we can presume that she conformed to this description.

In the ancient handbook of physiognomy *T'ai-ch'ing-ching*, the Yellow Emperor's sexual advisor Su-nü – known throughout Chinese literature as 'The Plain Girl' – also mentions that the girl's labia should be thick and enlarged and that her vagina should be rich in fluid. However, she also says that 'a suitable woman is naturally tender and docile and of gentle mien'. This was certainly not a description of Wu Chao. She was a well-known tomboy who wore boys' clothes as a child. Not for her the elaborated dresses fashionable in the early T'ang period. These looked like the kimonos later adopted by the Japanese, who added the large bow at the back. The dresses of T'ang China also had an apron on the front and a silk band under the breasts, like traditional Korean wear. Instead of these inhibiting garments, Wu Chao wore men's trousers under a long robe, which was single-layered in summer, quilted in winter. Boys' clothes were brighter than girls', since boys sought to attract attention when seen in public, while women were hidden away. Wu Chao's feet would not have been bound. Foot-binding was practised rarely if at all during the T'ang era. While there are some claims that the custom began in the Shang dynasty (1766–1122 BC), the first unequivocal reference to foot-binding appears in the literature during the Sung dynasty in AD 1130, though it only became widely practised among all classes during the Ming (1368–1644) and Ch'ing (1644–1911) dynasties. Then women had their feet painfully bound from girlhood. The ideal was to create tiny, three-inch lotus flowers, or 'golden lilies'.

Wu Chao may have been encouraged in her tomboy ways because her father died when she was ten and there was no restraining male influence in the household. This would have allowed her to go out of the house, a rare thing for women of her class at that time. But she was not a woman easily confined by conventions. She was made of sterner stuff. Years later she told a story of just how tough she had been as a young woman.

'The Emperor T'ai-tsung had a very wild horse no one could break,' she said. 'When I was a palace girl, standing by his side, I said, "I can master him, but I will need three things: a metal whip, an iron mace and a dagger. If the metal whip does not bring him to obedience, I shall use the mace to beat his head, and if that does not work I will use the dagger to cut his throat." T'ai-tsung understood what I meant by this.'

So shall we.

CHAPTER TWO

THE CHILD OF HEAVEN

WU CHAO WAS BORN IN 3262, the eighth year of the reign of the first T'ang Emperor, Kao-tsu – reign name Wu Te, which means 'Martial Virtue' – possibly on the twenty-third day of the first lunar month, Ren-shen, or 10 March 625 on the Gregorian calendar. According to local legend she was born in Kuang-yüan, Li county in Szechwan, where a festival commemorating her birth is held on that day at Li-chou. The late Tang poet Li Shang-yin enshrined the idea in a memorial poem and it was popularized in the 1960s by the dramatist Guo Moruo in his play *Wu Tse-tien* – the name by which Wu Chao is now better known. However, her father was not appointed governor-general of Li-chou until 628. Before that he worked in central government, so it seems she was born in either Ch'ang-an, the western capital, or Luoyang, the eastern capital.

Her given name Chao was well chosen. It means 'shine' or 'illuminate'. The upper half of the character contains the pictogram for the sun. Below it is the four-dot character for 'fire'. So she is associated with the imperial symbol of the sun. Her name would have been selected for her by her father, who would have given it to her at some point after her third month. By then he must already have been assured of her future greatness.

She also had the good fortune to be born in the year of the cock. The Chinese character for the sun is a cock in a circle, so the cock is consequently associated with the Emperor. According to Chinese mythology, the Tree of Life, a peach tree growing on the Happy Islands in the Eastern Ocean which stands three thousand miles tall, is surmounted by a gold cock that heralds the first rays of dawn. The cock stands for vigilance, custodianship and virility – the masculine yang element that brings warmth, strength and life – though, curiously, the year of the cock is itself a yin or feminine year. As the cock's crow brings with it the dawn, the cock is thought to dispel the darkness and evil spirits. This, unfortunately, was not the case with Wu Chao. However, people born in the year of the cock are supposed to be arrogant and domineering, with a natural distrust of others. They are also combative and pursue success at all costs.

Wu Chao's life has been considerably rewritten since the Communist takeover of China in 1949 and Marxist historians have made much of the fact that her father started out as a lowly timber merchant – hence Wu Chao's rise to power could be represented as an antediluvian Marxist revolution, with Wu Chao as the victor in a class struggle. In fact, her father, Wu Shih-huo, came from a wealthy family in northern China, though they may have had peasant origins. His name was Wu Shih-yue – 'yue' is a rare character composed of the two words *xun*, meaning 'seek', and *huo*, meaning 'found' or 'given'. But 'yue' is often mispronounced as 'huo' and he has come down in history as Wu Shih-huo. As the fourth son, he could not enter government service like his brothers, so he went into business selling timber instead. However, he did hold a minor post in the local militia organized by the ruling Sui dynasty and spent a great deal of time studying military matters. He predicted the failure of the Sui Emperor Yang-ti's expedition – the first of three – into Korea in 612 and, at the siege of Luoyang the following year, it was said that Wu Shih-huo's advice prevented the fall of the city.

The beginning of the seventh century was a time of great unrest in China. The first Sui Emperor Wen-ti had come to the throne in 581 and set about uniting China for the first time in four centuries. He raised a corps of pragmatic administrators and set about restoring the Confucian rituals that had last been use in government during the great Han dynasty that lasted from 206 BC to AD 220. But this period of stability was not to last. The second Sui Emperor Yang-ti came to the throne in 604 after assassinating his father and his elder brother. He then began costly programmes of construction and conquest. He rebuilt the eastern capital of Luoyang and the western capital Ch'ang-an – completing his father's work – and started the Grand Canal. This linked older canals into an extensive system 4,777 li – 1,569 miles – long to supply his troops along China's northern border. And he began rebuilding the Great Wall at prohibitive cost. The strain this put on the economy turned the people against him. There were numerous uprisings and Turkish nomads took advantage of Chinese weakness to raid across the border. One of the Sui's greatest generals Li Yüan, the Duke of T'ang, was sent to the north to resist the incursion of the Turks and suppress a peasant revolt there.

His family, the Li, claimed to be ethnically Chinese but, like many northerners, they had intermarried with the nomadic Xianbeis, a Turco-Mongolian tribe from Siberia, during a period called the Five Barbarians and Sixteen Kingdoms when the Chinese had been pushed south by barbarians from the north. In Fen and Chin, in Shansi province, Li Yüan met Wu Chao's father Wu Shih-huo. According to a biography of her father commissioned by Wu Chao in 699, it was Wu Shih-huo who spurred Li Yüan – the future Emperor Kao-tsu, founder of the T'ang dynasty – to rebel against the Sui.

'Bandits and rebels were as numerous as hornets and Shih-huo secretly urged him to raise troops to overthrow the Sui,' it says. Wu Shih-huo also gave Li Yüan a book on military tactics and told him that he had had an auspicious dream and heard voices predicting Li Yüan's success. These would have been seen as important omens at the time. Li Yüan, it was said, also had a birthmark the shape of an dragon under his left armpit, a sure sign that he would be Emperor. Even so, he urged caution.

'Please say no more,' he told Wu Shih-huo. 'Military books are forbidden, yet you give one to me. I understand the meaning only too well. Together we will prosper.'

It was recorded later that, in Wu Shih-huo's portentous dream foretelling the founding of the T'ang dynasty, Wu Shih-huo himself had also ascended to heaven and touched the sun and the moon. This was interpreted, after the event, as foretelling that Wu Shih-huo would himself go on to found a dynasty.

Wu Shih-huo had already earned the suspicions of the Sui because of his military expertise. Even his brothers had encouraged him to rebel, but, until he met Li Yüan, he had no confidence in the rebel leaders of the time. In the Duke of T'ang he recognized a true leader and sealed the alliance by inviting him to his home in T'ai-yüan when Li Yüan was on his way to Long-men to quash the rebellion there. Li Yüan was greatly pleased by the dream and the military book and when Li Yüan was appointed to head the army in T'ai-yüan to quell the Turks, Wu Shih-huo became a vital ally and confidant.

It is clear that Li Yüan already harboured the ambition to become Emperor. His mother was of the Tugu family and her father Tugu Hsin was a powerful nobleman who was forced to commit suicide for political reasons. Tugu Hsin had two other daughters. One became an Empress of the northern Chou dynasty, whose throne Wen-ti had seized; the other became Wen-ti's wife, the first Sui Empress consort, who always kept a watchful eye on who was visiting her husband's bed. Li Yüan's niece, Lady Wang, was in Yang-ti's harem. Her mother was Li Yüan's sister, who later became Grand Princess Tongan. The Emperor Yang-ti – Li Yüan's cousin – was already suspicious of such a powerfully connected man. One day Li Yüan was late and Yang-ti asked Lady Wang why her uncle was late for an audience. She said that he was ill. Yang-ti was amused by this and said, 'Ill? Will he die?'

Wu Chao's father also played a critical political roll, covering Li Yüan's tracks while he prepared to seize the throne. When members of the government became worried that some of the Imperial Guard might be disloyal, Wu Shih-huo persuaded them that, as the suspects were representatives of the Duke of T'ang, any move against them would risk splitting the country. And when a local garrison commander became concerned that troops were being raised that could be used in a rebellion, Wu Shih-huo assured him that they would be attached to the Duke of T'ang, who was still ostensibly loyal to the Sui Emperor Yang-ti.

The Sui dynasty was on its last legs because of Yang-ti's incompetence. He had squandered his military might in three unsuccessful campaigns against Korea, allowing uprisings to break out at home. Conscripting large numbers of men into his army left few at home to sow and harvest. Many of those who stayed at home were debilitated. To avoid conscription, men broke there own arms and legs, calling their injured limbs 'propitious paws' and 'fortunate feet', since they kept them out of the fighting. The result was famine. Then, while inspecting the building work along the Great Wall of China in the summer of 615, Yang-ti was surrounded by the Turks and besieged for a month. By the time the siege was broken, most of China was in open rebellion.

As a relative of the Sui family, Li Yüan was a reluctant rebel. But in 615 a ballad circulated that hinted that the next Emperor would have the surname Li. The omen, if not the ballad, was recorded by the writer Han Wu. He noted that Yang-ti had further depleted the imperial treasury by building the Western Park where he planned to spend his declining years surrounded by beautiful young women. In the park, it was said, there were 'sixteen places, five lakes and five seas surrounded by an abundance of flowers and trees'. However, one day Yang-ti was told that a number of plum trees had sprung up overnight. The Emperor was displeased. Shortly afterwards, in another courtyard of the palace, an arbutus or strawberry tree was in leaf. Yang-ti's surname is the same 'yang' character found in *yang-mei* – Chinese for 'strawberry tree' – while the Chinese for 'plum' is *li* – Li Yüan's family name. Later both the plum and the arbutus bore fruit at the same time. The Emperor was asked which tasted better. He replied that the fruit of the arbutus, although beautiful, was sour and not nearly as good as the 'jade plum'. Before long the arbutus had withered and died, so the Emperor would die too. The story foretold the fall of the Sui dynasty and the rise of the T'ang.

One aristocrat, Li Mi, seized on this tale and rebelled. Li Yüan encouraged this, while concealing his own ambition and assuring Li Mi that he had no higher ambition than to be the Duke of T'ang. Meanwhile Yang-ti began purging bearers of the surname Li. The powerful general Li Hun and thirty-two members of his clan were executed. More distant relatives were exiled. Initially Li Yüan escaped the purge, but must have feared his days were numbered. As it was, he was forced into action when his son, Li Shih-min, conspired with his father's best friend Pei Ji, the administrator of one of the Emperor's palaces in Chin-yang, to send two young women from Yang-ti's harem there to Li Yüan when he was drunk. Having sex with the Emperor's concubines, albeit unwittingly, was a capital offence and, after months of indecision, Li Yüan had little choice but to take up arms against the Emperor. Of course, this story may have been made up to defame Li Yüan when he, himself, was forced from power.

Having beat off the eastern Turks, Li Yüan made an alliance with his former foes, even signing his correspondence with the character 'ch'i' as if he were vassal to the Great Khan. With the Turks behind him, he became the most powerful leader in the north. And with Wu Shih-huo nominally his armourer, Li Yüan built an army of thirty thousand men in the mountainous region around T'ai-yüan. From there they set out to take over the country.

In the ensuing civil war, Wu Shih-huo proved a gifted military strategist. It is thought that the book on military tactics he gave Li Yüan he may have written himself. On more than one occasion, Wu Shih-huo's military skill in the field saved the day. Li Yüan's three sons rallied to the cause, along with his daughter Lady Li, who was one of the many strong women who abound in Chinese history. When she heard her father had rebelled, she fled to her estates west of Ch'ang-an, then she disposed of her property to recruit several hundred men who hid out in the mountains nearby. A young boy was sent to convince a highwayman who regularly killed and robbed his victims in a nearby bamboo grove to join their cause. Another servant convinced three more bandits and their bands of cut-throats to rally to the T'ang. Eventually her following, called the 'Lady's Army', numbered over a thousand and took over three prefectures. Lady Li later became the Princess of Ping-yang.

With Wu Shih-huo's help, Li Yüan crushed rivals in the north-west, forcing other rebel warlords to join him. In the face of the growing might of the T'ang, Yang-ti was forced to withdraw to Chiang-tu, the capital of the southern province where he had governed as prince before he seized the throne. This allowed his generals in the north to join the rebellion. Li Yüan took Ch'ang-an in 617 and Wu Shih-huo was rewarded with five thousand lengths of silk and three million cash. By then, Yang-ti knew the game was up. One day he sat looking into mirror and said to his wife, 'Such a fine head. Who will be the one to hack it off?' The Empress Hsiao then fell into the hands of the rebel Tou Chien-te and later found sanctuary with the eastern Turks.

As Li Yüan's army swept through the south, Yang-ti was murdered in his bathhouse and two of his grandsons who had been put on the throne in his place were swept aside and put to death. Li Yüan then proclaimed himself the first Emperor of the new T'ang dynasty, taking the reign name Wu Te. He is known to history under his temple name of Kao-tsu. After seizing the throne, he began consolidating his position. In 619, he invited the khan of the western Turks, an important ally in the civil war, to a banquet and, afterwards, let the legate of the eastern Turks kill him. Later, in 630, the eastern Turks were crushed by Kao-tsung's son Li Shih-min, who was then acknowledged as the 'Heavenly Khan'.

In the meantime Li Mi had been forced to surrender. Li Shih-min sought to impose T'ang rule in the regions formerly controlled by the warlord. However, the eastern capital Luoyang was occupied by the Sui general Wang Shih-ch'ung, who had also proclaimed himself Emperor. With him he had an army of 200,000 men, who had to be fed. The price of millet in Luoyang rose to forty thousand cash per bushel. No one could afford that. Instead they turned to cannibalism. Wan Shih-ch'ung got a large bell and turned it upside down to make a stewing pot of a capacity of 1,600 gallons to boil up the flesh of hapless women and children, which he divided among his officers. Soldiers also abducted children and boiled and ate them. Some even developed a taste for cannibalism. Wang Shih-ch'ung himself said, 'Of all the delicious things to eat, nothing is better than human flesh. And as long as there are people in the vicinity, we have nothing to fear from famine.'

Indeed, in medieval China, human flesh was thought to be good for you. One T'ang physician prescribed it for all ailments and dutiful children would carve off pieces of their own flesh to feed to ailing parents. In times of war and famine people would eat their own children, though in normal circumstances the punishment for cannibalism was to be beaten to death. One general slew all his concubines to feed his troops. Cannibalism was also provoked by a lust for vengeance. One son not only killed his father's murderer, but ate his heart and liver. Sometimes cannibalism was practised merely as a random act of cruelty. In the seventh century, a host in the south was offended by a effete young man who was serving the ale at his table and had him dragged out, murdered and served up as broth.

In 619, a T'ang envoy was sent to persuade a rebel prince to submit to T'ang rule. Over dinner he got drunk and taunted the prince.

'I hear that you, sir, are fond of eating human flesh,' he sneered. 'How does it taste?'

The prince rose to the insult. 'Eating the flesh of a drunkard is like eating pig meat marinated in the dregs of a brew.'

The envoy was outraged and upbraided the prince as a brigand. The prince responded by having the envoy and over twenty of the T'ang legation boiled and served to his men. He then fled to Luoyang and joined the other flesh-eating enemies of the T'ang.

In 621, Li Shih-min finally arrived at the walls of Luoyang and besieged the city. Those inside now ran short of easy victims to eat. They had already eaten all the leaves from trees and the roots of grass. When nothing was left, they made cakes out of mud and the residue of grain. But those who ate them found that their bodies swelled and their legs weakened and they died. The city finally fell and the cannibal prince was captured and beheaded.

As Emperor, Kao-tsu became, not just ruler of the Middle Kingdom, as China was known, but of 'all under heaven'. Thus, as ruler of the whole world, he was known, officially, as the 'Son of Heaven'. He rewarded Wu Shih-huo by making him President of the Board of Works. Later Wu Shih-huo was appointed governor-general of two important prefectures and made Duke of Ying with a fiefdom of eight hundred households who paid their taxes directly to him. Wu Shih-huo's brothers were also rewarded. The Emperor Kao-tsu paid Wu Shih-huo an even greater honour when, in 620, he selected a second wife for him from the Yang line of the Sui royal family, a cousin of the last Sui Emperor. The match was made by Kao-tsu's daughter, Princess Guiyang, and paid for by the government. Lady Yang was a sophisticated woman and the daughter of a former prime minister. Though she was already in her early forties, her marriage to Wu Shih-huo produced three daughters. Wu Chao was the second. As well as her two natural sisters, Wu Chao also had two half-brothers from her father's first marriage, Wu Yüan-shuang and Wu Yüan-ch'ing. Somewhat older than Wu Chao, they would have left the inner apartments where the women were confined by the time her father died at the age of fifty-nine. Wu Chao grew to dislike them as they mistreated her mother Lady Yang.

Wu Chao and her sisters would not have been a welcome addition to the household. Girl children were valued less highly than boys and, generally, the birth of a girl was greeted with a frown. The infanticide of girl children was common. Those who lived were treated harshly. As infants, girls were barely clothed and left on the floor with only a broken loom whorl to play with, symbolizing their future work of spinning. However, in some rare cases, fathers doted on their daughters.

Around the time Wu Chao was born, the reign of Emperor Kao-tsu was cut short. His ambitious son Li Shih-min murdered his two brothers at the palace's Hsüan Wu Gate – the northern-most gate that connected the palace to the Imperial Park. His justification was the accusation that they'd had illicit relations with the ladies of the imperial harem with whom the younger brother enjoyed particularly close ties. Li Shih-min then deposed his father in a coup, making himself Emperor with the temple name T'ai-tsung. Kao-tsu stayed on as 'Retired Emperor', but was left to swelter in the city while his neglectful son moved out to the summer palace. Eventually, T'ai-tsung started to build his father a summer palace of his own, but it was not completed by the time his father died in 635.

As Wu Chao was growing up, her father continued to enjoy the new Emperor's favour, putting down several rebellions. He was then appointed governor-general in Li-chou. There is a tradition that Wu Chao was born during his time there. But this would mean that she was three years younger than was generally believed, so she may have been as young as ten when she was inducted into the imperial harem.

The governor-general's house Wu Chao was brought up in would have been a grand affair. Such establisments had numerous halls, built around cloistered courtyards and private gardens. These were usually filled with an abundance of white flowers, or sometimes coloured flowers imported from India. There would be fruit trees and ponds stocked with fish and ducks. The various halls would be separate buildings, joined by porticos and covered walkways. They were self-contained so that parts could be closed off or rented out. The front or outer courtyard was the men's domain, where they received guests and did business. The rear or inner apartments were the women's realm and were off-limits to men unless they were family members. In larger households these would house harems and be guarded by eunuchs. That ended in 749 when the Emperor had so inflated his own harem that he decreed that all eunuchs in private houses be sent to the imperial palace.

Some of these residences were huge. The famous general Guo Ziyi had a house so large that you had to travel from one courtyard to the next by carriage or on horseback, while Imperial Grand Secretary Lisheng had to buy a piece of adjoining land to extend his house so that he could play polo – a game devised centuries before in ancient Persia – in his compound.

Alongside the family residence, the governor-general's compound would contain a reception hall, offices for minor officials, a prison with wardens guarding the inmates, and a school, complete with shrines to Confucius and his disciples. Here a teacher would instruct his pupils in the classics. The main hall of the residence would have faced on to the town square where Wu Chao's father would have read the imperial edicts despatched to him from the capital by mounted courier.

The walls of even the grandest buildings were made from compressed earth, which could turn to mud in heavy rain. During a rain storm in Ch'ang-an in 817, a pillar in one of the palaces collapsed, flooding the market with three feet of water and demolishing over two thousand homes. Walls were plastered inside and out, and roofs were made from glazed tiles, in an attempt to make them fireproof. There was no pane glass in T'ang China so windows were covered with paper, oiled to make it translucent – though wealthier houses used sheer silks. The paper or cloth was glued to wooden lattices to withstand the wind. Window frames were sometimes inlaid with small pieces of glass or mica that sparkled in sunlight. These lattices also adorned the top halves of doors. For privacy, both doors and windows were fitted with blinds made from slats of bamboo, which could be rolled upwards with cords to let in more light.

Officials of Wu Shih-huo's rank were allowed to decorate their houses. The beams and rafters would carry paintings and the roof tiles animal designs. Officials of the fifth grade and over could decorate their red front gates with a bird–head knocker. The fashion of having gate gods painted on the wood or paper attached to the gates began around that time. These deities were two T'ang generals who had volunteered to stand guard over the Emperor T'ai-tsung when he had fallen ill. Racked by guilt over murdering his brothers, he fancied that demons were throwing tiles and bricks at the door of his bedchamber. The two generals remained on guard night after night until the Emperor recovered. Afterwards he had portraits of the two generals glued to the door panels to prevent the demons entering and the fashion spread.

Outside the gates, as a prefect or governor-general, Wu Shih-huo would have lances carrying banners stuck in the ground. These were replaced by the Office of Military Arms every five years. Inside the house, the walls and ceilings would be covered with paintings and there would be screens decorated with examples of fine calligraphy. The floor would be covered with reed mats and Persian rugs. Shoes were removed on entering and indoors people wore thick-soled socks like Japanese *tabi*. During the cold winter, stoves or braziers would be ablaze with firewood or charcoal provided each month by the government for heating and cooking. Aromatics were added so the fires gave off a nice smell. The Emperor also provided a ration of meat and foodstuffs to everyone except the lowest in society. What you got, and how much of it, depended on your rank, so the Wu family would have been well provided for.

There were other ways to keep warm. Some patricians protected themselves from cold and drafts by surrounding themselves with their concubines. Literature records that they would commonly warm their hands on the women's breasts. At night, light was provided by lamps that burnt whale, seal or fish oil. Physicians discouraged the use of pork or bear fat because it was said to cause near-sightedness. Rich families like Wu Chao's would also have aromatic candles made from berries suspended in beeswax. In the summer bat dung mixed with cinnamon bark and frankincense was burned as a mosquito repellent.

During hot weather, wealthy hosts would cool their guests with blocks of ice carved into the shapes of phoenixes or other fabulous animals. Silk cloths soaked with water would be hung up on verandahs. One T'ang Emperor had an ice room built, complete with fan wheels to produce a cool breeze, while one of his ministers had a 'pavilion of automatic rain', where water cascaded from the eaves down all four walls as a form of air-conditioning. T'ang Emperors had massive ice pits built under the imperial parks in their capitals to store food. A thousand blocks, each three foot by three foot, were brought each year from frozen creeks in the north so the court could enjoy chilled melons and other delicacies year round. More lowly officials, such as Wu Chao's father, followed the imperial fashion and built underground refrigerators of their own.

Earlier Chinese houses were sparsely furnished. People sat on the floor and the only tables were low platforms about two inches high. These were essentially floor-mats raised on wooden frames. But by the time Wu Chao was growing up, folding chairs had been imported from Central Asia. There were cupboards and low benches made from carved and lacquered wood. And there were sofas standing two or three feet high, on which you could sit or recline.

A governor-general's residence would have had a separate bathhouse. This usually had a couch and a screen to protect women from men's gazes. The story is told that, in the fifth century, a Buddhist nun was staying at the home of a general who took the opportunity to spy on her naked as she was washing. While he watched, she took a knife, cut open her belly and removed her internal organs, then lopped off her feet and beheaded herself. He turned away in horror. Once he had averted his gaze, she reassembled herself.

Well away from the living quarters was a separate privy – a small shelter over a hole in the ground, which was sometimes fitted with a lid to hide the filth below. The smell was generally terrible and it was the custom to stuff jujubes – the fruit of the Chinese blackthorn – up your nostrils before using it. The muck was removed regularly by local ordure merchants. Privies were thought to be haunted. This would have appealed to Wu Chao, who was very superstitious. The principal deity of the privy was the Purple Maiden, the ghost of the chief wife of a provincial governor who had killed her in a fit of jealousy and had thrown her body down the privy during the Lantern Festival, on the fifteenth day of the first lunar month. On that day, it was the custom to welcome the Purple Maiden with the words, 'Your husband is out. His first wife is gone. So, young maiden, you many come out of the privy.' On the last day of the month, the householder would shine torches into all the privies and wells to expel the ghosts that abounded. The custom of welcoming and expelling the ghost of the Purple Maiden existed well into the twentieth century and is commemorated by the Cantonese saying, 'The third aunt of the toilet is easy to leave in but it is difficult to make her go.'

A well-to-do family like Wu Chao's would have used lavatory paper – another Chinese invention – though in poorer households people cleaned themselves with a stick. Upper-class people would wash their hands afterwards with water and a detergent made from the seeds of the soapbean tree. These were crushed, mixed with powdered minerals and perfumes and rolled into a ball. However, it must be said, Arab visitors were not impressed with the standards of Chinese personal hygiene and considered even the upper-class Chinese filthy.

Indoors chamber pots were used. These would be set beside curtained beds which had hard pillows made of wood, porcelain or stone – though one official who ran the government monopoly on salt and iron had a pillow encrusted with lapis lazuli to match the opulence of his gold bed. The pillows were low, since Taoists believed that high pillows shortened your life. One princess had a pillow made from a leopard's head to ward off evil.

Although the governor-general's compound contained a school, Wu Chao would have been educated at home. The mother of the household took charge of the education of the younger children, particularly their moral education. Private tutors were employed to give both boys and girls a literary education, though the number of educated girls remained relatively small. As girls grew older their mothers gave them a detailed education in the management of a household, and in courtesy and ceremony – everything that made Chinese society run smoothly. But it seems that Wu Chao was also educated in the classics to a high level. From her infancy she was seen as exceptional. She could certainly read and write. Forty-six existing poems have been ascribed to her, along with surviving fragments of literary criticism.

Wu Chao's father, Wu Shih-huo, died in 635. It is said that he died of grief at the death of the former Emperor Kao-tsu, the friend and confidant whom he had helped put in power. T'ai-tsung sent his own physicians to tend Wu Shih-huo on his deathbed. Wu Shih-huo was buried in his hometown Wenshui in Ping-chou. T'ai-tsung ordered the governor-general there, Li Chi, a famous general originally from the camp of Li Mi, to make the funeral arrangements. Later T'ai-tsung gave the family the inestimable honour of taking Wu Shih-huo's beautiful young daughter Wu Chao as his consort.

Wu Chao was about ten when her father died and it changed everything. Until then, she would have been considered a guest, or even an intruder, in her father's household. A girl child was not considered one of the family, but rather a member of the family of her future husband. A father was supposed to arrange a marriage for his daughters but, it seems, Wu Shih-huo died before he had secured Wu Chao's betrothal.

When there was a man in the house, he was the undisputed autocrat. But once Wu Shih-huo was dead, Wu Chao's mother reigned supreme as dowager. She brought a strong Buddhist influence to the household. Buddhism had spread into China from India and became the official state religion for the first time under the Sui. It overthrew the old Confucian idea of women being vastly inferior to men and, for women of the time, it was a liberation. Under the Sui, the Yang clan had been known for their generous patronage of the Buddhist *T'ien-t'ai* or Lotus Sect and Wu Chao's mother Lady Yang was renowned for her piety. She paid for the erection of votive images and the translation of Buddhist texts. It has even been suggested that, as a young girl, Wu Chao was educated in a Buddhist convent.

A greater liberation for Wu Chao would have been, with the death of her father, the removal of any male presence from the outer apartments of the house. This meant that the women of the household, normally confined to the inner apartments, would have unprecedented access to the outside world. As her guides, Wu Chao would have had the concubines and slave girls, who had considerably more freedom than the female members of the family. The concubines would have been kept on after her father's death out of respect for the departed.

As a tomboy, Wu Chao would hardly have been able to resist the temptation to explore the outside world. This would have been encouraged by Lady Yang: not only was she a woman who involved herself in the outside world; she also looked to the future. Years before, when Wu Chao was still a babe in arms, Lady Yang had welcomed into the house the noted face reader Yüan T'ien-kang, who had told Lady Yang that she had given birth to noble children. On seeing Wu Shih-huo's sons, neither of whom was the child of Lady Yang, Yüan T'ien-kang predicted that they would become provincial governors, but rise no higher. Wu Chao's older sister, later Lady Ho-lan, he said, would be honourably married but bring dishonour on her husband. Then he examined Wu, who was in the arms of her nurse but already dressed as a boy.

'The appearance of this boy is unusual and extraordinary,' said Yüan T'ien-kang, 'and not easy to comprehend.'

He then asked for the child to be put down so that it could walk. Yüan T'ien-kang was amazed and divined in the child 'the look of the sun's rays, the face of a dragon and the neck of a phoenix'. The child, he said, resembled Fu Hsi, China's mythical first Emperor, a divine being with a serpent's body who was born around the twenty-ninth century BC. And as the child tottered around the room, Yüan T'ien-kang said, 'If this child was a girl, she would rule the Empire.'

This must have seemed incredible to Lady Yang. No woman had ever ruled in China. It was against all the tenets of Confucianism, which confined women to an inferior role in the home. And certainly it would have been no cause for joy. Lady Yang knew all too well the fate of those involved in politics. Much of her family had died when the T'ang ousted the Sui and it was noted that, when Wu Chao left for the palace to become a concubine, her mother cried, despite the great honour being done to her family.

CHAPTER THREE

THE LOTUS
FLOWERS

THE TRIP TO THE CAPITAL would have been a rare expedition for Wu Chao. As she was going to the harem she would have been forced to abandoned men's dress. At that time women wore a kimono-style inner robe of embroidered silk, with a plain silk apron. Over it they wore a transparent garment. A brocade scarf covered the shoulders. Women's dresses at that time were low cut and a generous décolletage would have left much of her breasts exposed.

Her hair would have been put up in a high chignon, using simple hair-pins, and decorated with flowers and pearls. Her face would have been powdered porcelain pale. Rouge was applied to the lips and cheeks, and the eyebrows were shaved off and artificial ones painted on. When she went out to the carriage that would carry her to Ch'ang-an she would certainly have worn a veil or perhaps even the Chinese version of a burnoose – a piece of cloth draped over the head which covered the entire body down to the feet with only a small gap at the front to see through. This was the fashion among palace ladies at the time. And the blinds of the carriage would have been drawn down so that no one could see the faces of the women inside.

The journey to the capital was an arduous one. To the north of the city there was a semi-arid deeply eroded loess plateau. To the south the lofty and rugged Qin Ling mountains. Between lay the fertile valley of the river Wei where Chinese civilization had begun more than three thousand years before.

With a population of around two million, Ch'ang-an was the largest city in the world and it was six times the size of the modern city of Xian that occupies the site today. Approaching the city from the south, you would see a huge band of yellow earth. This was the new perimeter wall, a rampart of compacted earth nearly twenty feet high and some seventy li – twenty-three miles – long. Ten feet outside it was a moat thirty feet wide and twelve feet deep. The rampart had been begun by the first Sui Emperor, Sui Wen-ti, when he took over in 581, and was so big that it was still being built during the T'ang period.

Ch'ang-an had first become the capital of China during the Han dynasty eight hundred years before. It had taken over from the old capital of Hsien-yang just up the river on the opposite bank. But Ch'ang-an was destroyed in the fighting to remove the usurper Wang Ming in AD 23 and the Han moved their capital to Luoyang, over six hundred li, two hundred miles, to the east. When the barbarian Liu Yüan invaded in AD 316, during the Chinese equivalent of Europe's Dark Ages, he found less than a hundred families living in Ch'ang-an. Only four carts could be found in the entire city. Thorns and weeds grew in the streets and the officials had neither ceremonial robes nor seals of office. Instead, they had their names and ranks inscribed on tablets of mulberry wood. However, under the Wei dynasty, which ran from AD 386 to 534, thousands of families were moved into Ch'ang-an and the surrounding region. Then when Sui Wen-ti set about rebuilding Ch'ang-an as the administrative heart of his new Empire, he renamed it Daxing-cheng, which means the 'Walled City of Daxing'; under the preceding Chou dynasty Sui Wen-ti had been Duke of Daxing. It was laid out on a grid system like a modern American city and covered thirty-three square miles. To emphasize the celestial nature of the city, the streets and avenues were aligned along the cardinal axes, with the palace placed at the north end like the pole star. It was the still point that the rest of the universe revolved about. To emphasis this point, the palace was called the Taiji-gong, or the 'Palace of the Cosmic Ultimate'.

Before the fall of the Sui dynasty, the last Sui Emperor Yang-ti had created the Western Park, also known as the Fragrant Flower Park, the Forbidden Park and the Purple Park, which was two hundred li, or about sixty-six miles, in circumference. This was where the Emperor proposed to spend his declining years surrounded by beautiful women.

Among his many amazing constructions, Yang-ti built the Maze Palace which is described in *The Erotic Adventures of Sui Tang-ti*. The main palace was surrounded by thirty-six smaller palaces, all hidden in a forest of flowers:

> The magnificent main palace was a three-storey golden pagoda that glistened in the sunlight. Verandahs circled each storey. On them stood hundreds of palace maidens, smiling. They were clad in robes of the finest cicada-wing lace. With nothing underneath, their firm young breasts, slender waists and shapely legs could be seen – it was even more provocative than if they had been nude.
>
> Inside the palace there were numerous rooms. These were connected by intricate passageways. In the main chamber Yang-ti had four enormous silk tents named Intoxicating Passion, Sweet and Fragrant Night, Delight of Autumn Moon and End of Spring Sorrow. Inside each tent, there were thirty or forty naked girls who played games, talked and joked, or reclined on tiger-skin couches. Although the atmosphere was sedate, each of them secretly longed for the arrival of the Emperor, who would descend like a cloud.
>
> The walls of the chamber were lined with shiny bronze mirrors. They were hollow inside and incense was burnt in them. The room was full of the fragrance of jasmine, musk, peonies and orchids. Overhead were silk lanterns with pictures of naked beauties in provocative positions painted on them. They gave off the light of a faint moon and with candles inside them it looked like the naked beauties were about to descend any minute.
>
> When the Emperor arrived at the palace, he would be greeted by eight kneeling eunuchs. They would take his clothes and dress him in a leopard-skin loin cloth, lined with yellow silk. He would then wander about his palace, but he would always end up in the main chamber.
>
> When he entered the girls would cry, 'May the Emperor Live a Thousand Years.' He would then drink ginseng wine from a golden goblet until he felt his jade stem stir beneath his leopard-skin loin cloth. Then he would grab any woman in sight, though being slightly tipsy and surrounded by mirrors he would find it difficult to distinguish the real women from their images.
>
> Then he would enter one of the silk tents. With his eyes shut, he would let himself be guided by the women's voices. He found it more fun catching a woman this way. When he got hold of one, he would push her down on a bed, couch or tiger-skin mattress. Quickly he would throw aside his leopard-skin loin cloth and push his jade stem into her

moist jade gate, with a thrust that could have torn through an animal hide. The giggling and whispering of the other women would continue. And, though he had not yet satisfied the first woman, he would jump up and grab another, taking her in a different position or having her standing up. When he was thoroughly satisfied, he would doze off. And when he woke up the love game would start all over again. As the light in the chamber was artificial, you could not tell whether it was day or night. And Yang-ti did not care.

It is said that he had three thousand maidens in the palace and, when travelling, he took with him ten special wagons, each with a naked beauty inside lying on a red padded satin couch, awaiting his pleasure. However, such extravagance helped empty Yang-ti's treasury, already depleted by war and civil construction, leaving the Sui unable to resist the growing power of the T'ang.

The first T'ang Emperor Kao-tsu took over the city intact and restored the name Ch'ang-an – which means 'City of Everlasting Peace'. Finding the government granaries and treasuries empty, he reinstituted the old 'equal fields' system of agriculture which ensured a steady flow of tax revenue. The state parcelled out land, all of which the Emperor theoretically owned, in equal plots to the peasants. Every adult male between the age of seventeen and fifty-nine was allocated approximately thirteen-and-a-third acres. Local officials took a census every three years and redistributed the land. They reclaimed eighty per cent of the acreage from men who reached sixty and gave it to men who had reached the age of seventeen. Each man was then taxed two or three per cent of the annual harvest, while each woman had to hand over twenty-five feet of the linen or twenty feet of the silk she wove from the flax and silkworms she raised. Adult males also had to give the central government twenty days of compulsory or corvée labour on great construction projects and two months' special duty to local government, building roads, walls, bridges or dykes. During a time of famine these impositions were progressively lifted. If forty per cent of a peasant's crop was lost, he did not have to pay the grain tax. At a loss of sixty per cent, the cloth levy was also remitted and, at seventy per cent, forced labour was dropped.

The Sui dynasty had also left a debased currency. At the end of their rule, large-scale counterfeiting broke out. In 621, year four Wu Te, the

Emperor Kao-tsu ordered the minting of new coins of uniform weight, shape and metal content in government furnaces across China. Anyone caught minting coins privately would suffer the death penalty. The coins were made of copper, called *le* or *tsien* and known as 'cash'. They were small and round, with a square hole in the middle allowing them to be strung together. A string of one thousand coppers constituted the next highest unit of currency, called a *tael* or *liang*. However, cash was heavy and bulky and difficult to transport, so larger transactions were conducted in silver, gold or silk.

At first the T'ang made few alterations to Ch'ang-an, but, as the treasuries filled, T'ai-tsung built the Ta-ming Gong or Great Luminous Palace to the north-east as his father's summer residence. With twenty palace halls set in the imperial hunting park, it took twenty-eight years to complete. By then Kao-tsu was dead, but the vast palace was a fitting adornment to the capital. Political stability under T'ai-tsung had brought unprecedented prosperity and by the time Wu Chao arrived at Ch'ang-an it was, not just the biggest, but also the wealthiest city in the world.

As she approached the city from the south Wu Chao would have seen a few pagodas and the dark roofs of temple complexes and princely mansions protruding over the top of the rampart. Few buildings were higher than two storeys and most had just one. Wu herself would later change that. She was responsible for building the ten-storey Great Wild Goose Pagoda that could be seen from miles beyond the walls. Seven storeys of it are still standing. But now, as she approached the low city she inherited, she could see beyond it the rugged terrain of the great plateau across the Wei river to the north.

The main entrance to the city was the Mingde Gate, or the 'Gate of Luminous Virtue'. It had five entranceways instead of the customary three, each wide enough for two carts to pass. The central one remained closed and was reserved for the use of the Emperor. These gates were locked at dusk, when the curfew started, and were secured by cylinder locks. The gate and the surrounding wall was faced with red bricks. The tower above carried a wooden structure with huge pillars supporting a hip roof eleven spans wide and three spans deep. The Emperor would travel there to see off officials on the way to a distant posting or the funeral cortège of an eminent person bound for a tomb outside the city. The gate itself was manned by around a hundred men, housed in barracks on either side.

Once through the gateway, Wu Chao's carriage would take her up the Vermilion Bird Road. This was one of the city's six main thoroughfares, three running north–south, three east–west. Over five hundred feet wide, it was the width of a forty-five-lane highway. Although it was plenty wide enough for a race track, the punishment for speeding was fifty blows with a thin rod, unless the rider or coach driver was delivering an imperial decree or a doctor on the way to an emergency. There were worse punishments for driving without due care and attention. If a rider or coachman injured or killed someone they suffered sixty blows with a thick rod and death by strangulation.

The Vermilion Bird Road was lined with pagoda trees that grew up to seventy-five feet high. On either side of the roadway were low mud walls around ten feet beyond the line of the trees and separated from the road by a ditch that collected run-off and provided water for irrigation. At each intersection there were four bridges to span the four ditches. The water in these ditches was clean. They were not used as sewers and human waste was carted out of the city to be sold to farmers as fertilizer. The roadway itself was cambered to help water run off and slightly elevated, so Wu Chao would have had a good view of the houses beyond.

Immediately inside the city wall was a ring-road eighty feet wide which was used to move defenders around the ramparts if the city came under siege. The whole city was widely spaced, built along avenues one hundred and fifty feet wide. The roadways were made of compacted earth. These were dusty during the dry season and muddy in the snow and rain, so pathways of white sand – brought from the Chan river by oxcart – were laid. These were reserved for the officials who went to court on horseback. In the case of principal ministers, the sand ran all the way to their front doorstep. At every intersection there was a police post, manned by between five and thirty men of the Gold Bird Guard.

The southern section of the city was quiet and under-populated. Some of it was given over to cultivation and in the broad avenues to the left the picturesque willows, elms and pagoda trees used to line the city streets were replaced by fruit trees. In residential wards, the streets were lined with flowering trees. Beyond were more trees in the residential gardens.

A little way down the Vermilion Bird Road was the mansion of the ninth son of Kao-tsu, one of the Emperor T'ai-tsung's few remaining brothers, which took up an entire city block. Eighteen years later it would be turned into a Taoist temple in honour of T'ai-tsung. After that there were more Taoist, Buddhist and family temples, and the new university, which was flourishing two centuries before the first university in Europe was established at Salerno. To the left and right were the busy, walled West and East Markets, well stocked with goods from all over China, Central Asia and the South Seas. The East Market alone comprised two hundred and twenty streets, surrounded by warehouses. When just twelve streets burned down, four thousand shops were lost. The market's wide streets allowed carriages to pass the ox carts transporting goods and the pedestrians who flocked there. There were ironmongers, cloth dealers, printers, butchers, clothiers, and brush sellers. Stalls selling cakes and dumplings filled the air with appetizing smells. Wineshops hoisted banners advertising their wares. A company called Donkey Express rented jackasses – government regulations required that they were walked or ridden no more than fifty li, or seventeen miles, a day. Musicians, dancers and acrobats enlivened the atmosphere, performing in the small squares or on the stages set up there where priests prayed for rain during droughts. The market squares were also used for public executions; criminals' heads were left on the execution sites as a warning to others.

The East Market was closer to the homes of the wealthy and carried more upmarket items. It also tended to specialize in domestic goods. The West Market, by contrast, was the easternmost terminus of the Silk Road. There exotic goods were exchanged for local produce. The West Market had its own Persian bazaar that sold jewellery from all over the known world. Also on sale were more mundane items – measures and scales, low-grade silks, livestock, steaming bowls of porridge, ready-made clothes, bridles, saddles, and rush bags full of yellowy-red ants that fed on pests that attacked mandarin trees. Shops selling the same kind of merchandise congregated in certain streets. There was a brewer who sold Fu river ales called Old Woman's Clear Ale, Courtier's Clear Ale, Toad Tumulus and Melody – drunk warm like English beer – and an apothecary that sold acorns to arrest diarrhoea and all manner of plants, minerals, insects, and animal parts that were supposed to promote health. There an Emperor once ordered the ingredients for a Taoist elixir that guaranteed immortality. Restaurants and brothels vied for trade. The taverns were usually run by women, and drinkers drank ran a tab. Waiters were employed to make sure they paid up before they left. Inns also served snacks – such as deer's tongue, deer's tail, meat pies, rabbit's haunch, crab apple steeped in honey and cinnabar, pheasant's tail and jackals' lips – while white-skinned, green-eyed, blonde women from Central Asia sang to keep the drinkers spending freely. There were also ponds where passers-by could release fish to gain religious merit.

Early banks had been set up in the markets. There merchants could deposit money and gold and silver in return for a handy certificate that could be used in transactions. This was the forerunner of paper currency, another Chinese invention. These proto-banks did not make loans, though. Usury was controlled by Buddhist monasteries which also owned the oil presses, renting them out to sesame farmers. They also lent seed grain to peasants. If the peasant was one of the monastery's tenants, there was no interest to be paid, but the principal – the amount of grain they had borrowed – had to be returned within seven months. Other peasants had to pay interest at fifty per cent, returning one-and-a-half times the amount of grain they borrowed. The monasteries also lent money to people of higher status. These loans had to be repaid in six months and at the rate of an extortionate one hundred and twenty per cent – two hundred and forty per cent per annum. The rates were so high because it was relatively easy to default on the debt. Rates came down later when moneylending was taken over by the Uighur people of Central Asia, who did not share the Buddhists' qualms about the use of violence.

No official above the fifth rank was allowed to enter the markets and the shopping was done by servants from the palace and domestic slaves. There was strict segregation between government officials and the artisans and merchants, who were thought to be politically unreliable as they roamed the land talking freely to anyone they met on the way. Merchants and artisans were forbidden to ride horses or to sit the civil service examinations. Nor were they allocated land like peasants. However, they enjoyed certain tax advantages, only paying metropolitan taxes on their houses and property. While most remained humble pedlars, some grew very wealthy indeed, worth hundreds of millions of coppers. During the early T'ang period, they lent money to the government to pay civil service salaries, beginning the modern institution of the national debt.

At the centre of the markets were the Market Offices, which arbitrated in disputes. Then there was a Price Equalizing Office and a Price Regulating Office which were responsible for regulating the price of grain and other staples. The Market Director and his staff kept order, policed unfair trading practices, supervised weights and measures, inspected the quality of goods on sale, enforced the hours of trading, checked the quality of the money in circulation, regulated the traffic and issued certificates for the sale of livestock and slaves. Those slaves included Korean women, who were renowned for their beauty and fetched high prices from well-to-do men. Most slaves were foreigners, since it was a capital offence to sell a Chinese person into slavery against their will, though debtors and their children sometimes sold themselves as slaves, usually for a limited period, to clear their debts. The markets were so strictly regulated that they were only open a few hours a day. The noon opening was signalled with two hundred drumbeats. An hour and forty-five minutes before sunset, three beats of the gong announced the market was closing.

Right across the city, the individual wards were divided by walls with gates that were locked at night. During the curfew nobody was allowed out except in the case of an emergency. This system of walled wards had existed for eight hundred years. It was a method of social control that allowed the authorities to conscript soldiers or force labour with ease. Shih huang-ti of the Ch'in dynasty, who first unified China in the third century BC, had allowed only one entrance to each ward, to maintain absolute control over his people. Since then the authorities had loosened up a bit. Each ward had four gates – northern, southern, western, and eastern. The one hundred and nine residential wards were each subdivided into sixteen blocks that took their address from the position within the ward. So there was the north-west corner block, north-east corner block, south-west corner block and south-east corner block. Then there were the blocks to the west of the northern gate, to the east of the northern gate, to the north of the western gate, to the south of the western gate, to the north of the eastern gate, to the south of the eastern gate, to the west of the southern gate, and to the east of the southern gate. Then in the middle were the block north of the western cross street, the block north of the eastern cross street, the block south of the western cross street and the block south of the eastern cross street.

Frequent attempts to tear down the walls simply to build shopfronts on the major thoroughfare were brutally suppressed. Only the temples, monastic orders and officials above the third grade were excused the curfew and allowed to have entranceways that opened directly onto the main thoroughfare. Any ordinary citizens who tried to evade the system by scaling the walls – or anyone caught climbing the walls around the market or the city's ramparts – was punished with seventy strokes of the rod.

Before 636, the closing and opening of the gates was announced by soldiers shouting in the streets. However, two years before Wu Chao arrived in Ch'ang-an a new system was introduced. Drums were set up along the six major avenues. At sunset these were beaten eight hundred times before the gates were closed. From the second night watch, mounted soldiers did their rounds of the streets by the light of torches in silence. With the fifth watch, the drums were sounded again and the gates were opened so people could go about their normal day's business. But the rules were suspended for the New Year Lantern Festival on the fourteenth, fifteenth and sixteenth of the first lunar month when households hung banners from the top of bamboo poles and the populace was allowed to stroll the streets at night to enjoy the spectacle.

Under the T'ang dynasty, these strict regulations began to break down. Against the city regulations, the ten-foot walls were punctuated occasionally by private entranceways. Cook-shops and shops selling Turkish pastries began to spring up in the residential wards. Musicians played in the middle of the street, impeding traffic. And there was usually a huddle around the ward gates where notices were posted and crowds gathered to read them.

As Wu Chao travelled down the Vermilion Bird Road, she would have seen some magnificent buildings. On the left, around half a mile, or two blocks, beyond the temples was the Yongda ward, which was entirely taken up by the finance minister's huge pavilion and its garden laid out around an ornamental pond. Here the official banquet for those who had passed the civil service examinations was held. Those who had passed the triennial examinations on the Confucian classics for the grade of *chin-shih* also celebrated by hosting a dinner in the northern quarter, a district of restaurants, wine-shops and brothels abutting the palace wall. Unsuccessful candidates often stayed on to join the ranks of procurers, pimps, pawnbrokers, poets and artists seeking a patron, strong-arm men, political hustlers and the rest of the demimonde, rather than return home in disgrace to their parents.

The red light district in Ch'ang-an was in Ping-kang ward, not far from the East Market. The area was located in the north-eastern quarter of the ward and consisted of three winding lanes, the north, the middle and the south. The street determined the quality of the service the houses offered and the price the customer paid. Those in the northern lane enjoyed the highest status. A volume called *The Book of the Northern Lane* written in the late T'ang period and carrying gossip about a dozen courtesans at the time still survives.

All sorts of girls worked in the quarter. Some were illiterate peasants who had been kidnapped or sold into prostitution by poor families. But there were also educated courtesans who sang and danced, and in some cases achieved fame — or at least notoriety — writing poetry. Once in the quarter the girls were registered, then assigned to one of the walled compounds, which were ranked according to the status of the inmates. There girls were trained in the skills of their profession by madams — *chia-mu* or 'adopted' or 'fake mothers' — who did not spare the rod. They were allowed out to the Pao-t'ang-szû Buddhist temple nearby on festival days. There, dressed in their finery with their madams and maids, they would mix with the glittering youth of the city. Such prostitutes' parades took place in cities all over China, since, in those days, municipalities were inordinately proud of the beauty and skill of their working women. The only other time they left the quarter was to entertain at official banquets where the most cultivated courtesans and singing girls would attempt to outshine officials' wives and concubines. The one way for a woman to get out of prostitution was to befriend a wealthy man who might buy a courtesan and install her as his concubine. Rich men and important officials also kept singing girls alongside their wives and concubines as personal attendants, but while wives and concubines stayed at home the singing girls could go out with him to enliven the conversation when he met his friends.

Across the Vermilion Bird Road from the Yongda was the Lanling ward, where other career officials had their mansions. By the time Wu Chao had reached this point, almost halfway down the main avenue, there would have been a noticeable increase in traffic – although there was no possibility of a traffic jam on a road so wide. The broad avenue had been built for imperial spectacles and military parades. The Emperor, for example, might parade down Vermilion Bird Road on the first day of the lunar month to the Altar of Heaven by the Mingde Gate. The kings of client states, provincial governors, high-ranking eunuchs and other dignitaries also appeared in solemn procession. They were led by men holding great pieces of wood that were tolled like bells. No man was allowed to stand in the way of the procession of the Emperor, or even that of a prince or an official eunuch. If a resident was at his doorway when a procession approached, he would go inside and keep his door shut until it had gone by.

The Daxing-shan Monastery occupied the whole of the Jingshan ward to the east of the Vermilion Bird Road. It was one of the major Buddhist temple complexes and the first to introduce tantric Buddhism to China. It sat on the top of one of the six ridges that ran across the city. These had a special significance. The Sui architect Yü-wen K'ai, who had redesigned the capital in just nine months, chose the site because these ridges represented the six unbroken lines of the exclusively male *qian* hexagram from *I Ching* or *Book of Changes*, written by Wen-wang, father of the Chou dynasty (1111–255 BC), while he was imprisoned by the Shang from 1144 to 1147 BC. He was freed after paying a ransom of four chariots, a fine horse and a beautiful girl. His son, Wu-wang, or 'Martial Prince', then overthrew the Shang dynasty which had ruled since around the eighteenth century BC. In fact, the hexagrams of the *I Ching* have their original in the trigrams China's legendary first Emperor Fu Hsi discovered on the back of a tortoise in the twenty-ninth century BC and were used as the basis of Chinese writing. According to the *I Ching*, broken lines indicate the feminine, whereas solid lines are masculine. So the six unbroken lines of the *qian* are solidly male and represent the yang power of the capital city.

Yü-wen K'ai built the imperial palace on the second ridge and the imperial offices on the third. The Daxing-shan complex and several prominent Taoist temples were built on the fifth ridge, which was considered particularly noble. No private houses were allowed on this spur. The Daxing-shan temple was damaged by fire in AD 669 and fell into disuse. But when Wu Chao first passed it, thirty-one years earlier, nobles and gentry flocked to its courtyards. Among its halls, there was a pagoda, a sutra repository and a series of museums decorated with murals showing a history of the temples in the city.

On the other side of the Vermilion Bird Road was the Taoist temple of Yuandu, which took up much of the Chongye ward, sharing it only with another smaller Taoist temple, a Taoist convent and two family shrines. Its peach trees were famous and their blossoms were the subject of numerous T'ang poems. Along with local Taoist magicians and Buddhist priests from India who inhabited the complex, there were Zoroastrians who had fled from Persia and refugee Nestorian Christian monks from Syria.

Further up the road were wards where common people lived, along with the mansions of minor court officials, more temples and convents and shrines. Wu Chao's son, the future Emperor Chung-tsung, would also live there. When Wu Chao's husband, the Emperor Kao-tsung died, Chung-tsung turned his mansion into a temple and housed two hundred monks there to make offerings to the dead Emperor. It was called the Daxianfusi, or the Great Monastery of Offered Blessings, until it was renamed by Wu Chao when she seized the throne herself.

At the end of the Vermilion Bird Road lay the Imperial City, which, again, lay on a ridge. This meant the south gate to the Imperial City – the Zhuque Gate – was at the bottom of a slope, but the gate's size alone made it impressive. The walls surrounding the Imperial City and the Palace City beyond were thirty-four feet high. Like the Mingde Gate, the Zhuque Gate was heavily guarded and had a huge timber-framed pavilion over the gateway which was used for ceremonies because of its central position in the city. Other ceremonies took place in the tower over Danfeng Gate, which was the southern entrance to the still unfinished Ta-ming Palace. There, at nearly two hundred yards across, the road was even wider than the Vermilion Bird Road.

Before reaching the Zhuque Gate, Wu Chao crossed a bridge over a canal. Eight feet wide and ten feet deep, this canal brought water to the city from the tributaries of the Wei. Numerous other canals in the city watered the royal gardens and brought fuel and timber to the markets on barges. The canals were crossed by barrel-arched bridges and on their banks grew willows and flowers, greatly enhancing the beauty of the city.

Directly in front of the Zhuque Gate, the Vermilion Bird Road was crossed by the main lateral street that ran from the west gate of the city to the east gate and connected the West and East Markets. Excluding the ditches along either side, it was four hundred feet wide. Flanking the Zhuque seven hundred yards away in either direction were two more gates into the Imperial City.

To the west were hotels and hostelries that catered for silk merchants from Soochow and camel trains from Samarkand. Occasionally the narrow, bustling streets and alleyways opened out to reveal a landmark temple. There was also a Zoroastrian Temple there, founded in 621, and a Persian Manichean temple had moved there from another ward. To the north-west, where traders from the Silk Road entered through the Kaiyuanmen – the 'Gate Opening to the Distant Lands' – the streets were packed with more lodging houses, wine-shops, brothels, and temples for people from Central Asia. There were also extensive gardens cultivated around Han ruins, including the remains of the Han Imperial University, that had been built many centuries before.

Beyond that, to the north, was the Forbidden Park. Under the T'ang, it was primarily used for hunting with packs of dogs, or with hawks or eagles. However, there was also a zoo there, where leopards, lions, rhinoceroses and elephants, sent as tribute by foreign kings, were kept. The Forbidden Park also doubled as a botanical garden with rare plants from distant lands; eunuchs were often sent out to scour the Empire for new specimens.

To the east were an overspill of government offices, the Imperial University and a number of schools. And a little further to the north was the most fashionable residential district where top officials lived to be close to the Palace City. Even in these upmarket areas buildings were subject to strict regulations. For example, officials of the sixth grade and below could not have halls more than three spans in length or a front gate of more than one span, while officials of the third rank and above had to restrict themselves to halls of no more than five spans and gates of no more than three spans.

Passing through the gate to the Imperial City, the visitor reached the Empire's administrative centre. This again was built on a grid-iron plan with seven avenues running east and west and five running north and south. Various blocks were given over to the Ministry of Agriculture, a Department of Economic Affairs, the Capital Construction Administration, the Taxation Department and a Central Executive Department. It would be centuries before anything like this would be seen in Europe. Then there were the Imperial Stables, an Arms' Administrator, the Office of the Ancestral Temple and the Ancestral Temple itself, the Bureau of the Emperor's Horses and Carriages, the Office of the Imperial Heavenly Altar and the Imperial Heavenly Altar itself, the Department of the Palace Guard and units of the guard – divided into Right and Left guards, each subdivided into Mighty and Gallant – plus the Rites and Reception Bureau and the Sacrificial Ceremonies Bureau. The Crowned Prince also lived in the Imperial City and the Emperor came there to worship at the altars.

One day, all this administrative apparatus would fall into the hands of just one woman, Wu Chao. From here she would govern the country's thirty-nine superior prefectures. Some of these oversaw ten ordinary prefectures, while others, in remote regions, supervised just twenty thousand households. There were over three hundred and thirty prefectural seats. These lay at key points in their respective counties at intersections on the efficient system of trunk roads and waterways which allowed the power of the Emperor to be felt in every quarter of the land. Prefectures were subdivided into some sixteen thousand counties, each under the control of a magistrate. Some had more than fifty thousand people. Others had just a few thousand, but their small size generally robbed them of any political power on the national stage.

The county towns were market centres. These had good communications with the surrounding land, making it easy to collect local taxes. After the cost of local government had been deducted, the money was passed up the political chain. The prefecture and the province each took their administrative cut and the remainder was sent on to the imperial coffers.

At each level the seat of power was in a walled city or, in larger cities, a walled precinct within the city walls, designed to protect the state from rebellion. However, the provincial cities were not rebuilt in the modern grid-iron style. Many of them were hundreds of years old and had winding streets like old European cities. Nevertheless strict control of the local citizens was maintained everywhere.

In a centralized system perfected centuries before by the Han, the officials at every level were appointed by the throne and selected by examination. They owed their allegiance directly to the Emperor and the Emperor alone. Although China did have a hereditary aristocracy, noble birth did not convey political power or territorial rights, only wealth. Its power had been curbed by the first Emperor Ch'in Shih huang-ti. Higher titles were restricted to the imperial household. Lower ones were bestowed by the Emperor as a reward to ministers or generals, but they were rarely used. They lived by imperial largesse. The princes of the blood received the tax revenues of five thousand families. Fief princes, who were usually from collateral branches of the imperial household, got the revenues from three thousand families. Dukes got the revenues from one thousand or two thousand families, marquises one thousand, counts seven hundred, viscounts five hundred and barons three hundred.

The organization of government was similarly sophisticated. The First Minister was the President of the Department of State Affairs. Under him were two Vice Presidents and the ministers and deputy ministers of the six executive boards that ran the apparatus of the state. The Board of Revenue raised taxes, controlled the treasury, administered the budget, oversaw the granaries, ran censuses, registered births, deaths and marriages, and ran the land registry. The Board of Works built and maintained public buildings, monuments and military facilities, and controlled the rivers, canals and irrigation systems. The Board of War ran the army. The Board of Justice acted both as a justice department and as the judiciary. The Board of Rites controlled ceremonies, rituals and sacrifices, as well as operating as a foreign ministry – a minor concern to most Chinese Emperors, who conducted most of their foreign policy with the army. And the Board of the Civil Service ran the civil service examination and recommended hirings and firings, and promotions and demotions.

Then there was the Secretariat, which also had a President and two Vice Presidents. It prepared proclamations and edicts, recorded all acts of state and compiled the annals that were used, later, when the dynastic history was written. It was the duty of each new dynasty to write the history of the preceding one.

The third arm of the state was the Chancellery, which had two Presidents and two Vice Presidents. Its duty was to transmit imperial decrees and make sure they were carried out. The Department of State Affairs, the Secretariat and the Chancellery were the three great levers of state that Wu Chao would one day have at her disposal. Lower down the pecking order were smaller departments that ran the imperial palace, the stables, the guard, the Crown Prince's palace and other imperial institutions.

The Presidents of the Department of State, the Secretariat and the Chancellery, and sometimes ministers from the six boards, were given the title Tsai Hsiang – or First Minister – and formed an inner cabinet that ran the government. Below them were the mandarins who had such grand titles as Bearer of the Golden Seal with the Purple, or Grandee of the Radiant Emolument. They wore different-coloured robes. Ministers and mandarins were also awarded civil titles, such as duke or marquis, and given land and the tax revenue from fifty to two thousand households. They were powerful men because of the influence they could bring to bear, but it was the Emperor alone who ruled.

Alongside the government there was an independent Censorate, whose job was to criticize government policy, expose wrongdoing, report irregularities and offer advice. It comprised three courts – Palace Affairs, General Affairs and External Affairs – which dealt with complaints from the provinces and problems in the army, and followed its campaigns. Being a censor was a sensitive job, since it was an imperial appointment and the Emperor could demote or dismiss a censor at will. However, the Emperor did not have an entirely free hand. The civil service was a powerful institution. An Emperor could not function without it and there was a long tradition of government by moral persuasion as taught by the political philosopher Confucius who lived in the fifth and sixth centuries BC. His works were the basis of the examinations candidates sat to join the civil service.

Beyond the Imperial City and its administrative hub was the Palace City, known as 'the Centre', 'the Great Within' or 'the Forbidden'. On the south side abutting the Imperial City were the outer ceremonial courts with a wide gate leading to each. These were laid out with the same rigid right angles as the rest of the city. Beyond these was a marble terrace, topped by the Halls of Audience – the main one being the Taiji-dian, or the 'Hall of the Cosmic Ultimate'. This was where government ministers would have an audience with the Emperor to conduct government business. It was a grand stage where the affairs of state were played out with proper imperial pomp and ceremony.

These buildings were huge, designed to intimidate anyone summoned into the imperial presence. Massive pillars decorated with paintings or lacquer supported the high yellow-tiled roofs that curved elegantly from ridge to eaves. These jutted out far beyond the walls to provide shade from the high summer sun, while allowing the low winter light to penetrate the depths of the halls. The roof beams and ceilings were decorated with paintings and inlaid with gold leaf. However, there were other, more frivolous, buildings in the compound. One pavilion, which could seat two hundred guests, revolved.

Beyond the Halls of Audience was the huge royal courtyard, two hundred and forty yards wide and five-and-a-half li, or 1.8 miles, long. This was used for military and ritual purposes. Here the Emperor greeted foreign dignitaries, announced amnesties and conducted rituals on the Winter Solstice and the first day of the lunar year. Beyond that was the walled city of the Inner or Back Palace where the Emperor T'ai-tsung lived with his Empress, the three thousand women of his harem, the five thousand female servants at his beck and call, his eunuchs, and his younger children. Only rarely was anyone else allowed to enter. Even the Emperor's sons were moved out into their own mansions once they were old enough to be separated from their mothers. The Crown Prince lived in an adjoining residence known as the Eastern Palace. The imperial children would visit their mother and father in the palace under strict conditions and would not normally be allowed to spend the night there.

Wu Chao was bound for this secluded world where, in theory at least, no man's eyes would alight on her, except those of the Emperor and his eunuchs, who numbered no more than five thousand. Most had been sold by their parents, castrated and sent to the capital. The majority were illiterate and performed menial tasks around the palace. However, those who had an education were employed teaching the ladies of the palace.

The Inner City itself was a maze of lanes and courtyards, great halls and mansions, temples and shrines, pleasure gardens, pavilions and ponds. There Wu Chao would be housed in an apartment of sumptuously decorated rooms, though the most lavish compounds would be reserved for senior consorts. The whole place was run by rigid etiquette, policed by the *nü-shih*. Like all the other women there, Wu Chao would never leave the confines of the Back Palace while the Emperor lived. Her only contact with the seething city outside would be through the courtesans, singing girls and dancers, who performed scantily clad, often topless and sometimes naked at the Emperor's numerous drunken feasts and banquets. Even at court – in the Emperor's presence – both men and women would appear drunk and uninhibited. The Emperor's women were rarely allowed to join in these sumptuous entertainments, though they were allowed to watch from behind a screen. Apart from these entertainers, no one else was allowed to enter the palace precincts.

Palace women came in many varieties. As well as senior wives from dynastic families, there would be girls offered as tribute by the provinces, as well as those provided by foreign and vassal countries. Then there would be girls offered by prominent families, keen on securing imperial favour, and girls recruited by palace agents. They would scour the Empire for girls of exceptional beauty or abilities, even taking them from government or commercial brothels. Once in the palace they would be sorted out by the *nü-shih* and eunuchs. The best-looking were kept for the harem. Any showing artistic skills were sent to the *chiao-fang*, training centres where they were coached as the musicians, dancers, singers and acrobats needed to entertain at feasts. Along with the Chinese girls trained there, there were numerous Indian, Indochinese, Korean and Central Asian performers. The rest were assigned to tending mulberry bushes to make silk and menial tasks around the palace so that, wherever he looked, the Emperor's eye would fall on beautiful, nubile young women.

Among the Emperor's consorts there was a strict hierarchy. At the top was the Empress, who was usually from a noble house. Normally only her children could succeed. However, childless Empresses sometimes adopted the children of other consorts to secure the succession, though this practice was disapproved of. Next in rank were four imperial consorts of the first grade. Sometimes, in extremis, their sons could succeed. The Four Ladies, or *fu ren*, were known as Noble, Pure, Virtuous, and Good. Below them were nine consorts of the second grade, or *pin*, with nine different titles. Nine *jie yu*, Graces or Selects, made up the third grade. The fourth grade comprised nine Beauties, or *mei ren*; the fifth grade nine *cal ren* or Talented Ones. Beyond that there were twenty-seven *bao lin* in the sixth grade, twenty-seven *yu nu* in the seventh grade and twenty-seven *cai nu* in the eighth grade. This hierarchy was organized according to *The Rites of Chou*. These were the Ladies of the Back Palace, whom the Emperor honoured with his favours – though there were plenty more besides who held no official title but were employed for their beauty and other accomplishments. The organization of this massive female household mirrored the structure of government and had six departments including the *nü-shih*. And there was a parallel system of eunuchs.

When Wu Chao entered the palace, at least three of her cousins already graced T'ai-tsung's harem. There were two Lady Yangs, one of whom was the former Princess of Chi, widow of T'ai-tsung's younger brother Li Yuan-chi, whom he had murdered at Hsüan Wu Gate. The third, Lady Yan, bore T'ai-tsung a son, who became Prince of Yue Li Chen.

The reason for all these consorts was not to satisfy the Emperor's lusts, but to promote his health. According to the Taoists of the Green Buffalo, 'A man benefits greatly if he frequently changes the women he has sex with. It is best if he can have sex with more than ten women in a single night. If he always copulates with one woman, her vital essence will gradually grow weaker. Eventually she will be in no condition to benefit the man and she, herself, will become burnt out.' The master P'êng-Tsu concurred, saying, 'One cannot achieve one's aim of preserving health and prolonging life with just one woman. You have to make love to three, nine or eleven women a night – the more the better.'

It also produced robust heirs. Taoists maintained that a man absorbed female yin energy from a woman's saliva, nipples and vaginal secretion, while he expended his male yang energy with his semen. His aim was to absorb as much yin energy as possible from his lower-grade concubines and expend it only with his higher-grade consorts – particularly the Empress.

The Emperor would have sex with ten to twelve women a night, taking care to make them come so that he would benefit from as much of their yin energy as possible, while not coming himself. Ideally, he would come just once a month when the sun – the Emperor – slept with the moon – the Empress. That way, they would ensure that their offspring were as healthy as possible. Such restraint was not always possible, of course, and other consorts did fall pregnant. However, the system did mean that, despite all the sex that the Emperor was having, few babies were produced and the imperial family remained relatively small.

In any event, the expending of semen was discouraged. According to the seventh-century physician Li Tung Hsuan, 'A man should develop the art of holding back his ejaculation until his partner is completely satisfied. He must find out and regulate his perfect rate of ejaculation. It should be no more than two or three times in ten coitions.' Sun Ssu-mo, the most prominent physician of the T'ang dynasty, said in his *Priceless Recipe*, 'When a man squanders his semen, he will be sick and if he carelessly exhausts his semen he will die. And for a man this is the most important point to remember.' Born in AD 581, Sun Ssu-mo lived for one hundred and one years. In that time, he invented an inoculation for smallpox and discovered that tuberculosis was caused by tiny creatures eating away at the lungs. He also divided tumours into five types and developed a treatment for each. During his lifetime the Emperor gave him the title Chen-jen – Man of Wisdom – and after his death he was known as Jo Hwang – King of Medicine.

Sun Ssu-mo recommended that a man should ideally ejaculate only once every hundred times he makes love. This, he realized, was impossible for most men, but if a man could keep his ejaculations down to twice a month, with good food and exercise he could still live a long life. And he laid out a formula related to age: 'A twenty-year-old man should ejaculate once every four days. A thirty-year-old once every eight days. A forty-year-old once every ten days. A fifty-year-old once every twenty days. A sixty-year-old should not ejaculate at all unless he is particularly strong, then he can do it once a month.'

If a man is particularly strong and fit, Sun Ssu-mo continued, too much restraint can be harmful, and boils and pimples would appear if he went without ejaculating for too long. However, spiritual people should avoid emission altogether, although they should not give up sex.

'When a couple are like immortals,' he said, 'they can unite deeply, without moving so that the semen will not be disturbed. They should imagine that they had a red ball the size of a hen's egg between their navels. Then they can thrust very gently. But if they get excited, they should hold back. In one day, the couple can do this dozens of times. It will ensure a long life.'

The Tao master Liu Chang also believed that retaining the semen encouraged longevity: 'In the spring, a man should ejaculate just once in three days; in summer and autumn, twice a month. In a cold winter, a man should not ejaculate at all. The path of heaven is to retain as much yang as possible in winter. This way a man will increase his lifespan. One ejaculation in winter is a hundred times more harmful than one in springtime.'

Although ejaculation needs to be rationed, doing without sex simply is not an option. Sun Ssu-mo wrote, 'A woman cannot live happily without a man. A man cannot live long without a woman. He will crave a woman all the time and this will wear out his spirit. Of course, if he truly does not crave a woman, he may still live long, but such men are extremely rare. If a man tries to suppress his natural urge to ejaculate for long, it becomes hard to retain it. He may squander it in his sleep and when he pisses. He will dream that he is having sex with ghosts. Losing his semen this way is a hundred times more harmful.'

It was also said, 'In this world no one can completely free themselves from the Seven Feelings and Six Desires. There is no escape from the fatal circle of wine and women, and wealth and ambition ... Experience shows that of these four evils woman and wealth bring the most disaster.'

For a woman's perspective, we must turn to *The Secrets of the Jade Chamber*, a book produced under the Sui but attributed to the Yellow Emperor's sexual mentor Su-nü. It says, 'After ejaculation, a man is worn out. There is a buzzing in his ears. His eyes are heavy and he wants to go to sleep. His mouth is dry and his arms and legs are stiff and heavy. For the brief seconds of pleasure he experiences in ejaculation, he suffers long hours of weariness. However, if he learns to hold back and keep his emissions to an absolute minimum, his body retains its strength. His mind is set at ease, and his sight and hearing are improved. Although the man has denied himself the pleasure of ejaculation his love for his woman will greatly increase. He can never have enough of her. And that is a lasting pleasure.'

The book also lays out the health benefits: 'When a man makes love once without ejaculating, he strengthens his body. Twice and his sight and hearing become more acute. Three times and all his diseases will be cured. Four times, his soul will be at peace. Five times, his heart and circulation with be rejuvenated. Six times, his loins will be strengthened. Seven times, his buttocks and thighs will become stronger. Eight times, his skin will become smoother. Nine times, he will increase his life span. Ten times, he will become immortal.'

Plainly it was important for an Emperor to learn this, if he was going to join the immortals. Wu Chao herself also grew interested in immortality towards the end of her life.

Two ways for a man to stop himself ejaculating were outlined in the Sui classic *Important Guidelines of the Jade Room*: 'The minute you feel the seed moving, put the index and second finger of your left hand on your groin and press hard. At the same time, open your mouth and breathe out heavily. Then grind your teeth together thirty or fifty times. This way, the seed will drain back to their source down the jade stem.' Or: 'When trying to benefit yang from yin during sex, and you feel you are coming, quickly raise your head and open your eyes wide. Look left and right, up and down. At the same time, contract the muscles of your lower abdomen. This done, the discharge will cease.'

When the Emperor was with the Empress or one of his senior consorts, he did not have to be so careful and the master Tung Hsuan-tzu spelt out exactly what to do in that situation:

> Before intercourse, the woman should sit, then lie down to the left of the man. After resting, the man should ask the woman to lie flat on her back, open her legs wide and stretch out her arms. Then he should cover her body with his own, taking the weight on his knees which should be placed between her open thighs. He should rub his jade stem gently but unrelentingly against the outside of her jade gate, like a lone pine standing proudly at the mouth of a mountain cave. While he is rubbing her this way, he should open his mouth and suck in her tongue. He

should fondle her breasts or private parts with his hands, looking at her face or her jade gate. Once her secretions begin to flood out, he should hurl his jade stem through her gate, coming immediately so that the seed and secretions mingle. Then he should continue thrusting unmercifully until the woman begs him to spare her. At this point, he should pull his jade stem out, wipe it with a piece of silk – then put it back in again, making nine shallow thrusts, followed by one deep one. He should vary his movements – sometimes fast, sometimes slow; sometimes vigorous, sometimes gentle. After inhaling and exhaling twenty-one times, the woman will be ready to climax. The man should then push his penis into the depth of five inches, stabbing quickly and rubbing both sides of her flowery path. She will get very wet and feel satisfied. Then he should pull out his jade stem before he comes a second time. Should he come a second time, it will be bad for his health and he must be very careful not to.

However, one must go about these things with due caution and respect for the laws of heaven and earth.

'The heavens turn to the left; the earth to the right,' Tung Hsuan-tzu said. 'Man sings; woman echoes. This is the law of nature. If a man stirs and a woman does not respond, or a woman initiates and a man refuses, both will be harmed. So the man must turn to the left and the woman to the right. He descends from above; she receives from below. This is the union of heaven and earth.'

CHAPTER FOUR
THE ART OF THE BEDROOM

To help the Emperor with the mammoth sexual task that befell him every night, the *nü-shih* instructed him on the sexual requirements of the women who were brought to his bed. This knowledge was sometimes gained first-hand, since casual lesbianism was common in the harem, where it was known as 'mirror-rubbing' – the idea was that when two women rubbed their vulvas together it looked like each was mating with its mirror image. While male homosexuality was looked down on in Chinese culture, mirror-rubbing was not, since it did not involve the loss of any yin energy. In fact, a woman who had been brought to orgasm this way would have more yin to pass on. Chinese dildos, made from leather and attached to the heel, were also in common use in the harem. While male masturbation was seen as harmful, women's masturbation was encouraged.

To pique the Emperor's interest when he had no immediate prospect of the full measure of pleasure, the women chosen for his harem had to be both beautiful and adept. They were also trained for the task. Although Wu Chao was, at most, thirteen when she entered the imperial harem, she was made a junior concubine fifth class, a *cai ren* or Talented One. Her duties outside the bedroom were to look after the Emperor's wardrobe, but she would also be trained in the ways of the bedchamber. As part of her training she would be given lavishly illustrated books showing the various sexual positions and other ways to stimulate a man.

One famous book was based on the T'ang poem 'Spring Reigns in All the Thirty-Six Palaces', which was later illustrated by the famous Mongol painter Chao Meng-fu. It contained thirty-six pictures of a couple naked in various positions and in one rare edition these were accompanied by captions explaining the scene represented and its merits.

The first picture was called 'The butterfly flutters about, searching for flowery scents'. Its caption read, 'She sits waiting with parted legs on a rock by the shore of a garden pond. He, first carefully feeling out the terrain, takes pain to insert his nephrite proboscis into the depths of her calyx. Because the battle has only begun and the region of bliss is still far off, both still show a relatively normal expression, their eyes are wide open.'

The second picture showed 'The queen bee making honey'. The caption read, 'She lies on her back, cushioned in pillows, her parted legs raised as though hanging in mid-air, her hands pressed against 'the fruit', guiding his nephrite proboscis to the entrance of her calyx, helping it to find the right path and not to stray. At this moment her face shows an expression of hunger and thirst, while his features reveal the most intense excitement, with which the viewer becomes infected. All this is brought out by the artist with remarkable subtlety.'

The third picture was 'The little bird that had gone astray finds its way back to its nest in the thicket'. The caption read, 'She lies slightly to one side, dug into the thicket of cushions, one leg stretched high, and clutches his thigh with both hands as though his obedient vassal had finally found its way to the right place, her most sensitive spot, and she feared it might go off and get lost again. This accounts for the shadow of anxiety on her otherwise happy face. Both parties are in full swing, quite preoccupied by the spasmodic thrill of the "flying brush" and the "dancing ink".'

The fourth picture showed 'The hungry steed galloping to the feed crib'. The caption read, 'She, flat on her back, presses his body to her breast with both hands. Her feet propped up on his shoulders, he has sunk his yak whisk into her calyx to the shaft. Both of them are approaching ecstasy. The way in which the artist pictures their physical and mental state at this moment, their eyes veiled beneath half-closed lids, their tongues enlaced, reveals the master of the brush.'

The fifth picture showed the position called 'Two Dragons Tired of Flight'. And the caption read, 'The woman's head rests on the pillow. Her arms lie by her side, limp like a string of silk. The man is resting his head on the side of the woman's neck, his entire body limp, as numb as cotton. After the orgasm, their souls seem to have left their bodies and now they are on their way to beautiful dreams. After the violent passion they have come to rest. The barest thread of life is discernible. If the artist had not added this subtle touch, the couple would seem to be dead, two lovers in one coffin and one grave. The picture brings home to us the sublimity of bliss savoured to the very end.'

And so on.

These books were sometimes taken into the bedroom, as a somewhat later text explained:

> You should look at spring [erotic] pictures before you start to act, while both parties are fully dressed. While still treating each other as host and guest, look at one picture, for when discussing its finer points the feelings will naturally be aroused, and before any action has been taken the male member will have raised itself, and the fluid of desire will have started to flow. But one should ignore these things, and wait instead until after you have seen more than ten, and absolutely prohibit doing anything even then, but wait for one to be fully aroused, for only then does one feel the full power of the spring palace.

Further instruction could be gleaned from the 'Joyful Buddhas' in the palace, which were probably Mongol in origin. These were pairs of richly adorned Buddhas who embrace each other with their genitals linked. Some had movable sexual organs, plainly visible, and were used in sex education. When a prince got married, the couple were first led to the hall. After they had knelt and worshipped, both the bride and groom must feel the genitals of the statues with their fingers, so that they learnt, without words, about sexual intercourse. Only after this ceremony were they allowed to drink the wedding cup.

The new girls in the palace would be taught the four basic positions for making love outlined by seventh-century Chinese physician Li T'ung Hsuan. They were:

1. Close union – man on top.
2. Unicorn horn – woman on top.
3. Intimate attachment – side by side.
4. Sunning fish – rear entry.

He then detailed the twenty-four variations on these basic positions, each of which has a poetic name, some of which defy translation. The variations on the 'close union' are:

1. Silkworm spinning a cocoon – The woman wraps her legs around the man's body and clasps his neck with her hands.
2. Turning dragon – With his left hand, the man holds the woman's feet up above her breasts. With his right hand, he guides his jade stem into her jade gate.
3. Loving swallows – The man lies flat on the woman's belly. She holds his waist. He holds her neck.
4. United kingfishers – With the woman on her back, the man kneels between her legs and supports her waist with his hands.
5. Dwarf pine tree – The woman crosses her legs around the man and they hold on to each other's waist.
6. Dance of the two phoenixes.
7. Phoenix holding her chicken.
8. Flying seagulls – The man stands beside the bed, holding the woman's legs while he enters her.
9. Leaping wild horses – The woman rests her feet on the man's shoulders while he penetrates her deeply.
10. Galloping steed – The man squats with one hand supporting the woman's neck, the other supporting her feet.
11. Horse's hooves – The woman puts one of her feet on the man's shoulder, letting the other dangle.
12. A giant bird soaring over a dark sea – The man holds the woman's waist and supports her legs on his upper arm.

The variations on the 'unicorn horn' are:

1. A pair of flying ducks – The woman turns around so that she is facing the man's feet.
2. A singing monkey holding a tree – The man sits up with the woman on his lap, facing him. She holds him while he supports her buttocks with one hand. He supports himself with the other.

3. Cat and mice share a hole – The woman lies flat on top of the man, giving deep penetration.
4. Flying butterflies.

The 'dance of the two phoenixes' can also be performed with the woman on top, apparently. A variation on 'intimate attachment' is:

Two fishes side by side – The man and woman lie face to face and kiss, while the man uses one hand to support the woman's feet.

And the variations on the 'sunning fish' are:

1. Mandarin ducks entwined – The couple lie on one side with the woman facing away from the man. She curls her legs so that he can enter her from the rear.
2. Flying white tiger – The woman kneels on the bed with her face on the pillow. The man kneels behind her and pulls her on to him by holding her waist.
3. Dark cicada clings to a branch – The woman lies flat on the bed with her legs spread. The man holds her shoulders.
4. Goat facing a tree – The man sits in a chair. The woman sits on his lap with her back towards him.
5. Late spring donkey – The standing woman bends over and supports herself on her hands. The man stands behind her and holds her waist.

Despite this detailed analysis, Li T'ung Hsuan admitted that there are two other positions that do not really count as variations on the basic four:

1. Bamboos near the altar – The man and woman stand face to face.
2. Autumn dog – The woman and man kneel on all fours, pressing their buttocks against each other's. The man bobs down, takes his jade stem with one hand, bends it backwards and inserts into her jade gate.

Then there were the three peaks, the four attainments, the five desires and the nine essences – the secrets of love play – to be learned about, along with playing the jade flute and drinking at the jade fountain.

The Emperor had to do his part too. Su-nü said that to sustain an erection throughout a long night there were seven things a man must do:

1. His five organs must be kept in good order.
2. He must learn to feel the woman's nine erogenous zones.
3. He must appreciate the woman's five beautiful qualities.
4. He must learn to arouse her so that he can drink in her yin essence.
5. He must drink in her saliva so that his semen and her breath are in harmony.
6. He must elude the seven injuries.
7. He must perform the eight worthwhile deeds.

And, like the palace women, the Emperor would have to be trained according to the principles laid out in the Han sex manual *The Art of the Bedchamber*.

> The principle of the art of the bedchamber is very simple, yet few use it. A man must have sex with ten different women at night without emitting a single drop of semen. This is the essence of the art of the bedchamber ... A man must not engage in sexual intercourse merely to satisfy his lust. He must try to regulate his sexual desire and thus nurture his vital essence. He must not force himself to extravagant action during sex, giving free rein to his passion, just to enjoy carnal pleasure. Instead, he must think of how the sexual act will benefit his health and keep him free from disease. This is the subtle secret of the art of the bedchamber.

Learning these things was important, not just for sexual satisfaction, but because they were a religious duty. Taoists believed that love and the whole of life were about the balance of the yang – or male essence – and the yin or female essence. As the compiler of the Han book *The Art of the Bedchamber* wrote,

> The art of the bedchamber forms the pinnacle of human emotions, encompassing the Tao [or Supreme Way]. The ancient rulers regulated man's outer pleasures to control his inner passions and made detailed rules for sexual intercourse. It is written: 'Sexual pleasure was created by the ancients to govern all human affairs.' If you control your sexual pleasure, you will be at peace and live to a great age. But if you abandon yourself to pleasure, disregarding the rules as laid out here, you will become sick and endanger your life ... If the yin and yang are balanced, the souls find a place where they can merge. The yang spirit is the soul of the sun; the yin spirit is the soul of the moon. When the sun and the moon come

together, they form a house. Man's nature is governed internally and makes a shape. Man's passion is governed from without and forms the walls of the house. Once these walls have been established, the two people can safely go ahead. Passion unites the *ch'ien* and the *k'un*. The *ch'ien* moves and is strong, his vital essence spreads out and his semen is stirred. The *k'un* remains still and harmonious. She is a haven for Tao. When the hard has shed its essence, the soft dissolves in moisture. Nine times returning, seven times resuming, eight times coming back, six times staying. The man is white, the woman is red. When the metal has mixed with the fire, the fire is extinguished by the water.

Once the young women of the palace were well versed in these matters, they were encouraged to take the initiative in the bedchamber and to be inventive in their love-play. Su-nü, sexual adviser to the Yellow Emperor, was said to have written, 'All men's illness can be attributed to the incorrect exercise of the sexual act. Woman is superior to man in the way water is to fire. Those who are expert in sexual intercourse are like good cooks who know how to blend the five flavours into tasty broth. Those who know the art of yin and yang can blend the five pleasures. Those who do not will die an untimely death, without really having tasted the pleasure of the sexual act.'

Being literate, Wu Chao would have also been able to give herself a sentimental education by studying the erotic poetry and books that abounded in medieval Chinese literature. These works express the beauty and poignancy of erotic love. In his essay 'On a Beautiful Woman' the Han-dynasty writer Szu Hsaing-ju described this lovely girl in her room, reclining on a couch, like a strange flower of unsurpassed elegance. And while she waited, longing for a lover, she sang,

> By myself in the bedroom, it seems unbearably lonely.
> Dreaming of a handsome man, my feelings hurt me.
> Why does the delightful stranger delay his arrival?
> Time is fast running out, this flower will wither –
> I would entrust my body to him, for eternal love.

She was in luck. A handsome stranger did arrive. She poured a drink for him, and while he drank it she sang another song, accompanying herself on the lute. Then:

She stuck one of her hairpins under his cap and her long silk sleeve brushed over his robe. The sun was setting and the room filled with shadows. A cold breeze blew outside and snow flakes started falling. But inside the bedroom you could not hear a single sound. Then she prepared the bed with luxurious bedding, even scenting the quilt with a bronze incense burner. With the mattresses, quilts and pillows prepared, she let down the curtains that surrounded the bed. She took off her robe and her undergarments, revealing a white body with thin bones and soft flesh. When they made love, her body was as soft and moist as ointment.

As well as reading erotic books, Wu Chao would have received some more practical instruction involving the Emperor himself. T'ai-tsung liked the ladies of the Back Palace to bathe naked with him in the palace ponds. This would take place, according to T'ang custom, on the tenth, twentieth and final day of each lunar month – that is, once every week, since the Chinese week had ten days. Beyond the needs of hygiene, T'ai-tsung's bathtime frolics plainly had erotic purposes. The Chinese – particularly northerners like the T'ang – disapproved of the communal bathing, with men and women together, that was practised in Cambodia and Korea.

When Wu Chao began menstruating, the *nü-shih* would note this down as the beginning of the 'red flood' or the 'peach-flower fluid'. Then she would be considered ready for sex and would wait her turn to be summoned to the imperial bedchamber. When the day came, the *nü-shih* would give her a silver ring to put on her right hand. T'ai-tsung was afraid of assassination – not unreasonably, since he had killed two of his brothers to take the throne – and he felt particularly vulnerable at night alone with a lover. So stringent security measures were enforced. When Wu Chao was summoned to serve the Emperor on the dragon bed, she would be stripped naked and checked for concealed weapons. Then she would be wrapped in silk and carried to the imperial presence over the shoulder of a eunuch.

Wu Chao may not have been entirely naked. Some jewellery was probably allowed. Chinese woman often wore bracelets around the ankles with tiny bells on them which tinkled during love-making. They also adopted the Burmese habit of putting small bells inside the vagina to increase their pleasure. These were said to contain the semen of a mythical bird called the P'eng, which was extremely lascivious and liked to have sex with Burmese women. The aborigines there made straw puppets and dressed them in women's clothing to collect the sperm, which they dried and rolled into a small pellet. If this pellet was inserted in a man's urethra, it would greatly increase his potency. Otherwise, the pellet was enclosed in a gold ball and inserted in the vagina.

We can only guess at what making love to the Emperor after such an intense build-up would have been like for Wu Chao. How would it compare with the literature she had read? Around AD 100 the Chinese poet Chang Heng wrote a poem about the joys of the first encounter:

> Let us now lock the door with its lock of gold
> And light the lamp to fill the bedroom with illumination.
> I will take off my clothes and my make-up
> And roll out the book by my pillow.
> Let the Plain Girl be my teacher.
> We will practise all the various positions
> That ordinary husbands rarely see,
> Like those taught to the Yellow Emperor by T'ion-lao
> No pleasure shall rival those of this first night.
> We will never forget them, no matter how old we grow.

While they made love, Wu Chao and the Emperor would not be alone. There might be other women there to assist or observe. Sometimes two naked handmaidens would be employed to stimulate both parties before the act itself. And the *nü-shih* would be there to make notes. She would make a detailed record of what occurred, right down to the number of thrusts the Emperor made with his penis. This information would be used to provide more detailed sex tips for the couple to improve their sexual compatibility.

The notes taken by the *nü-shih* were written up as sex manuals for the Emperor to study. These began in the Han dynasty but had their greatest flowering under the Sui, who produced many of the Chinese sexual classics. Su-nü was the supposed author another Sui sex manual called *The Plain Girl's Secret Way* which Mao Tse-tung used to give to his myriad lovers. It outlined the Taoist way of sex, in which the man must retain his masculine yang essence by controlling his ejaculation. At the same time, he must drink in as much of the female yin essence as possible. This he can get from the woman's lips, her breasts and her vaginal secretion. To obtain the greatest advantage from these he must give the woman full satisfaction. To do that, the Emperor was told, the man must put aside his own needs desires and concentrate all his attention on the woman. According to *The Plain Girl's Secret Way*, the signs he must look for in his partner begin with a flushed face and hot ears, which show that teasing shallow penetration can begin. Then sweat on the nose and hard nipples show he can now enter to the depth of five inches. Next, her voice becomes lowered and hoarse, and she begins to pant. Here full penetration is recommended. After this, her vulva will be richly lubricated and each thrust will cause the juices to overflow. The man should now withdraw to the 'Valley of the Water-Chestnut Teeth' at a depth of about two inches, and begin to vary the timing and direction of his thrusting. When the woman wraps her legs tightly around the man and clutches his shoulders and back, he can thrust deeply into the 'Valley of the Deep Chamber' to give her ecstasy.

There are another ten indicators that Su-nü says the man must look for:

1. Her hand holds his back. The lower part of her body is moving. She licks him. This indicates that she is aroused.
2. Her delicate body is supine. Her limbs lie straight and still, but she is breathing heavily through the nose. This indicates that he should resume his thrusting.
3. She plays with the sleeping man's jade hammer with her hands. This indicates that she wants him.
4. Her eyes flicker. Her throat makes guttural sounds or she whispers terms of endearment. This means she is greatly aroused.
5. She holds her feet and opens her jade gate widely. She is enjoying him greatly.
6. Her tongue hangs out as if she is half-drunk or half-asleep. This means her vulva is ready for a succession of shallow and deep thrusts at great frequency.
7. She stretches out her feet and toes and tries to hold his jade hammer inside her, though she does not know which way she wants him to thrust. Meanwhile, she murmurs in a low voice. The tide of yin is about to come.

8. Although she has come, she turns her waist, sweats slightly and smiles. This means that she is not ready for him to ejaculate because she wants more.
9. The tide of yin has arrived, but she still holds on tightly. This means that her satisfaction is not yet complete.
10. Her body is hot and wet with sweat. Her limbs are relaxed. She is now thoroughly satisfied.

Another female adviser, Lady Purity, told the Yellow Emperor,

> When a woman's face flushes, approach her gently. When her nose sweats and her breasts swell, enter her slowly. When her voice is husky and she swallows her saliva, shake your jade stem gently. When she gets wet inside, push your jade stem in as deeply as it will go. When her fluids overflow and run down her backside, guide them back to her jade gate.

The man must constantly monitor the woman's response:

> When the woman is ready, she gets short of breath and inhales hard. When she wants it, her mouth opens and the nostrils flare. When she wants more, she flings her arms around you. When she is within sight of contentment, she sweats all over. When she reaches contentment, her body stretches and her eyes become fixed.

Su-nü believed that the depth of the thrust was all-important, and she divided the vagina into eight valleys: the Lute String Valley, the Water-Chestnut Teeth Valley, the Little Stream Valley, the Black Pearl Valley, the Valley Proper, the Deep Chamber, the Inner Door and the North Pole, at depths of one to eight inches, respectively.

Her formula for successful intercourse was simple:

> A man must notice what the woman's needs are and at the same time retain his precious semen. He should rub his hands together to make them warm and grip the jade stem firmly. Then he should use the method of 'shallow draw' and 'deep thrust'. The longer he does this, the more the couple will become aroused. The pace must be neither too fast, nor too slow. Nor should he thrust too deeply in case he injures the woman. First try several thrusts to the Lute String Valley, then strike energetically at the Water-Chestnut Teeth. When the woman nears orgasm she will unconsciously clench her teeth. She will sweat and begin to pant. She will close

her eyes and her face will flush. Her jade gate will open widely and her essence will flood out. The man can then see that she is enjoying it very much.

So there was plenty for the Emperor to think about.

The fact that Wu Chao was so much younger than T'ai-tsung would not have mattered to Su-nü. She recommended relationships of unequal ages:

If an old man and an old woman mate, even if they do manage to have a child, it will not live long. But if a man of eighty makes love to a girl of eighteen, or even fifteen, they will have children that will live long. And a woman of fifty can often still have a child, if she had sex with a young man.

There were plenty of sources of advice for the Emperor too. Wu Hsien, a Tao master writing during the Han dynasty, taught that this control did not come easily and that men must spend their time learning it. He spelt out the principles:

One must love one's partner to get the greatest pleasure. However, when practising ejaculation control, you must try to fain indifference ... The novice should thrust slowly and gently, first in one set of thrusts, then two and three. Between sets, he should stop and compose himself, before resuming again ... He must be kind and gentle with his partner to help her orgasm quickly. If he feels he is about to lose control, he should withdraw so that only the tip of his penis is inside the jade gate.

Wu Hsien also gave detailed practical advice on how this could be achieved:

1. A beginner should avoid getting too excited or too passionate.
2. He should start with a woman who is not very attractive and whose jade gate is fairly loose. That way it is easier for him to learn to control himself. If she is not very beautiful, he will not lose his head. And if her vagina is not too tight, he will not find it too stimulating.
3. The beginner should aim to go in soft and come out hard.
4. He should try to give three shallow thrusts, followed by one deep. This should be repeated eighty-one times.

5. If he becomes too excited, he should withdraw his penis until there is only one inch of it inside the woman. He should wait there until this has calmed down, then resume his three shallow thrusts, followed by one deep.
6. Then he should try five shallow thrusts, followed by one deep.
7. Eventually, he should work up to nine shallow thrusts, followed by one deep.
8. A great deal of patience is required to learn ejaculation control.

Li T'ung Hsuan spelt out the six styles of penile thrust. These included moving the jade stalk to and fro over the lute strings like a saw, as if prising open an oyster in the hope of finding a pearl; hitting the golden gully as if cleaving a stone to find its jade kernel; hitting the jewel terrace, like a pestle against a mortar; moving in and out, left and right, like a hammer shaping iron; milling around the sacred field and deep vale, like a farmer hoeing his field in autumn; and letting the two peaks inhabited by the gods rub against each other until the two mighty mountains crumble into one.

Then nine styles of movement: striking out to the left and right like a soldier trying to break through the enemy; rearing up and down like a wild horse crossing a swift river; moving outwards and inwards like seagulls swooping among the waves; using shallow teasing thrusts, followed by deep ones, like a bird pecking leftover rice from a pot; making shallow strokes, then deeper ones, like a rock sinking in deep water; pushing slowly, like a snake slithering into its burrow to hibernate; thrusting quickly like a scared rat running into a hole; circling high, then swooping, like an eagle catching a hare; and rising high, then plunging, like a ship in a gale.

Li T'ung Hsuan said the best stratagem was to use a combination of these thrusts: 'Shallow and deep, fast and slow, straight and slanting. Each has its own special effect. A slow stroke should have the jerky movement of a carp on a hook. A fast stroke should have the movement of a flock of birds flying against the wind. Up and down, in and out, left and right, slowly or in rapid succession, these movements should be choreographed. At each moment one should use the movement most appropriate, rather than stubbornly stick to one style.'

There were other games to be learnt, such as 'Throwing Feathers through the Arch', 'Flying Arrows with a Living Target', 'Carrying Fire over the Mountains' and 'Striking the Silver Swan with a Golden Ball'.

The practice of using three deep thrusts to one shallow, followed by five deep thrusts to one shallow, followed by seven and then nine, was recommended in the *Yellow Book*, the sex manual of the Yellow Turbans, a rebel group that sprang up during the fall of the Han dynasty. It says, 'When the dragon and tiger play together according to the rules of the 3–5–7–9 strokes, the heavenly and the earthly unite. Open the red gate, insert the jade stalk. The yang will imagine the mother of yin white like jade, the yin will imagine the father of yang fondling and encouraging her with his hands.'

And the Taoist Chen Luan wrote in AD 570, 'When I was twenty, I was fond of Taoist studies and enrolled in a Taoist monastery. We were taught sexual intercourse by the *Yellow Book* and to practise the 3–5–7–9. In pairs of "four eyes and two tongues" we practised Tao in the cinnabar field [the body below the navel]. We were taught that this was the way to overcome obstacles and prolong life. Husbands and wives exchanged carnal pleasure. They were not ashamed to do these things even under the eyes of their fathers and elder brothers. They called this "the true art of obtaining vital essence".'

Kissing was all important, since it was a way to drink in the yin essence. In his discourse 'The Libation of the Twin Peaks' the master Wu Hsien ranked the various types of kisses:

The 'Red Lotus Peak' – on the lips – is the highest kiss. The 'Jade Spring' gushes from two holes under the woman's tongue. The libation floods out when the man licks it with his own tongue. It is transparent and is very good for the man.

The 'Twin Peaks' – on the breasts – is the next highest kiss. 'White Snow' comes from the woman's nipples. It is sweet to taste and white in colour. Although it is good for the man, it helps the woman even more. It strengthens her circulation and regulates her menstruation, relaxing her body and putting her at ease. It also helps produce more libation in her 'Flowery Pool', or mouth, and 'Dark Gate', or vagina. Of the three libations, 'White Snow' is the best. If a woman has not borne a child and her breasts give no milk, the effect is even better.

The 'Purple Mushroom Peak' is the lowest of the three peaks. It is also known as the 'White Tiger's Cave' or the 'Dark Gate'. The lubricating libation which comes from it is called 'Moon Flower'. It is when a woman is excited to the point where her face is red and she starts murmuring does the libation flood out.

Mastering the art of the bedchamber was especially important at T'ai-tsung's age. It was said, 'Until a man reaches his fortieth year he is full of fiery passion. But when he has passed forty he will notice his potency decreasing. Then diseases will swoop on him like a swarm of bees. If this is allowed to continue, he will find himself beyond cure. So at forty a man must learn the art of the bedchamber.'

As using these the techniques of the art of the bedchamber robbed women of the yin essence without giving any yang in return, it was vital that the ladies of harem were not let into these secrets. The sixth-century Tao master Chung Ho Tzu wrote, 'A man must not let the woman know about his technique if he wishes to nurture his yang essence. If the woman finds out, the technique would not only be useless, but quite harmful. It would be like giving your enemy your most deadly weapon.'

Su-nü also acknowledged the danger: 'When facing the enemy, a man should consider her rock or slate, while his essence is precious like gold or jade. If he feels in danger of losing his semen, he must withdraw immediately. Sex with a woman is like galloping on a horse with reins that are rotten, or walking along the edge of a pit filled with sharp spikes. But a man who has learned to treasure his semen is quite safe with a woman.'

As we shall see, the Emperor's semen was not safe with Wu Chao. She learned the art of the bedchamber and used it as a weapon to deadly effect throughout her life.

After Wu Chao's first sexual encounter with the Emperor, the silver ring would be moved from her right hand to her left and the details of the copulation would be entered in the records, along with the day and hour of the union. If the Emperor could not restrain himself and came, and the girl fell pregnant, she would be given a gold ring to replace the silver one. With so many women passing through the Emperor's bedchamber, it was difficult to keep track of their identities. Later every woman who had sex with the Emperor got a stamp on her arms which read, 'Wind and moon' – that is, sexual dalliance – 'is forever new.' A cinnamon oil was used to make this stamp indelible and no one in the harem could claim to have slept with the Emperor unless they had this stamp.

Though Wu Chao entered the palace in a lowly position, there were opportunities for advancement. The harem was a hotbed of intrigue, every one using their beauty and their womanly wiles to attract the favours of the Emperor. And relations between the palace women were not without jealousy, as demonstrated when Emperor T'ai-tsung endowed two palace women on one of his Chief Ministers, Fang Hsuan-ling, the Duke of Liang. The Duke's wife, Madame Liu, was a jealous woman and burned the hair of the two women's heads. So T'ai-tsung sent Madame Liu a gold pitcher full of ale with note that read, 'Drink this and you will die immediately. Your husband is an official of the third grade, so it is fitting that he has concubines. If you continue to be jealous, drink this. But if you cease being jealous, do not.' As it was, Madame Liu decided to drink it, but survived. The pitcher did not contain poison, just vinegar. 'Drinking vinegar' is a Chinese expression for being jealous. Afterwards T'ai-tsung provided the two palace women with a separate residence where Fang Hsuan-ling could visit them and they would be safe from the predations of Madame Liu.

Naturally, the palace ladies had a great deal of time to spend on their appearance and they paid particular attention to the condition of their skin. Face creams were made from chicken's eggs steeped in ale and sealed in a pot for twenty-eight days or from boiled apricot pips, pulverized and fried with sesame seed, then mixed with powdered hemp seed to make the skin glow creamy white. Bat brains were applied to remove black heads and women smeared the blood of a black-boned, silky bird on their face and bodies on the seventh day of the seventh lunar month to smooth their skin. Other concoctions were taken internally. Peach blossom mixed with white melon seeds and pulverized dried tangerine peel, then strained through a sieve and mixed with ale, was taken three times a day to improve the complexion and slim the waistline.

T'ang poets praised the 'lead face' or 'lead flower' look. Ceruse, or lead oxide, was applied to the face and breasts to whiten the skin. Cloves were added to make the powder smell nice. Safflower, vermilion or crushed lac insects from Vietnam or Cambodia were used as a rouge. This was brushed on the cheeks, directly under the eyes. Cinnabar, or mercuric sulphide, was applied to the lips to redden then. And massicot – another form of lead oxide – was used to colour the forehead yellow, since the T'ang believed a yellow aura around the forehead was auspicious. Eyebrows were plucked and redrawn, often in the shape of an insect's wing, with cobalt. Make-up was applied in front of burnished bronze mirrors, which were decorated on the back with mythical beasts, the constellations, patterns or occult symbols. Palace women drenched themselves in perfume and the imperial cortège could be smelt for miles. They ate herbs so that their bodies exuded sweet smells and hung bags of herbs under their armpits to take away their body odour, which was considered barbarian. One courtesan was said to smell so sweet that bees and butterflies pursued her in the streets. Any hint of bad breath was dealt with by chewing cloves or olives. Palace women also spent a great deal of time on their hair, coiling it into elaborate shapes, binding it with ribbons and decorating it with ornaments and combs made of gold, silver, rhinoceros horn, ivory and jade. They wore as many as twelve combs to keep their hair in place.

But there were other things to do in the harem apart from beautify yourself, study the arts of the bedchamber and wait to attract the attention of the Emperor. For unversed young women, the harem could be a university. Eunuchs were employed to teach the palace women music, Taoist philosophy, the Confucian classics, poetry, mathematics, history, calligraphy, law and board games, such as *weiqi*, now known by the Japanese name 'go', or the Confucian game of pitch pot, played to the accompaniment of zither music. From what we know of Wu Chao's later life, she took full advantage of these educational opportunities.

Wu Chao was close to T'ai-tsung. She was, after all, in a position to offer the Emperor advice on breaking a horse. She was plainly a favourite, though generally T'ai-tsung favoured soft and feminine women. Certainly he was delighted by her looks and called her 'Beauty Wu'. But her brutal attitude may have frightened him, for she never progressed beyond the fifth grade. Generally, he liked delicate, light-skinned women who were frivolous and entertaining. A poet from the Ming dynasty perfectly explained his preferences:

I think you are totally adorable
Your skirt reveals your thighs
Stirring painful passion in me
I think your waist is like a willow tree
Your smell is like an orchid
Your face its flower

Another poet, Shen Mao-hseuh, took these ideas of female beauty into the bedroom:

Shrouded by the lace bed curtains,
She is beautiful and shapely in the nude.
The heart of the flower is ruby red,
Almost as red as rouge.
So fragrant, she melts like the snow.
'You reckless devil, do not crush
The flowers in my hair.'
She fondly blames my growing vigour.

Though able and clear-headed, Wu Chao had a flat, squarish face with a broad forehead and, in character, was altogether rather too formidable in character to rise to prominence among T'ai-tsung's mistresses.

CHAPTER FIVE

THE DEW OF HEAVEN

T'AI-TSUNG'S EMPRESS WEN-TE was a member of the Chang-sun family, which was descended from the imperial house of the Wei dynasty. She had given him three sons and three daughters. One of them, the Princess Jinyang, was T'ai-tsung's favourite and she would accompany him as far as the Chienhua Gate when he went to attend court. But she died when she was twelve. After her death, T'ai-tsung wept copiously and starved himself for a month.

T'ai-tsung had eleven other sons with senior consorts, but only the three by Wen-te were strictly eligible to succeed. The eldest, Crown Prince Li Cheng-chien, was intelligent and competent and was allowed to take care of routine business when his father was out of the capital. But as he grew older he began to hang out with actors and boys. Worse. He rejected his Chinese heritage, dressed in Turkish clothes, surrounded himself with Tartars and spoke Turkish. He lived in a tent in the palace, surrounded by banners emblazoned with the wolf's head – a Turkish emblem – and roasted sheep whole. Expressing a wish to live free on the Mongolian steppes, he enacted a right called the 'Funeral of the Khan'. He would lie on the ground pretending to be dead while his entourage rode around him, howling in lamentation. He was also lame, through illness or injury, and consequently considered unsuitable for high office. Despite having an expensive education lavished on him, the best tutors in China could not turn him into an Emperor-in-waiting.

Wen-te's second son Li T'ai, Prince of Wei, was a much better bet. He was a serious scholar, an accomplished writer and handsome with it. However, it is thought that Li T'ai might not have been the son of the Empress, but rather the son of one of T'ai-tsung's concubines, which should have ruled him out of the succession. Whatever the case, T'ai-tsung had privately decided to make Li T'ai his heir, and gave him a greater allowance than the Crown Prince. In the normal course of events, he should have been given a governor-generalship and sent out to the provinces. Instead he was kept in Ch'ang-an and was moved into apartments close to the throne room. This, predictably, caused a feud between the two brothers and T'ai-tsung feared that one of them might take matters into their own hands as he had, himself, at the Hsüan Wu Gate.

Things came to a head when T'ai-tsung executed Li Cheng-chien's lover, a handsome thirteen-year-old singing boy called Ch'eng Hsin, whose name means 'As Your Heart Wishes'. Li Cheng-chien fell ill with grief. He had a statue of the boy installed in one of his halls and made libations to it as an act of mourning. Li Cheng-chien suspected that it was Li T'ai who had told their father of the homosexual relationship. Supported by T'ai-tsung's own brother, the Prince of Han, a drunken libertine whose backing was secured by the promise of all the girl and boy musicians in the palace, Li Cheng-chien took a leaf out of his father's book. He planned to murder Li T'ai, depose his father and seize the throne. But before he could act, the plan was discovered when another son, Li Yu, Prince of Ch'I, rebelled. Li Cheng-chien was stripped of his titles and banished to a remote town in southern Szechwan province, where he died the following year. The Prince of Han was ordered to kill himself, and Li Cheng-chien's other followers were beheaded, though, in a rare display of leniency for the times, their wives and families were spared.

The succession was now open to Li T'ai. However, his elevation was opposed by T'ai-tsung's most trusted advisor Chang-sun Wu-chi, who was the brother of the late Empress Wen-te. He was also the first of the Twenty-Four Founding Knights who were commemorated in a painting on the palace's Lingyen Tower by the court painter and minister Yan Li-ben. This mural depicted those who had fought to establish the T'ang dynasty, including those who had helped T'ai-tsung seize power at the Hsüan Wu Gate. Chang-sun Wu-chi had been one of the conspirators.

Chang-sun Wu-chi proposed that, instead of Li T'ai, T'ai-tsung's third son Li Chih, Prince of Chin, should succeed. It was said that Li T'ai was not the son of Wen-te, so if he became Emperor the influence of the Chang-sun family would be diminished. More likely he was too learned and mature to be controlled by Chang-sun Wu-chi – he was already the editor-in-chief of five hundred scrolls of geographical records. The matter was resolved when it came to light that Li T'ai had been intimidating Li Chih on the grounds he had been close to his disgraced uncle, the Prince of Han, in the hope of winning the succession. Such a display of imperial ambition while the current incumbent was still alive was considered tantamount to treason.

'Whoever covets a post is unworthy to occupy it,' ruled T'ai-tsung

Li T'ai was degraded to the lower ranks of princes and banished. He died in exile two years later.

The incident left T'ai-tsung distraught. He felt he had now been betrayed by two of his sons and a brother. Reminded, again, of the fratricide that brought him to power, T'ai-tsung became so agitated that he grabbed a sword from his rack on the wall and threatened to kill himself, but he was restrained by his counsellor Ch'ü Sui-liang, a famous calligrapher whose work is admired to this day.

It was urgent that the succession be settled, so Li Chih was made Crown Prince and an edict was issued saying that anyone who raised the question of the succession again would be summarily put to death. However, T'ai-tsung himself had his doubts about Li Chih, believing him to be nervous, timid and none too bright. He suggested replacing him with another of his sons, Li K'o, Prince of Wu, whose mother was the daughter of the Sui Emperor Yang-ti. However, as Li K'o was not of the Chang-sun family, Chang-sun Wu-chi opposed the change. Instead he persuaded T'ai-tsung that Li Chih might be able to rule effectively if he had the right wife. They picked the daughter of one of his officials, whose family had intermarried with the imperial house. From the same prefecture as Wu Chao, the future Empress Wang was famed for her virtue. Her great aunt was Emperor Kao-tsu's sister the Grand Princess Tongan, who seems to have brokered the marriage. T'ai-tsung then spent much of his remaining years writing the *Ti-fan* – or 'Plan for An Emperor' – as a political guide for his son. Li Chih was also put under the tutelage of an elderly statesman to teach him statecraft and he remained Crown Prince despite his father's misgivings.

The conspiracies over the succession cast a shadow over the last years of T'ai-tsung's reign. His invasion of Korea in 645 ended in disaster and he was beset with illness and criticism. Then in the middle of 648 there was a strange portent. The planet Venus appeared repeatedly visible during the daytime. The court's Grand Astrologer took this as a sign that a woman would soon ascend to the throne. The rumour circulated that, after three generations, the T'ang dynasty would fall and be replaced by a woman Emperor named, once again, the 'Martial Prince' – or Wu-wang. Again this was hard to believe since, though in China's long history there had been powerful dowager Empresses and Empress consorts, the dragon throne had never been occupied by a woman.

One night, while T'ai-tsung was drinking with his generals, the topic of conversation came around to the nicknames each of them had borne as a child. One general replied, 'Wu Niang,' meaning, 'Fifth Girl.' The Emperor laughed and said, 'What kind of girl are you, who is so strong and brave?'

However, the general had the 'Wu' character in his name and the Emperor grew suspicious that he might be the 'Martial Prince' of the prophecy. The general was banished to a provincial post and when a censor reported that there were fresh conspiracies afoot the poor man was executed.

But still the rumours would not go away. T'ai-tsung consulted his Grand Astrologer, only to be told that within forty years the house of T'ang would be almost wiped out. Worse, the woman responsible had already entered the palace. T'ai-tsung asked what would happen if he had all possible suspects killed. The Grand Astrologer replied that the will of heaven was not to be thwarted so easily. The perpetrator would probably survive while many innocent people died. Besides, if the perpetrator lived, in forty years' time, they would have mellowed with age, which might mitigate the disaster for the T'ang. But if the person responsible was killed, another would replace them who might wipe out the T'ang altogether. So the matter was dropped.

Through all this, no suspicion fell on Wu Chao. Although her surname was Wu, it was not the common character for 'Wu' and she occupied such a lowly place in the palace hierarchy that she escaped notice altogether. But Wu Chao must have known of the portent. Coming on top of the prophecy of the face reader Yüan T'ien-kang when she was a child, it would have nurtured her long-held ambition.

And it cannot have escaped her notice that, with the Emperor T'ai-tsung growing old and feeble, any chance of advancement lay with the Crown Prince Li Chih.

Wu Chao had probably known Li Chih since he was a child. He had been ten when she had come to the palace and, according to one account, T'ai-tsung kept him in the palace close to him because the boy's mother had died when he was just eight. Li Chih only moved out to the Eastern Palace, as was traditional, when he was appointed Crown Prince at the age of fifteen. Wu Chao and Li Chih would have come into contact again when the Crown Prince was in his twenties. As T'ai-tsung grew infirm after the disastrous campaign in Korea, he moved his son into living quarters next to his own, contrary to custom, and Li Chih visited his father frequently during his final illness. Wu Chao was also in attendance. The official histories say, tersely, that the Crown Prince met and admired Wu Chao at that time. Rumours hint that they were lovers while T'ai-tsung was still alive. But there is a more romantic tale. One day, while visiting his father, Li Chih had to relieve himself. Wu went with him. It was common for a serving girl to accompany a man to the toilet to wash him afterwards. The tale is told of a wealthy official in Shih Ch'ung named Wang Tun who would take ten beauties with him when he 'changed clothes' – a common euphemism for urination – and was happy to strip naked in front of them.

It is not known in what state of undress Li Chih was in the bathroom. However, when he had finished peeing, Wu Chao was ready with a bowl of water. She fell to her knees and, as she proffered the bowl, some of the water splashed on Wu Chao's face. Li Chih apologized for spoiling her powder.

'I humbly receive the favour of the rain and mist,' Wu Chao replied. This reply was loaded with innuendo, since 'clouds and rain' is a common Chinese poetic phrase for sexual intercourse.

In another version, Wu Chao said, 'It is an honour to be splashed by the dew of heaven.'

Again, the phraseology is loaded with sexual overtones. This tale was told during Wu Chao's lifetime. Indeed, when she was planning to usurp the throne, she was accused of using the 'occasion when the Crown Prince was "changing his clothes" to fornicate with him'. Throughout his life Li Chih was known to be a weak-willed man, free with the bottle and his body. It is unlikely that he would have resisted such an obvious invitation from such a beautiful woman as Wu Chao, even if she was his father's concubine and the penalty for having sex with your father's mistress was death by strangulation.

After T'ai-tsung came back from the Korean campaign and before his death, a royal scandal broke out which shows just how dangerous it could be for Wu Chao to begin an affair with Crowned Prince Li Chih. Princess Gaoyang, the seventeenth of T'ai-tsung's twenty-one daughters and his favourite surviving child, was married to Fang Yi-ai, the second son of the minister Fang Hsüan-ling. By this time, the great monk Hsüan-tsang had returned to Ch'ang-an after nineteen years of travelling and brought back a large number of Buddhist scriptures from India. He was granted government funding and support for the translation of them. At the same time, he employed a young monk named Bian-ji as his scribe to write an account of his travels through southern Asia. Bian-ji's study was a hut inside the boundaries of Princess Gaoyang's estate. One day when the princess was hunting with her husband she met Bian-ji. Soon after they became lovers. To ensure her husband's quiescence, she gave him two slave girls and countless treasure. Bian-ji was also rewarded. Later when a gold pillow was reported missing from the palace, the authorities found it in Bian-ji's hut. He explained that the pillow had been given to him by Princess Gaoyang as a present. As a consequence, their affair was discovered. The princess was banished from court by her angry father and Bian-ji was executed, together with the slave girls Princess Gaoyang had given her husband. However, Bian-ji had completed Hsüan-tsang's book before he died. It became an important piece of early travel writing, recording the cultures of various peoples that lived between China and India. Later, the legend of the Monkey King, imported from India, became fused with the travels of Hsüan-tsang, as ghostwritten by Bian-ji, as a favourite of popular storytelling. This tale then appeared as a long novel called *Journey to the West* by Wu Chengen in the Ming dynasty. It has since appeared on TV as *The Monkey King*.

Whatever went on between the Crown Prince and Wu Chao, in the bathroom or elsewhere, made little difference in the short term. Palace protocol demanded that, when the Emperor died, all the consorts who had served him on the dragon bed had their heads shaved and were sent to convents, though this may only have applied to women who had borne him no children. So when T'ai-tsung died in 649, year twenty-three Chen Kuan, at the age of fifty-five, Wu Chao and all her companions were shorn of their hair and sent to nunneries where they were expected to live in seclusion for the rest of their days. Wu Chao arrived in the Buddhist convent of Kan Yeh, bald-headed and with few prospects ahead of her. She was just twenty-four. But life in a Buddhist convent in those days in China was not as dreary as it sounds. Early Buddhist nuns in China were given lavish robes and gifts. In the late Ch'i and Liang dynasties the nuns gave away all donations they received and wore only straw sandals and clothes made of hemp. But at the time Wu Chao entered the convent, nuns wore ordinary clothing and were supported by the order, unlike their sisters in India who maintained their poor and simple life by begging for food. Indeed, during the T'ang dynasty, many Buddhist and Taoist nunneries in China had doubtful reputations. They were not havens for pious virgins, but rather the repository for divorcees and widows who had no family to return to. Women who wanted to take lovers without registering as prostitutes also lodged there. Some took their vows so they would be patronized by the royal house for life. Others, like the T'ang poetess Yu Xuanji, operated as courtesans from the convent. The religious authorities generously provided food and liquor and there were regular dinner and drinking parties. These provided an opportunity for a divorcee or a widow to be taken on as a concubine by some wealthy man and to return to family life.

By all accounts these parties were bibulous affairs. Although there were twenty-six varieties of water available – including melted frost, which was recommended for hang-overs, jade water that prevented hair going grey, water from pig's troughs which cured snake bites, and fruit and vinegar waters – the Chinese preferred alcohol. Most Chinese lacked the enzyme to digest milk and tea was only drunk as a beverage in the south in the seventh century. There was a small native variety of grape and black, yellow and white grapes had been imported into China centuries before, but a new purple variety had just arrived from Central Asia. This was the 'mare's teat' grape, so called because of its elongated shape. The T'ang knew how to make wine – a simple process, since vine moulds naturally break down the grape's sugar to make alcohol – but it did not catch on. Southerners preferred a wine made from bananas, Chinese strawberries, betel nut or myrobalan – a plant used for making dye in India – while T'ang and other northerners, because of their Turkish background, preferred koumiss, fermented mare's milk. More commonly, for everyday drinking, northerners would use millet and the southerners rice in the more complicated process of brewing ale or rice wine. Black pepper ale was drunk on New Year's Day, when ale was mulled with ginger and pepper. In the height of summer, fish ale was popular – a 'fish' fashioned from camphor was thrown into the mix. Lotus, honey, bamboo leaves, and pomegranate juice were also added. There was also a certain amount of home brewing, which was thought to produced a superior ale. Even a prince got in on the act, producing an ale called 'sweet dew'. There was a great deal of drinking at both ceremonial and social functions and no stigma was attached to drunkenness under the T'ang, even in court. On a cold winter's day, drinking began before breakfast and continued throughout the day.

Even though alcohol was technically banned under Buddhism, drink was consumed in monasteries and convents. Indeed, on some occasions – such as an imperial birthday – it was practically compulsory. T'ang medical books overflow with hangover cures, dubious additives to prevent inebriation and revolting concoctions – involving horse's sweat and the skin from rats' heads – which were guaranteed to make drunkards give up the booze.

While in the convent of Kan Yeh – which means, aptly, 'realizing one's own doing in life' – Wu Chao seems to have had her mind on the world outside its walls. Indeed, she was lovelorn. One of her surviving poems, thought to have been written at the time she was cloistered after Emperor T'ai-tsung's death, seems to be addressed to Li Chih, who was now the Son of Heaven, reigning as Emperor with the temple name Kao-tsung. It read,

Watching red turn to green, my thoughts are tangled and scattered,
I am dishevelled and torn from my longing for you, my lord.
If you fail to believe that lately I have shed tears constantly,
Open my chest and look for the skirt of pomegranate-red.

And there was hope for Wu Chao. At the time, there were machinations afoot in the palace which would rescue her from a life of contemplation, frustration and drunkenness in the convent. Kao-tsung had fallen in love a woman who was not his wife. Named Hsiao, she was a highborn consort of the first rank, probably from the royal line of the Chi or Liang dynasties in southern China who owed their positions in government to intermarriage. The last Sui Empress Hsiao, Yang-ti's wife, was a Liang princess and member of the same family. In the imperial harem, this Hsiao had borne the title *shu fei*, or Pure Consort, the second of the Four Ladies of the First Grade. Having been his concubine before he came to the throne, Hsiao had already borne Kao-tsung two daughters and a son and, in hope of securing the succession for him, she was trying to depose the childless Empress Wang and replace her. The Empress Wang responded by adopting Li Chung, Prince of Che'en, the son of a concubine of low rank, who then became Crown Prince with the backing of Chang-sun Wu-chi. But this only intensified the struggle between the two women, who competed over whose son would eventually take the throne.

On the anniversary of the death of T'ai-tsung, Kao-tsung paid a ceremonial visit to the convent at Kan Yen, where Wu Chao was confined, to honour the spirit of his father. It was not very far away, being situated in the vast royal park to the north of the palace. (A primary school now occupies the site.) There, perhaps by chance, he saw Wu Chao. It was said that they wept at the sight of each other, which indicates that something had been going on between them when he was Crown Prince and she was his father's concubine. The Empress heard of this and hatched a plan to oust her rival Hsiao from the affections of the Emperor. She sent word for Wu Chao to grow her hair back. Then she urged the Emperor to follow his instincts and take Wu Chao back into the palace and, against all rules of propriety, into his harem. In another version of the story, the Empress Wang herself ordered Wu Chao's return. Then, at a banquet in honour of the Emperor, Wu Chao was presented, dressed seductively and showing off her newly grown, long-flowing hair. The Emperor, being a man of sensual tastes, immediately retired with her to the bedchamber, leaving the Empress to rejoice that she had replaced her rival Hsiao in her husband's heart with Wu Chao, a woman she took to be an ally. As a result of this very public bedding, Wu Chao was later accused of incest, having slept with both father and son. In order to quench her jealousy, it was said, the Empress Wang 'loosed a tiger on the mountain'.

Wu Chao's behaviour was anything but tiger-like, at first. As a concubine of the former Emperor, her position in the palace was improper if not immoral and she could not afford to make enemies. With the Empress Wang, she was subservient and compliant. But in the bedchamber she quickly earned the favours of the Emperor, who soon promoted her to *chao-i* – which means 'Luminous Demeanour' – the first of the nine consorts of the second grade. He also elevated the posthumous titles of thirteen ministers who had been some of Kao-tsu's earliest followers, thereby enhancing her father's prestige. The motive for this would not have gone unnoticed at court.

The fact that Kao-tsung's liaison with Wu Chao was incestuous would have drawn criticism, particularly from southerners who were more purely ethnically Chinese. Among northerners with a Turkish heritage like the Li family, such dubious entanglements were not uncommon. In the biographies of the early Lis there are several examples of men marrying their brother's widows and of sisters sharing the same husband. T'ai-tsung himself took over the concubine of his cousin Li Yuan, Prince of Lujiang, and tried to raise the consort of a brother to the position of Empress, before being persuaded to drop the matter. This was Lady Yang, former Princess of Chi, widow of Li Yuan-chi whom T'ai-tsung had murdered at the Hsüan Wu Gate – and Wu Chao's own cousin. Nevertheless, some attempt had to be made to obscure Wu Chao's relationship with Kao-tsung's father out of deference to his ethnically Chinese ministers. But generally all manner of sexual misdemeanours were tolerated in Kao-tsung's court.

The disgraced Princess Gaoyang had returned from exile and had been rehabilitated after her brother came to the throne. She then began a court case to dispute her husband's elder brother's inheritance of the dukedom of their late father. At some point she even accused the brother of having behaved 'improperly' with her. Even so, at the end of 652, the princess was honoured by her brother with a royal visit at her home.

The long-serving Chang-sun Wu-chi was asked to deal with the case and, within a couple of months, Princess Gaoyang was accused of plotting against the throne, along with her sister, their husbands and two uncles. They were found guilty of treason. The men were beheaded while the women were ordered to kill themselves. It seems they had been supporters of Kao-tsung's elder brother Li Tai, who had died the month before. Chang-sun Wu-chi used this as an opportunity to clear the court of all opposition to Kao-tsung. He managed to implicate in the plot the Emperor's half-brother Li K'o, whose mother was the last Sui Emperor Yang-ti's daughter. In all likelihood he was completely innocent but, because he had the blood of two royal houses in his veins, he was highly regarded by many people and, consequently, a potential threat to the throne. He was sentenced to death and many mourned him. On the execution ground, Li K'o was said to have uttered a curse invoking Chang-sun Wu-Chi's downfall. Soon Chang-sun Wu-chi would fall victim to Wu Chao.

Having established her own position in the Emperor's affections, Wu Chao succeeded in ousting both the Pure Concubine Hsiao and the Empress Wang. It seems she did this by pandering to Kao-tsung's unusual sexual tastes. Wu Chao, it was said, 'abased her body and bore shame to provide the Emperor his satisfaction'. This may refer to anal sex, which appears frequently in Chinese erotic literature, but seldom in the sex manuals of the period. Despite this omission, it should be noted that the Chinese rarely condemned anything that went on between a man and a woman in the bedchamber.

'The world is based upon the interaction of the male and the female principles,' said Wang Shih-chen in *The Golden Lotus*, 'and it is natural for men and women to be drawn together. One cannot say that anything we do is out of depravity and evil passion.'

In 652, year three of Kao-tsung's reign name Yung Hui – 'Forever Glory' – Wu Chao gave birth to a son – possibly two – while Hsiao bore no more children. Wu Chao had plainly learnt the secret of the yin–yang energy and overcame any attempts Kao-tsung made to restrain his ejaculation, reversing the flow of *ch'i*. The Emperor was certainly coming with her and probably not with the Pure Concubine Hsiao or the Empress Wang. Wu Chao was taking Kao-tsung's masculine yang essence and drinking in the Emperor's potent reserve of energy and power. An ambitious woman, she now had the opportunity for advancement. With a son of her own, Wu Chao was in a position to make a bid to become Empress herself and put her offspring on the throne. And she made no secret of her aim. After the birth of her second son, she finished writing the *Nü Tse*, or 'Rules of Conduct for Women'. This replaced the former *Nü Hsün*, or 'Instructions for Women', the official handbook on court conduct written by the Empress Wen-te. She was implicitly comparing herself to the beloved wife of the Emperor T'ai-tsung and coveting her position.

Wu Chao also took practical steps to secure her advancement. She bribed other concubines to spy on the Empress Wang and Hsiao. She then reported what her two rivals did and said, with an unfavourable spin, to the Emperor. In this the Empress Wang played into her hands. She was arrogant and discourteous with the other ladies of the palace. Her mother, Lady Liu of Wei, and her uncle, the President of the Secretariat Liu Shih, were haughty and rude on their frequent visits to the palace. They were powerful 'Lius of the east of the river', with family connections to famous politicians and the Grand Princess Tongan. With her ear to the ground, Wu Chao sought out those the Empress and her family had offended and rewarded them with favours and gifts that the Emperor had bestowed on her. By the time the Empress and Hsiao realized what was going on and joined forces to counter their formidable rival, they found they had no support among the courtiers. Their complaints to the Emperor fell on deaf ears. Meanwhile, Wu Chao secured her position in the Emperor's favour by introducing him to her older sister, who had been married to an imperial official named Ho-lan, but was now a widow with two young children. Kao-tsung could not resist. He and Lady Ho-lan became lovers and it is thought that Wu Chao's older sister was the mother of Kao-tsung's sixth son, Li Hsien, born in 654, year five of Yung Hui. However, the boy was given the title Prince of Yung and passed off as Wu Chao's. That year, Wu Chao herself gave birth to a daughter, which presented her with a new opportunity for advancement.

Although the Empress Wang had been effectively sidelined, Kao-tsung showed no intention of deposing her. Being childless was alone sufficient grounds to obtain a divorce under T'ang law, but the imperial family considered the bonds of matrimony to be sacred and it would have been considered unfilial to put aside a wife that Kao-tung's father had personally selected for him for her virtue. She was a member of the powerful and well-connected Wang clan and any move against her would be fraught with political dangers. To remove the Empress Wang, the Emperor would need just cause – and Wu Chao knew how to give it to him. The childless Empress came to visit Wu Chao's newborn daughter. After the Empress left, possibly within hours of the birth, Wu Chao smothered the infant. When the Emperor arrived, Wu Chao told him the child was well and feigned shock when he discovered that his baby daughter was dead. Servants informed Kao-tsung that the Empress had just been there and he was left to draw his own conclusions. After all, the Empress had already exhibited intense jealousy over Hsiao.

There may, of course, have been other explanations. Although Wu Chao became more murderous as she gained power, she usually spared her own children even when there were legitimate charges against them. In medieval China, infant mortality was high. The child could have perished in an innocent cot death. There is another theory that the baby died of carbon monoxide poisoning in the poorly ventilated rooms. But even if the child had died of natural causes Wu Chao was unscrupulous enough to seize the death of her own baby as an opportunity for advancement. Even the Emperor does not seem to have been entirely convinced that his wife had murdered Wu Chao's child, since he never made the charges public. Nevertheless, he now had a legitimate excuse to move against the Empress Wang.

First Kao-tsung attempted to raise Wu Chao to the rank of concubine first class. But all four such positions were filled, one – the Pure Concubine – by Hsiao. So Kao-tsung proposed the new title of Imperial Concubine. This was opposed by Lai Chi, President of the Secretariat, and Han Yüan, President of the Chancellery, on the grounds there had been no such post in former times. Many in government saw the position of Imperial Concubine as a direct threat to the authority of the Empress and the matter was quietly dropped.

Chief among the opponents of Wu Chao's elevation was Chang-sun Wu-chi, now Supreme Commander of the Army, who championed the Empress Wang as a restraining influence on Kao-tsung and had backed her adopted son Li Chung as Kao-tsung's successor. To talk him round, Kao-tsung plied him with cartloads of treasure. Kao-tsung and Wu Chao paid him a royal visit. Even Wu Chao's Lady Yang dropped by for a chat and the sons of his favourite concubine were given government positions. Other supporters tried to talk Chang-sun Wu-chi around, to no avail.

However, Chang-sun Wu-chi had an enemy – the Chief Secretary of the Secretariat, Li I-fu. He was the loser in an interdepartmental political struggle and an order had been drawn up demoting him and exiling him to Szechwan. To maintain his position in the capital, Li I-fu sought to ingratiate himself with the Emperor. He drew up a petition asking Kao-tsung to depose the Empress Wang and elevate Wu Chao 'in deference to the will of the people'. Kao-tsung granted him an audience, rescinded his banishment and promoted him to Vice President of the Secretariat. Meanwhile, the Empress Wang was further isolated when her mother, Lady Liu of Wei, was accused of practising sorcery against Wu Chao and banned from the Inner Palace, while Lady Liu's brother Liu Shih, the President of the Secretariat, was demoted and exiled. These moves sent out a clear signal to the rest of the political class – oppose Wu Chao at your peril. Younger, ambitious ministers rallied to Wu Chao's cause, but the elder statesmen, led by Chang-sun Wu-chi and Ch'ü Sui-liang, who had served under the Sui, as well as the rebel Hsueh Ju and the T'ang, still remained loyal to the Empress Wang.

However, Li I-fu's petition had put the deposition of the Empress Wang and the elevation of Wu Chao on the political agenda. Kao-tsung maintained that changing Empresses made dynastic sense, since Wu Chao had borne him sons while the Empress Wang was barren. Ch'ü Sui-liang argued that the Empress Wang came from a noble family and, as T'ai-tsung had recommended the match, he was in no position to defy the will of the late Emperor. When Crown Prince Li Chih and Lady Wang had visited T'ai-tsung's deathbed to bid him farewell, the Emperor had turned to his Chief Ministers, including Chang-sun Wu-chi and Ch'ü Sui-liang, and said, 'We entrust our son and daughter-in-law to you all.'

When Ch'ü Sui-liang was consulted he asked what crime the Empress Wang was supposed to have committed that earned her deposition. No one mentioned the dead baby.

Later Ch'ü Sui-liang modified his position, saying that, if Kao-tsung insisted on changing Empresses, he should pick a new wife from among the daughters of the noble families of China, rather than Wu Chao, who everybody knew had been the concubine of his father. Kao-tsung should bear in mind what people would think of him a thousand years later. Then he conceded, 'In opposing Your Highness' wishes I have committed a crime worthy of death.'

He returned the cap and rod of office and kowtowed until blood ran from his brow, begging merely to be demoted and exiled, though he would not withdraw his opposition to the match. In the face of such open defiance, Kao-tsung had Ch'ü Sui-liang dragged from the Hall of Audience. Wu Chao, who had taken to listening to the debates of the council of ministers from behind a screen, was heard to say, 'Why not have him executed?' But Chang-sun Wu-chi rallied to Ch'ü Sui-liang's defence, saying that he could not be punished for obeying the will of the late Emperor.

The President of the Chancellery, Han Yüan, urged that the Emperor revere the marriage bond as it was respected by the common people. The wife of the legendary Yellow Emperor, he said, had been ugly, but she had helped him rule wisely, and the beautiful wife of the last Shang Emperor had brought about the downfall of the dynasty. He also noted that the ancient King of the Wu had not listened to his ministers and had, consequently, found his capital city laid in ruins. The new President of the Secretariat, Lai Chi, was also against the match. He warned Kao-tsung to consider the judgement of posterity and that he should not risk leaving no one to offer sacrifices at his ancestral temple. There on the anniversary of an ancestor's death and on the Cold Food Festival on the fifth day of the fourth month, Ding-hai, incest was burnt and a meal of pork, chicken, fish and ale was provide for the deceased. Both Han Yüan and Lai Chi were demoted and exiled.

However, they were small fry. The only minister of a similar standing to Chang-sun Wu-chi was the Controller of Works, Li Chi. He too had been a general in the civil war that had put the T'ang on the throne and had been in government ever since. Originally, his name had been Hsü, but he had been honoured by having the T'ang surname Li conferred on him. He was also the man, as governor-general of Ping-chou, who had buried Wu Chao's father on the instructions of the Emperor T'ai-tsung. A practical politician, Li Chi said simply that the Emperor's choice of a wife was a private matter, not a matter for the government. This turned the tide in favour of Wu Chao, starting a bandwagon that others leapt on to. The President of the Board of Rites, Hsü Ching-tsung, found himself a leader of the growing faction whose interest lay in opposing the old guard by championing Wu Chao and he announced simply, 'When an old farmer harvests an extra ten bushels of wheat, he wants to change his wife. So when the Son of Heaven wants to change his Empress, why should he seek the permission of others?'

Ch'ü Sui-liang was demoted and sent as governor-general to a prefecture in modern-day Hunan and on the thirteenth day of the tenth month, Xin-si, year six of Yung Hui – 16 November 655 – an edict was issued declaring that the Empress Wang and the Pure Concubine Hsiao were guilty of plotting to poison the Emperor, a charge that had not been mentioned before. They were to be stripped of all titles and were to be imprisoned in the Inner Palace, while their relatives were to be demoted and exiled to Ling-nan. This was the southernmost province of the Empire, comprising what is now north Vietnam and the island of Hai-nan. Referred to in imperial decrees as a 'distant, evil place', it was hot, disease-ridden and full of venomous snakes. The aborigines there attacked incomers and the region was regularly devastated by typhoons. The pestilential fogs and mosquito-infested swamps meant that few northerners exiled there ever returned.

Six days after the downfall of the Empress Wang, Wu Chao was raised to the rank of Empress by a decree that read,

> The Lady Wu comes from an eminent and honourable family from a region famed for its soldiers and scholars. She was picked to enter the palace for her ability and virtue. She earned the respect and friendship of women of her own rank and served those set above her with distinction. When We were Crown Prince and visited Our late mother, the Lady Wu was at her side both day and night ... Noting her good qualities, the late Emperor praised and honoured her, and bestowed her on Us. It is thus fitting that she be raised to the rank of Empress.

It was not true that Wu Chao had served the Empress Wen-te, since she had died before Wu Chao entered the palace. The canard that T'ai-tsung had 'bestowed' Wu Chao on his son was added to cover the fact that Kao-tsung had incestuously adopted one of his father's concubines and to justify Wu Chao's return to the palace from the convent.

Further, Wu Chao's firstborn son, Li Hung, was made Crown Prince instead of the former Empress Wang's adopted son Li Chung, although Li Hung was only three years old – two by Western reckoning – and plainly too young to inherit the throne. Soon after Wu Chao gave birth to another son, Li Che, Prince of Ying, also known as Li Hsien, like the son of her sister whom she had taken as her own. Although the name Hsien sounds the same in both cases – and is thus the same when romanized – the character and intonation are different. However, the boy is known to history by his temple name Chung-tsung. His date of birth the second day, Geng-chen of the eleventh month, Jia-wu, of the seventh year of Kao-tsung's reign – 26 November 656 – was officially recorded because, unlike his brothers, he was born the son of a reigning Empress. This was not the seventh year of Yu Hui, but year one of Hsien Ch'ing. Emperors sometimes changed reign name for political reasons. It could be done to mark a new beginning if, say, something had gone disastrously wrong or something momentous had happened. In this case, Wu Chao had come to the throne. She sat beside the Emperor during audiences with his ministers, though, in deference to the Confucian tenet that women should have no part in government, she remained hidden by a curtain.

Those who had supported Wu Chao in her struggle to become Empress were soon elevated. Hsü Ching-tsung became a First Minister and took over the role of elder statesman previously occupied by Chang-sun Wu-chi. Meanwhile Wu Chao exacted revenge on those who had opposed her. Ch'ü Sui-liang was exiled permanently, despite his long service. He wrote protesting that it was he along with Chang-sun Wu-chi who had promoted Kao-tsung's cause against that of Li Tai in the succession battle of 643, year seventeen Chen Kuan. The Emperor did not even bother to read his letter. After Ch'ü Sui-liang died he was stripped of his titles. Liu Shih and Han Yüan were accused of conspiring with Ch'ü Sui-liang to poison the Emperor and banned from ever returning to court.

Then one of the librarians of the former Crown Prince's library was accused of forming an illegal society. When the matter was investigated by Hsü Ching-tsung, the man tried to commit suicide. Hsü Ching-tsung then announced that he had discovered a plot by Chang-sun Wu-chi to seize power and recommended that he be banished, even though he was the Emperor's uncle. Kao-tsung balked, but Hsü Ching-tsung pointed out that any delay might prove fatal. Chang-sun Wu-chi had been a First Minister and Supreme Commander of the Army for thirty years and, if he moved against the Emperor, Kao-tsung would not have the power to resist him. He had also backed the appointment of Li Chung as Crown Prince, who had now been replaced by Wu Chao's son Li Hung, so the new Empress certainly did not want him around. Chang-sun Wu-chi was banished along with his family without even being granted an audience with the Emperor. He was stripped of his titles and taken into exile under armed guard. His sons were murdered on the road. Later his case was reopened and Chang-sun Wu-chi was forced to commit suicide in his place of exile.

The former Empress Wang's uncle Liu Shih and Han Yüan were eventually recalled to face accusations of conspiracy. On the journey, they were forced to wear the heavy wooden frames around their necks worn by common criminals in medieval China. They were still on their way to the capital when word was sent that they were to be executed at the place where the message arrived. Liu Shih was duly put to death on the road, along with Chang-sun Wu-chi's nephew. However, by this time, Han Yüan was already dead from the privations of the journey, though the messenger demanded that the coffin be opened to verify the fact. It was noted in the dynastic history that, 'after the deaths of Han Yüan and Ch'u Sui-lang, frank speech was avoided, both inside and outside the court, for almost twenty years'.

Any threat from the former Crown Prince Li Chung was also dealt with. After he had been deposed, he had been exiled to the provinces. As he heard the news from the court, he became more fearful that the Empress Wu would send assassins to murder him. He was beset by nightmares and became so paranoid that he took to wearing his wife's clothing in the hope of confusing any would-be killer. When this got back to court, it was used as excuse to demote him to the rank of commoner. He was then banished to southern Szechwan, to be held in the house where his uncle, another former Crown Prince, T'ai-tsung's eldest son Li Cheng-chien, had spent his last years.

Wu Chao's treatment of all those who opposed her, including Kao-tsung's kin, was ruthless. But Kao-tsung was sanguine.

'My family is unlucky,' he said. 'There is constant trouble with my relatives.'

However, the standard sources say that he became more debilitated in spirit and morale by the deaths of those close to him and he wept openly at the fate of the Empress Wang and his uncle Chang-sun Wu-chi. Even so, there is evidence that he continued to be a competent and energetic ruler. His armies conquered the western Turks, vastly expanding his Empire, and he began a biennial census of those who lived within the Great Wall. But with Wu Chao on the throne beside him – ruling, in effect, from behind a curtain – these things could be said to be her doing.

Li I-fu, whose petition had helped the Empress Wu to power, was appointed a First Minister. He was notoriously corrupt, selling government posts to the highest bidder, and he was soon mired in a sex sandal. It seems that he had put pressure on the governor of a jail named Bi to release an attractive female prisoner into his custody and made her his concubine. When the President of the Supreme Court of Justice got to hear of this, he reported the fact to the Emperor and an investigation was ordered under the auspices of the Grand Secretary of the Chancellery. Fearing discovery and disgrace, Li I-fu turned his wrath on the prisoner governor, who hanged himself in his own jail.

The censor, who was supposed to be an independent watchdog on government corruption, claimed that Li I-fu had used his authority to have the prison governor killed, then claimed it was suicide. That way he had disposed of the only witness against him. In the imperial system, the Emperor had the exclusive power of life or death over his subjects. Li I-fu had usurped that power for private ends, the censor said. This was little short of treason. It was one of the Ten Abominations, the most heinous crimes against state and society, and must be punished if Kao-tsung were to keep his authority. The Emperor could not ignore the accusation of the censor, particularly one of this gravity. He summoned Li I-fu into the imperial presence.

Even though the censor feared for his life and that of his family for moving against an ally of the Empress Wu, he ordered Li I-fu to kneel before the Emperor and confess his crime. Li I-fu did not move. Three times the censor repeated the order, but Li I-fu did nothing. He then withdrew, confident that he had the Emperor's protection – and that of the Empress. The censor was reprimanded for making malicious accusations. He was demoted and sent to the provinces. It was now clear to everyone that you did not cross Li I-fu. He became known as 'the Leopard' and was said to have 'the smile of a dagger'.

The excesses of his family eventually brought Li I-fu down in 663 – year three Lung Shuo, as the reign name had changed again. By that time Li I-fu had become more of a liability than an asset. After eight years as Empress, Wu Chao's position was relatively secure and she made no attempt to save him. Li I-fu had grown so arrogant that he did not even beg for the Emperor's pardon and was banished to a disease-ridden area of southern China where he died three years later.

CHAPTER SIX
THE HEAVENLY EMPRESS

THE EMPRESS WU was formally enthroned on the nineteenth day of the tenth month, year six Yung Hui – 12 December 655. With all due pomp and circumstance, she held an audience in full imperial regalia for the entire court at the Su I Gate, the inner gate of the palace that led to the women's quarters. This was attended not only by the court, but also by the ministers and foreign ambassadors. Then, in an unprecedented move, all the wives of the courtiers were ordered to pay their respects to their new sovereign. Wu Chao then visited the T'ao Miao or Temple of the Imperial Ancestors, an act that made her formally a member of the imperial family.

Her father was posthumously ennobled as the Duke of Chou and honoured with the titles Filial and Loyal. Her mother, Lady Yang, was also honoured and given the title Lady of Jung. The Wu families were given the revenues of a thousand families and the new policy of Hsien Ching – Illustrious Celebration – was proclaimed, prompting another change in reign name. Even Wu Chao's two half brothers, Wu Yüan-shuang and Wu Yüan-ch'ing, were given court appointments. However, there had always been a rivalry in the family, since Lady Yang's stepsons had treated her with scant respect, especially after their father died. At a banquet at the newly ennobled Lady of Jung's house one night, Wu Wei-liang, the son of Wu Shih-huo's brother, got drunk. When she asked him what he thought of her good fortune, in his cups he ventured the opinion, 'Deserving officials should be in court, but they should not be there because of family connections. That is dishonourable and wrong.' The Lady of Jung told the Empress Wu what he had said. The Empress promptly despatched the Wus, her two half-brothers and their families to distant postings in pestilential provinces. Both brothers died in their far-flung posts.

Although Kao-tsung was now completely under the thrall of Wu Chao, he had not forgotten about the former Empress Wang and Hsiao. One day he was passing the apartment where they were incarcerated and found the door bricked up with only a small hole left through which they were served food. Perhaps feeling a twinge of remorse, he called through the hole, 'Empress, Pure Concubine, how are you?'

The two women wept. They said that they were condemned criminals and had been reduced to a rank lower than that of palace slaves, so why was the Emperor honouring them by addressing them with their old titles? Through their tears, they said, 'We feel blessed by your highness remembering the good old days. You have changed death into life for us and we can see the sun and moon again.' And they begged Kao-tsung to rename the place they were incarcerated as the Courtyard of Remembrance.

The Emperor promised that he would do so.

Hearing of this, Wu Chao sent executioners to the women's apartment. The former Empress Wang and the Pure Concubine were beaten. Each was given a hundred blows. Then their hands and feet were cut off and they were thrown in a wine vat.

'Let the two hags get drunk to their bones,' said Wu Chao.

The former Empress Wang and the Pure Concubine were left there to bleed to death. They died in agony a few days later. Then their corpses were decapitated and their bodies hacked to pieces.

It is said that the Empress Wang accepted her fate. When the executioners arrived, she bowed low and said, 'Long live His Majesty. Wu Chao has gained favour, while I achieved death.'

Hsiao was less sanguine and cursed Wu Chao.

'Wu is a deceitful fox, who had sealed my fate,' she said. 'I pray that in all my future lives I will come back as a cat, and she as a mouse. Then in each life I will tear her throat out.'

After hearing this, Wu would allow no cats in the imperial palaces. As a Buddhist, she believed that Hsiao might easily return as a cat and take her revenge, so she took further steps to prevent this. In medieval China, both royalty and commoners were often given a posthumous name to honour the accomplishments they made in their lifetime. Wu Chao ordered that the former Empress Wang and Hsiao be known posthumously as Snake and Owl. Then they might be reincarnated as a snake and an owl. Both were considered creatures of ill-omen and were shunned by all men. These posthumous names were also an effective piece of propaganda that smeared the two women's characters during their lifetime.

Even so the Empress Wu was still troubled by the bloodthirsty end of her rivals. It is said that their ghosts haunted her, appearing with their hair unkempt and dripping with blood. She insisted that the court move into the Ta-ming Gong, the Great Luminous Palace begun by T'ai-tsung for his father, the retired Emperor Kao-tsu. When they moved, the palace was not even finished. Building work was only completed in 662, year two Lung Sho – 'Days of the Dragon' – and seven years after Wu Chao came to the throne. By then the Emperor Kao-tsung, the Empress Wu and the entire court had abandoned Ch'ang-an in favour of the eastern capital Luoyang, which was substantially rebuilt; they only returned to Ch'ang-an occasionally when it was absolutely necessary for administrative purposes.

There were good political reasons for this move. Many of the old guard who had supported the Empress Wang came from the north-west, whereas Wu Chao's supporters were outsiders from the north-east who saw backing her as a way of advancement. They soon outnumbered the old guard in court and moving the government to the eastern capital was one way of rewarding them. It also made it very clear politically that the ascendancy of the north-west was now over.

There may have also been economic reasons for the move. Ch'ang-an was in a traditionally poor area that often suffered droughts. Shipping grain in from other parts of China was costly. Luoyang could be supplied more easily had it had direct access to the extensive canal system built by the Sui. However, there were instances, during the time the court was in Luoyang, when the eastern capital found itself in the grip of a famine, while Ch'ang-an remained prosperous. Consequently, traditional chroniclers have always maintained that the reason the court was moved out of Ch'ang-an was so that the Empress Wu could escape the ghosts of the Empress Wang and Hsiao that plagued her.

The cost of this move was enormous. Duplicated ministries were set up in both capitals and a caretaker government nominally under Wu Chao's six-year-old son, the Crown Prince Li Hung, was left behind in Ch'ang-an. Even so, during Kao-tsung's reign the court was frequently called back to Ch'ang-an to conduct official business. On these occasions the Empress Wu refused to occupy the imperial palace inside the city where the former Empress Wang and the Pure Concubine had been murdered. Instead, she and Kao-tsung stayed at the Chiu Ch'eng Kung – the Palace of the Nine Perfections – their summer palace outside the city among the beautiful mountains along the border of the Shensi and Kansu provinces.

The vast imperial entourage traipsed the eight hundred and sixty-five li, or two hundred and eighty-five miles, from Ch'ang-an to Luoyang and back again no less than seven times during Kao-tsung's reign. The journey took twenty-five days. All the men, women, baggage and paraphernalia needed for the journey were carried on horses and camels. Just feeding and housing the imperial retinue along the way caused huge disruption and places on the route were given long periods of tax exemption in recognition of this. And the journey was dangerous. Even with an armed escort, the imperial entourage was not safe from bandits. Things got so bad during a famine in 682, year one Yung Jun – 'Forever Pure' – that Kao-tsung appointed a special censor to take charge. The Emperor released an eloquent bandit leader from jail, removed his fetters, dressed him in a cap and gown and got him to lead the procession. By the time ten-thousand-strong entourage reached Luoyang, not a single copper had been lost, though a large number of people had died of hunger. After Kao-tsung died in 683, year one Hung Tao – 'Broaden the Way' – Wu Chao established the capital permanently at Luoyang, where it remained until 701, year one Ch'ang-an. The reign name then borrowed from the city of Ch'ang-an means 'Peace and Stability for a Long Time'.

The eastern capital Luoyang had been founded nearly nine hundred li, or three hundred miles, to the east of Ch'ang-an in 605, the second year of his reign, by the penultimate Sui Emperor Yang-ti. Unlike the celestial city of Ch'ang-an, it was not aligned precisely to the cardinal points. Instead its major axis lay along a line connecting the peak of Mount Mang in the north to that of Yi Que in the south. Covering twenty-five square miles, the city was, again, laid out on a grid, though the Imperial City was separated from the rest of the town by the meandering Luo river, which periodically flooded – once destroying nearly a fifth of the city.

The Palace City occupied the high ground beyond and was enclosed on three sides by the walls of the Imperial City and on the fourth by the Imperial Gardens. The palace and administrative complex was more easily defensible than in Ch'ang-an and had an immense network of underground granaries. Even so, when the court of Wu Chao and Kao-tsung moved there, extensive building work had to be done.

As in Ch'ang-an the northernmost gate which connected the Palace City to the Imperial Gardens was called the Hsüan Wu Gate. It was the highest gate and the spot where the Palace City was most vulnerable, so it was the most heavily guarded of all the entrances. However, if you could bribe the guards at the Hsüan Wu Gate, or otherwise get them on your side – as T'ai-tsung had done in Ch'ang-an – it was easily possible to storm the palace. All coups began at the Hsüan Wu Gate.

The northern half of the city was further subdivided by the Chan, a tributary of the Luo. The rivers fed a network of canals that criss-crossed the city and were themselves crossed by numerous bridges. The most prominent of them was the Tien-tsin Bridge, one of three bridges across the Luo. It had two towers at each end and was supported by several large barges chained together.

The major avenue, the Dingdingmenjie, ran parallel to the Mang-Yi Que axis but, owing to the topography of the city, it was offset to the west. However, like the Vermilion Bird Road, it led from the city's main south entranceway – the Dingding Gate – to the gate of the Imperial City and on to the Palace City beyond. Used for ceremonial processions, Dingdingmenjie was one hundred and sixty yards across. It was lined with willow, elm and fruit trees, and had a canal running down one side. It was crossed by five major avenues one hundred to one hundred and twenty yards across and smaller streets fifty yards wide.

Although it was smaller than Ch'ang-an, Luoyang was of greater economic importance and had three markets – the West Market near the Houzai Gate to the south and the North and South Markets either side of the Luo river, which was a major trading route. The South Market was the biggest of the three. It covered one hundred and twenty streets, and contained four hundred warehouses and three thousand shops. It was served both by the river and by a canal that ran along its eastern edge. Further canals supplied the West Market with its one hundred and forty-one warehouses and sixty-six streets. During Wu Chao's time in the city the North Market was moved to be near the Chan river and the Cao Canal, which had been dug during the reign of Emperor Yang-ti and was said to have been jammed by 'more than ten thousand boats from all over China'. As in Ch'ang-an, the markets were strictly regulated and walled. The earthen perimeter of the West Market alone ran for twelve li, or four miles, and had four gates in it.

Luoyang was divided into one hundred and three wards each of one square li. A wall about quarter of a mile long ran along each side. Two roads forty-six feet wide divided the ward into quarters. Under the T'ang the quarters were then subdivided again, giving sixteen sectors in all. This meant the same address system could be used as was used in Ch'ang-an. It was also applied to other Chinese cities under the T'ang.

The aristocracy lived along the southern wall of the Imperial City to be near court, while high officials preferred the south-east of the city, which was quieter. There they tended vast gardens with man-made hills, lakes, islands, and pavilions, which were allotted to them according to their rank.

The northern part of the city was much busier. Workshops filled the wards just north of the Luo river and hotels surrounded the North Market. There were two Zoroastrian temples there, with another two by the South Market, to cater for the religious needs of visitors from Persia.

Buddhist monasteries ran public bathhouses in T'ang cities. A monk ran one in Luoyang which was open for the first five days of each lunar month. It attracted thousands of customers, both the wealthy and the destitute, the laity and the clergy.

Like southern Ch'ang-an, Luoyang was so spread out that it had a semi-rural appearance. With broad streets and walled wards, the city was easy to control politically, which suited the Empress Wu. And, like Ch'ang-an, Luoyang was a very flat city with few buildings more than two storeys high. Again, the Empress Wu was to change all that with her Celestial Pillar, which was built in 694, year one Yen Tsai – 'Prolonging the Years' – to mark the change of dynasty from T'ang to Chou. At over a hundred feet high, it could be seen for miles.

Once the court was ensconced in Luoyang and stuffed with her supporters, Wu Chao was politically unassailable. However, since the murder of the former Empress Wang and the Pure Concubine, she became prey to superstition and the occult. While she dismissed the advice of seasoned statesmen, she often paid heed to the words of necromancers. As precedent and the Confucian tradition were against her, she looked for omens and signs to lend divine authority to her rule. Both Kao-tsu and T'ai-tsung had kept a single reign name for their period of office, but during Kao-tsung's period of office the reign name changed thirteen times, with year one of one reign followed by year one of the next. The reign name was changed another thirteen times before Wu Chao was deposed and died. And with each change of reign name, she believed, her reign was transformed.

If an Emperor thought his reign had been one of supreme achievement he would perform the *feng-shan* sacrifice at the foot and summit of China's principal holy mountain T'ai-shan in Shandong. The Emperor was the Son of Heaven who interceded between the heavens above and his people below and, in the ceremony, he reported to both earth and heaven that his duties on earth had been done. This was such a momentous claim that few Emperors risked the accusation of being vainglorious by staging the sacrifices. In fact, they had only been performed six times before in the whole of Chinese history. The last time had been in AD 56. T'ai-tsung had planned to perform the sacrifices in 632, just five years after becoming Emperor, but had been talked out of it by his First Minister Wei Cheng. He tried again in 641, year fifteen Chen Kuan, and was on his way to T'ai-shan when a comet appeared. This was thought to be a bad omen, so he returned to Ch'ang-an. A third attempt in 648, year twenty-two Chen Kuan, was washed out by flood. As it could then be said that both heaven and earth were against T'ai-tsung making the *feng-shan* sacrifices, the excuse was given that he could not afford to stage them, since he had spent so much on building four new palaces – the Hsiang-ch'eng palace alone involved nearly two million man-days of labour. In 659, year four Hsien Ch'ing, the Empress Wu got Hsü Ching-tsung to write to the Emperor formally requesting that he perform the *feng-shan* sacrifices. The matter was agreed in principle, but as the sacrifices had not been performed for over six hundred years it took some time to discover what the ceremonies might be and then to organize them. Meanwhile, the Empress made other efforts to secure her position.

Under T'ai-tsung, an attempt had been made to list all the prominent clans of the Empire in the *Chen-kuan shih-tsu-chih* – 'Compendium of Clans and Lineages of the Chen-Kuan Period' – which had been completed in 638, year twelve Chen Kuan. Unfortunately there had been a grave omission. The Wu clan had been deemed so insignificant they had not made the listing. Clearly, this had to be put right. In 659, year four Hsien Ch'ing – four years after the Empress Wu had come to the throne, the Emperor commissioned a new work called the *Hsing-shih lu* – 'Record of Surnames and Clans' – with a new system of classification. Not surprisingly the Empress Wu's family and the clans of the other imperial consorts made the first rank. This new methodology was endorsed by Kao-tsung, who wrote a preface for the book. The new compendium ran to two hundred chapters, broadening the official ruling class to the parvenus who had supported Wu Chao in her struggle to become Empress and further diminishing the rank of the old aristocracy, particularly the 'four-surnames' clans of the Shan-tung who maintained their power by intermarriage and were still influential.

In medieval China, an Emperor's prowess was judged as much by his artistic achievements as by his political and military successes. Under Kao-tsung, great literary endeavours that had been started under T'ai-tsung were completed and others were begun. These included revisions to the standard commentaries on the works of Confucius, a thousand-chapter literary anthology and other works of comparable length. And in 657 the Emperor published the first pharmacopeia in Chinese history. It contains some remarkable cures. In one, a man whose testicles had been bitten off by a horse had them restored by a doctor who pushed them back inside the body cavity, sewed up the laceration with fine mulberry bark thread, then treated the wound with the finely minced liver of a black chicken.

Another cure told of a wounded general from the early seventh century who had an arrow lodged in his jaw. He summoned a doctor, who told him that the arrowhead had penetrated so deep that it could not be removed. The general had the doctor beheaded. A second doctor was called. He said that removing the arrowhead would be excruciatingly painful. He too was executed. A third doctor realized that he had better try something, so he drilled a hole in the general's jaw, alongside the embedded arrowhead. Then he forced a wedge into the hole, cracking open the jaw until there was a gap an inch wide and he could remove the arrowhead. He was rewarded with a lavish feast and entertained by singing girls.

State sponsorship was extended to the Taoist and Buddhist clergy, even though Kao-tsung was hostile to Buddhism, which had continued to flourish in China during his father's reign. He even issued an edict insisting that Buddhist and Taoist monks and nuns show deference both to the Emperor and to their parents. After all, he argued, Buddhism, Taoism and Confucianism were all, at heart, the same thing, so Buddhists and Taoists should show their respect to Confucian institutions – the family and the state. Buddhist clerics were outraged. Being ordained, they believed they had withdrawn from the world into a transcendental state where their ancestors and the Emperor had no jurisdiction. Kao-tsung argued that they owed a duty to the state that protected them and allowed them to practise their religion unmolested. His power, or *te*, he insisted was absolute and spanned all worlds, temporal and transcendental, present and future. And he argued that respecting parents and the worship of ancestors were the very basis of Chinese civilization.

Countering this, the clerics reminded the Kao-tsung that, as he worshipped his ancestors, it was his duty to respect the spirits. Since Buddha was a spirit, the Emperor should show respect to his representatives, rather than the other way around. Besides, several sutras had specifically forbidden deference towards secular authorities and warned that anyone who accepted homage from a monk or nun did themselves harm.

A great debate ensued that was attended by over a thousand people. Kao-tsung found himself ranged against powerful people, including the Empress Wu's mother, the Lady of Jung, who was a passionate Buddhist. At the end of the debate he was outvoted, even though the Empress Wu had sought to fix the ballot behind the scenes. Kao-tsung was forced to compromise and he decreed that, in future, Buddhist and Taoists must honour their ancestors, but not necessarily the Emperor.

Despite his enmity towards Buddhism, Kao-tsung continued funding the Buddhist convert Hsüan-tang to translate the Sanskrit scriptures that he had brought back from India. The Empress Wu was, of course, an avowed Buddhist. She sponsored two sea voyages to India by another scholar named I-Ching, who brought back over four hundred Buddhist texts. She soon took over as the principal patron of Buddhism and she later used the precepts of Mahameghan Buddhism to justify her imperium.

In the tenth month of 660, year five Hsien Ch'ing, Kao-tsung fell ill, probably suffering from a stroke said to have been brought on by his guilt over the deaths of the former Empress Wang and his uncle Chang-sun Wu-chi. Kao-tsung's vision was impaired and he suffered incapacitating bouts of dizziness. As the Emperor was unable to work, the Empress Wu took over his state duties and proved herself an able administrator. As, under Confucianism, women should not govern and, thus, could not be good at it, her abilities could not be acknowledged by dynastic chroniclers. Instead, they characterized her skill at running government as a naked attempt to usurp power and accused her of wanting the Emperor dead. The story was told that, when Kao-tsung fell ill, he had been examined by the imperial physicians, led by the Taoist healer named Sun Ssu-mo. He was one of the twenty senior doctors of the Office of Supreme Medicine, which also boasted a hundred junior medics, ten practitioners of acupuncture, four master masseurs, sixteen practitioners of massage and twelve hundred years of medical records.

According to Wu Chao's official biography, the royal physicians Zhang Wenzhong and Qin Minghe diagnosed an 'unnatural wind rising in the body', though other sources say that the diagnosis came from Sun Ssu-mo himself. This, they said, could be cured by drawing blood from the head with a needle.

'How dare you propose letting blood from the head of the Emperor,' the Empress Wu said from behind her customary screen. 'Such talk deserves death.'

The physicians threw themselves to the ground and begged for forgiveness. But Kao-tsung intervened.

'How can we blame the doctors when they offer their advice on disease?' he said. 'My headaches have become unbearable. Let them do what they recommend.'

The physician carried out the bleeding and, after a while, Kao-tsung said, 'My sight is now clear.'

'Heaven has sent these doctors,' said the Empress Wu, bowing low. And she gave them lavish gifts of jewels and a hundred lengths of multicoloured silk.

It is likely that Wu Chao was ignorant of the medical practices of the time and the idea of bleeding the patient frightened her. Indeed if the physician had been performing the standard Chinese cure of the T'ang period – that of piercing the 'brain's door' at the base of the cranium – and had pushed the needle just a little bit too far the result would have been instant death. However, she may well have wanted the Emperor dead. She now had a seven-year-old son who was Crown Prince. If Kao-tsung died, she would have taken over as regent. On the other hand, Kao-tsung was a feckless drunk with an eye for the women. Wu Chao was now thirty-five and had given birth to a least three children. At any time she might loose her power and position to the machinations of any young woman who turned the Emperor's head. After all, she had deposed the previous Empress by her beauty and her abilities in the bedchamber.

CHAPTER SEVEN
THE TIGER AND
THE LAMB

ONE OF THE EMPRESS Wu's first acts in government was to invade Korea, China's only neighbour that could boast a comparable civilization. China was often under attack from the Turks and the Tibetans – and, earlier, the Mongols – but these were all nomadic peoples. The Chinese knew of the civilization in India, but it was a distant land on the other side of the Himalayas and hard to get to. Persia and Byzantium were also far away and Japan lay beyond the sea, which the Chinese considered to be the boundary of their Empire. Korea had been part of China under the Han dynasty eight hundred years before. Retaking it would bring the regime huge prestige, especially since Sui Yang-ti and T'ai-tsung had so conspicuously failed to do so. So Wu Chao came up with a plan. Instead of attacking across the Liao river, which then formed the border between China and Korea, and the Yalu, which is Korea's current border with Manchuria, the Empress Wu planned to send 100,000 troops by sea to take Paekche, the southernmost of the three kingdoms that then occupied the Korean peninsula, with the aid of Silla, the middle of the three kingdoms. From there, with the aid of Silla, the Chinese could attack the kingdom of Korea itself from both sides.

Kao-tsung wanted to head the army in Korea, but Wu opposed it, ostensibly on the grounds of health. It is true that Kao-tsung suffered from ill-health for the remaining twenty-three years of life, but he had recovered enough from his stroke by 660, year five Hsien Ch'ing, to father two more children by the Empress Wu. These were her youngest son Li Tan, born in the seventh month of 662 – Ren-yin, year two Lung Sho – and her only surviving daughter, Princess Tai-ping, a year or two later. The dates of birth of the Emperor's daughters were not recorded, unlike the sons born while he reigned. However, Tai-ping was married in 681, probably when she was aged sixteen or seventeen, which meant she was born in 663 or 664, year three Lung Sho or year one Lin Te – *Te* means 'virtue' while *Lin* is a mythical beast that resembles a deer. The name Tai-ping means 'Peace'; possibly she was so named because she was born during the Korean war when her parents would have been craving the return of peace. However, given her turbulent later life, the name carries a certain irony.

Kao-tsung was also well enough to travel extensively and the imperial couple visited the province of Shensi, the ancestral home of both their clans. However, Kao-tsung was never strong enough to take over the reins of powers again and remained Emperor now only in name. Keeping the Emperor away from the war also had a sound political motive. If the invasion failed, Kao-tsung would be blamed, possibly resulting in him being ousted from power, as Sui Yang-ti had been, and taking Wu Chao with him. But if it succeeded, he would take all the credit and, emboldened, those around him might make renewed attempts to bring her down. As it was, while the war in Korea dragged on, one last attempt was made to dislodge her. At the time, she favoured a certain Taoist priest who had been given the run of the palace. He performed certain rites that could easily be construed as sorcery – a powerful charge that had brought about the downfall of Lady Liu of Wei and Liu Shih. A eunuch, who had previously served in the household of the deposed Crown Prince Li Chung, heard about this and reported it to the Vice President of the Secretariat Shang-kuan I, who had also served Li Chung and was the last official to have any ties to the old guard. He told the Emperor and advised him to depose the Empress Wu. Perhaps because he was tired of being Wu Chao's puppet, Kao-tsung complied and Shang-kuan I drafted a decree deposing her. But the palace was full of Wu Chao's spies. Before the Emperor could issue the decree, the Empress Wu went to him, whereupon, the dynastic history records, 'the Emperor repented and, fearing her anger, told her that it had been done on the advice of Shang-kuan I'.

Shang-kuan I and his eunuch informant were sent to prison, where they died. Shang-kuan I's property was forfeit and his family were taken into the palace as slaves, a common fate for the family of a disgraced official. His granddaughter Shang-kuan Wan-erh became a favourite of the Empress Wu and she later rose to a position of great influence under the Empress Wei, consort of Wu Chao's son Li Che, later Emperor Chung-tsung. But despite the political skills she learned at Wu Chao's side, she met a tragic end, as we shall see later.

As both Shang-kuan I and the eunuch had worked for the former Crown Prince Li Chung, he too was implicated and was forced to committed suicide in his place of exile. Of the Emperor's sons, only two who were not Wu Chao's remained alive. One was Li Su-chieh, the son of the Pure Concubine; the other Li Shang-chin, born of a lowly concubine. Neither could be considered a threat.

By this time the Chinese army had won several great victories in Korea and destroyed the Japanese armada that had come to the aid of Paekche. In the process four hundred ships had been burnt, leaving 'the heavens black with smoke and the sea red with blood'. Now the army was tired and wanted to return home, but there were fears that the returning army could be used in a coup to oust the Empress Wu and they were ordered to finish the job in Korea. The veteran Li Chi, then nearly eighty, was sent on what was to be China's seventh and last campaign against Korea in the seventh century. As a result, three years later, in the ninth lunar month of 668 – Bing-chen, year one Tsung Chang, or 'Chief Protocol' – the Korean capital Pyongyang was burnt to the ground, destroying the records of the seven-hundred-and-five-year-old kingdom. Four million Koreans became subjects of China, two hundred thousand of them as slaves, taken as prisoners of war. The war had lasted eight long years, with numerous reverses, but the Empress Wu's strategy triumphed in the end and the Chinese Empire under the T'ang reached now its greatest extent, running from the Korean peninsula to the borders of Persia and Kashmir.

The Empress Wu had good reason to be afraid of the army. Professional soldiers came from large, well-off families and served from the age of twenty-one to sixty. They were well educated and well trained. In the autumn and winter, the slack farming seasons, they participated in huge formal exercises as well as the winter hunt. Exempt from taxes and compulsory labour, professional soldiers were seconded into the twelve imperial guards and the six guards of the Crown Prince, where they served as the capital's garrison. So they were a force to be reckoned with and never far from home. In 664, year one Lin Te, Wu Chao cancelled the Great Shoots that had been instituted in 619. Traditionally the Emperor had been carried out of the palace on his throne to watch his soldiers show off their prowess with seven types of crossbow. Plainly, this was a risky business. A single stray arrow loosed by a disaffected soldier could have changed the course of history. The Great Shoots were not revived again until 711, six years after Wu Chao's death.

Wu Chao had now been Empress for ten years and many of those who had helped her to power had grown old and retired. The government was whittled down to two generals who spent most of their time away on military campaigns. The downfall of Shang-kuan I gave the Empress Wu a free hand and she took over the running of the government completely, in her husband's name. According to the dynastic history,

> From this event, whenever the Emperor attended to business, the Empress hung a curtain and listened from behind it. There was no matter of government, great or small, she did not hear. The whole sovereign power of the Empire passed into her hands. Life and death, reward or punishment were hers to decide. The Son of Heaven sat on the throne and folded his hands, that is all. In court and in the country, they were called the Two Sages.

Still Wu longed to have the legality of her rule endorsed by divine authority and, in 665, year two Lin Te, she decreed that the time for the *feng-shan* sacrifices had now arrived. No one pointed out that for Kao-tsung to stage this momentous ceremony, claiming that his work on earth was done so early in his reign, could only be viewed as hubris. Ironically the ceremony is supposed to symbolize the complete pacification of the Empire and its contented submission to the rule of the Emperor. Instead, fighting in Korea had been renewed and there were still political intrigues in court that attempted to bring down the real ruler of the Empire – the Empress. But the people were happy. Five successive bumper harvests had made everyone in China well off and the presence at the ceremony of foreign delegations from as far away as Persia and Japan demonstrated China's military and diplomatic prowess. Even the son of the dictator of Korea, Ch'uan Kai-Su-Wen, was there, during a brief hiatus in the war. Besides, the celebration was to be accompanied by a promotion for all officials, the distribution of titles and gifts, a general amnesty, alms for the aged and generous donations to the people of the

Shandong and the places the imperial procession passed through on the way to the holy mountain at T'ai-shan.

Nor did anyone object to the participation of the Empress Wu, even though no woman had had any part in the ceremony before. Nevertheless, Wu had made a thorough study of the ceremony and petitioned the Emperor, saying that there was no reason that, as a woman, she should not take part. It was almost imperative.

'According to the doctrines laid out in traditional books, the male and female ceremonials are distinct,' she wrote. 'There is a female altar because that is the sex of the Earth goddess the divinity sex of the Earth ... besides, one invites the spirits of late Empresses to take part in this important festival, so why are only senior male officials allowed to be involved with these sacrifices to a woman? This defies logic and creates disharmony where there should be order.'

T'ai-shan was one thousand and eighty-two li, or three hundred and fifty-seven miles, from Luoyang and the journey took forty days. The cortège spread for sixty miles. It comprised military leaders, government officials, soldiers, servants and foreign legates of Turks, Persians, Indians, Koreans, Japanese and others, each with their own entourages. They took sheep and cattle with them to eat on the way and slept in tents and felt yurts. To bolster the Wu contingent in the ceremony, Wu Wei–liang and his brother Wu Huai-yün, sons of her half-brother Wu Yüan-ch'ing, turned up for the ceremony, though they would have been wiser to have remained in obscurity in the provinces. Also present was T'ai-tsung's former consort, Wu Chao's cousin Lady Yan, now the Princess Dowager Yue, who, as oldest surviving royal woman of the clan, was Wu Chao's assistant.

The sacrifices began at the foot of T'ai-shan on New Year's Day, year one of Ch'ien Feng – 10 February 666 – with the Empress Wu playing the part of the First Assistant. During the ceremony the mountain itself was 'to be given a title', which is what the *Feng* in the reign name means. The other part, *Ch'ien*, is the sign of the male or yang element in *The Book of Changes*. Taking the male element on herself, Wu Chao then led the second procession to the summit, where the sacrifices were completed the following morning without any unfavourable portents being observed. However, five years after Wu Chao's death the sage Chang Yüeh said the Emperor had committed sacrilege by allowing the Empress

Wu to participate. This, he said, had led to the fall of the T'ang and the rise of the Chou dynasty.

After the ceremony the imperial cortège toured Shandong, visiting the birthplace of Confucius and the supposed birthplace of Lao-tzu, the founder of Taoism who wrote a two-part book of five thousand characters about the Tao – 'the Way' or 'Supreme Principle' – and the *te* – or 'virtue'. He was much more spiritual than Confucius, who was a practical philosopher. After writing the *Tao-te Ching*, Lao-tzu was said to have disappeared, though it was thought that he had lived as a recluse for one hundred and fifty to two hundred years and had appeared in other guises down the ages. Once during his lifetime he was said to have met Confucius and berated him for his pride and ambition. Confucius, on the other hand, was so impressed by Lao-tzu that he compared him to a flying dragon that rides on the clouds and wind.

Living in the sixth century BC, Lao-tzu was said to have had the surname Li. This came about because, it was said, after seventy-two years in the womb, he was born through his mother's flank at the foot of a plum tree. So *Li*, the Chinese for 'plum', was chosen as his surname. Consequently he was claimed by the T'ang – whose family name was Li – as an ancestor in a proclamation made by T'ai-tsung as early as 637, year eleven Chen Kuan, in an effort to dissociate the T'ang from the Buddhism of the Sui dynasty. During the visit of Kao-tsung and Wu Chao to his putative birthplace, Lao-tzu was honoured with imperial rank and given the lengthy title Supreme Emperor of Mysterious Origin. A memorial hall was erected on the supposed site of his birth to be supervised by two government officials. The surrounding county was named the County of the True Source and all those with the surname Li were excused paying taxes for a year.

After four months travelling, the imperial entourage returned to the capital, along with Wu Wei-liang and Wu Huai-yün. It was then that the Empress Wu's worst fears were realized. Despite her amorous abilities, Wu Chao knew that the lecherous Kao-tsung might replace her with a younger model at any time. Now the Emperor had fallen for her own niece Ho-lan Kuo-ch'u, daughter of Wu Chao's sister Lady Ho-lan, now Duchess of Han, who had already enjoyed the sexual favours of the Emperor herself. Her name Kuo-ch'u comes from the phrase *yi-nu-kuo-ch'u* which means 'daughter and national beauty'. Ho-lan Kuo-ch'u regularly visited the palace, ostensibly to see her aunt, the Empress Wu, but in fact to carry on an illicit affair with the Emperor. He had already ennobled the girl, making her Duchess of Wei, while her mother was alive. Now he wanted to introduce her into the upper ranks of the imperial concubines. The Empress Wu was now forty-one and the mother of five. She could not hope to compete with a fresh-faced, nubile young woman half her age.

Nevertheless Wu Chao tried to maintain her grip on Kao-tsung by providing him with new and exciting sexual variations. She had mirrors installed around the couch where she used to sport with him in the day-time. One day General Liu Jen-kuei came for an audience. He was hor-rified to see the Emperor sitting alone, flanked by two mirrors, and said, 'There are not two suns in the sky, nor two rulers on the earth. Now your servants see numerous Sons of Heaven. Is this not a sinister omen?' The Emperor had the mirrors removed. But Wu Chao had them reinstalled for her own pleasure after his death.

Now some more drastic method of removing the Empress Wu's rival Ho-lan Kuo-ch'u was called for. At a banquet given by Wu Chao's mother the Lady of Jung in honour of the Emperor and Empress, Ho-lan Kuo-ch'u collapsed in convulsions and died. The Empress Wu's nephews Wu Wei-liang and Wu Huai-yün were accused of poisoning her and executed, and the remains of their side of the family were struck off the clan register and exiled to the south. There is some doubt about who was responsible. The Lady of Jung could have done it to secure her position as mother-in-law of the Emperor and, simultaneously, to rid herself of the stepfamily she hated. Another theory is that Wu Wei-lian and Wu Huai-yün did it, aiming to poison Wu Chao and put Hol-lan Kuo-ch'u on the throne in her place. But the dynastic chroniclers say that it was the Empress Wu who laced Ho-lan Kuo-chu's food with a lethal compound of clay. In the long history of China, other Empresses had risen to power as Wu Chao had, but they had always done it with the backing of a powerful family. Wu Chao had done it in spite of her family. Only her mother could be relied on.

The Empress Wu's father Wu Shih-huo was now left without a descendent of the male line to make sacrifices in his ancestral shrine, so the murdered Ho-lan Kuo-ch'u's brother – and thus the Lady of Jung's grandson – Ho-lan Min-chih was honoured with the Wu surname, so that he could perform the ancestral rites. But Ho-lan Min-chih proved to be a bad choice. A ne'er-do-well, he lived with his grandmother and, when the Empress Wu's daughter the Princess Tai-ping visited the Lady of Jung with a number of palace women in attendance, he set about seducing all of them. Then he abducted and raped a noted beauty, the daughter of Yang Ssu-chien, who had been selected to be the consort of the Crown Prince. This was a serious offence.

Up until this point Ho-lan Min-chih had been protected by his grandmother, who doted on him. But that protection was lost when the Lady of Jung died in 670, year one Hsien Heng, which means 'all prosper' or 'everything goes smoothly'. She was given a lavish state funeral with military escorts, musicians and flag carriers. At that time there had been a drought in northern China and the crops had failed. In the face of famine, the Lady of Jung's opulent send-off caused resentment against the whole Wu family. To atone, the Empress Wu offered to abdicate, but, as the Emperor was increasingly unfit to govern, this was an empty gesture. Instead, the Empress Wu decided to sacrifice one of her relatives. She already believed that Ho-lan Min-chih suspected her of the murder of his sister, Ho-lan Kuo-ch'u, and moved against him. With the Lady of Jung dead, he was without a benefactor. A wayward youth, he crassly ignored the mourning laws. These stipulated that a grandson must mourn for twenty-seven months – during that time he should don austere cloths, eschew music and dancing and refrain from sex. Casting aside the regulation sackcloth, Ho-lan Min-chih continued his regular round of debauched entertainments. The Empress Wu promptly charged him with unfilial conduct and stripped him of his honorific surname Wu. He was banished, but killed himself – or was killed – on the road to exile and his known associates were purged. This left Wu Chao's father, Wu Shih-huo, without a male descendant to perform his ancestral rites once again, so his remaining grandsons, Wu Ch'eng-ssu and Wu San-ssu, the surviving sons of Wu Chao's two dead half-brothers, were recalled from exile – ch'eng-ssu means 'to succeed as heir' and san-ssu means 'to think twice'. Both became key confidants of their aunt, the Empress Wu, and were key players in her elevation and downfall.

After the death of the Lady of Jung in 670, the Empress Wu and the Kao-tsung went to visit a Shaolin temple in the Songshan mountains, around a hundred li, or thirty-three miles, from Luoyang. There Wu Chao wrote, 'On seeing the place my dead mother once patronized, the loneliness deepens in my heart, and I feel sad recalling my longing for her. So I composed this poem to express my sorrow:

> Accompanying my Emperor, I tour the restricted gardens,
> Granted this favour to leave the fragrant chambers.
> Clouds lay shrouding the mountain peaks.
> A rosy mist descends, pierced by waving banners.
> The Sun Palace leads to a scene of riverside homes.
> The Moon Hall opens out to a view of houses perched on cliffs.
> Golden wheels spin over the golden land.
> In chambers of incense, long, fragrant robes move.
> Bells sound, the hum of Buddhist chants rises lightly,
> Banners flap, the mists gradually disperse.
> Once it met with the disaster of fire,
> A mountain of fire engulfed the crowded fields.
> There is no trace left of the Flower Terrace,
> But the Lotus Tower remains in all its glory.
> Truly it depends on those with benevolent means
> To aid the Almighty to perfect the world.
> Compassion gives rise to good fortune.
> At this place I linger with dutiful thoughts,
> But a branch in the wind cannot find peace.
> Even tears of blood will not bring her back.

Although the murderous, power-crazed Wu Chao often appears heartless, she was plainly a woman of great feeling. Her utter ruthlessness must be seen in the great sweep of Chinese history, where individual lives and, sometimes, the lives of millions have been sacrificed on the altar of political expediency.

But the sense of mortality that comes with the death of a beloved parent did not curb the Empress Wu's political ambitions. It seemed to sharpen them. Not content with one *feng-shan* ceremony, Wu tried to stage another on Sung-shan, the holy mountain near Luoyang, and other more distant peaks. The sacrifices on Sung-shan scheduled for the winter of 676, year one Yi Feng – 'Appears Like a Phoenix' – was postponed when Tibet invaded. Three years later, in year one Tiao Lu – 'To Mediate' or or 'To Harmonize with Dew' – they were postponed again when the Turks started causing trouble. However, an inscription was left on the Sung-shan that year commemorating Hsia-hou Ch'i, the mother of an early ruler of the Hsia dynasty of around twenty centuries BC, who had been metamorphosed into a large rock on the mountain. She was one of the powerful female figures of Chinese mythology. Finally in 683, year one Hung Tao, one last attempt to stage a second round of *feng-shan* sacrifices was cancelled because of the Kao-tsung's terminal ill-heath. He died later that year. However, the plans for the ceremony had already been laid and the rites that year were to have been divided equally between male and female deities, including the mother of Ch'i and Hsi-wang Mu, the Queen Mother of the West.

Hsi-wang Mu was the queen of the immortals, ruling over the female spirits who lived in a fairyland called Hsi Hua – 'West Flower'. Her fairyland garden was full of exotic birds and rare flowers. The *p'an-t'ao*, the flat peach of immortality, also grew there. Her popularity overshadowed her husband and male counterpart, a mere prince who oversaw the males in Tung Hua – 'East Flower'. Originally Hsi-wang Mu was a mountain spirit, a humanoid with a tiger's teeth and a leopard's tail, who was transformed into a beautiful woman. Her birthday was celebrated by the Pa Hsien – 'the Eight Immortals' – with a great banquet where Hsi-wang Mu served dragon's liver, monkeys' lips and the paws of bears. *P'an-t'ao* was served as dessert.

According to Taoist legend, Hsi-wang Mu visited Wu-ti, the great Han Emperor of the late second and early first century BC, and gave him the fabulous peach of immortality. Wu-ti wanted to plant the stone, but Hsi-wang Mu dissuaded him, for the soil of China was not rich enough to grow such an exotic fruit. Besides, the tree of the *p'an-t'ao* only blossomed once every three thousand years. Nevertheless, Wu-ti held on to the stone. When Hung-wu, the first Emperor of the Ming dynasty, came to the throne in AD 1368, he was presented with the stone of the *p'an-t'ao* which had been found in the treasure house of the preceding Yüan dynasty. Ten engraved symbols identified it as the stone of the peach Hsi-wang Mu had given to Wu-ti some fifteen hundred years before. It is not known where the stone of the *p'an-t'ao* was in the Empress Wu's time, but it was clearly in her interests to promote such powerful female deities.

For the superstitious Wu Chao, ceremony was power and, throughout her time on the throne, she promoted huge public spectacles where she would be centre-stage. In 668–9, years one and two Tsung Chang, she tried also tried reviving the ancient custom of the building a *Ming-t'ang*, or 'Hall of Illumination'. This was a special audience hall used for ceremonial purposes, dedicated to Shang-ti, the supreme deity and the oldest god in the Chinese pantheon, who was worshipped long before the invention of Taoism. Rites performed there would have stressed the Emperor's – and therefore the Empress's – earthly power and harmonious relations with the heavens. However, scholars could not agree on how the hall should be built and its construction was postponed until after Kao-tsung had died and Wu Chao came to power in her own right. Despite these setbacks, in 674, year one Shang Yuan, the Empress Wu did succeed in having Kao-tsung and herself named T'ien-huang – 'Celestial Emperor' – and T'ien-hou – 'Celestial Empress', the first time these titles had been bestowed in Chinese history.

The Empress Wu knew that for a government to win support in China it must gain the respect of the scholar class, so she became a literary patron in her own right. Scholars from the State University established in Luoyang in 662, year two Lung Shuo, were gathered together in court. They produced the *Lieh-nü chuan* – a collection of biographies of famous women – for her, along with the *Ch'en kuei*, a book expressing her philosophy of government which would later became required reading for all candidates for the civil service examinations. She also commissioned another political book called *Pao-liao hsin-chieh* – 'New Admonitions for the Hundred Officials' – and a huge book on music and ritual called the *Yüeh shu*. More than a thousand other volumes were produced reflecting her wide interests. But her literary endeavours had a more sinister purpose. From the late 660s, a group of these scholars – known as the Scholars of the Northern Gate because their quarters were near the northern gate of the Palace City – were enrolled as her private secretariat. This was standard practice for those seeking power in imperial China. T'ai-tsung had gathered the Eighteen Scholars of the Prince of Chin around him before seizing power at the Hsüan Wu Gate, and his son Li Tai had gathered a group of scholars to produce his five hundred scrolls of geographical treatise before he fell from grace. Wu Chao's scholars examined all documents submitted to the Emperor, thus preventing any petitions that might be harmful to her reaching him and greatly increasing her grip on government.

A shrewd politician, the Empress Wu further secured her position by a severe crackdown on top officials, while taking a more lenient approach to their juniors, being liberal to society at large and positively generous to the lower orders. Towards the end of 674, year one Shang Yuan – 'Above the First One' – she made a bid for popularity by introducing a twelve-point plan for reform:

1. Taxes were slashed on agriculture and silk production and the conscription of those involved in those industries was stopped.
2. Metropolitan taxes were cut and the cultivation of lands formerly left fallow around the walls of the palace was permitted.
3. With the war against Korea now over, she demobbed most of the army, declaring that she intended now to follow a policy of peace and thus transform the Empire through religion and virtue.
4. The Department of Public Works was to stop extravagant spending on the decorations of palaces, temples and monasteries.
5. The budget for building works was to be slashed, even when it employed compulsory or corvée labour.
6. The channels for citizens to express their opinions and represent them to the throne were to be broadened.
7. This new freedom of expression was to be balanced by an edict 'to shut the mouths of slandering minions'.
8. Everyone, including princes and dukes, was to study the *Tao-te ching* – 'The Classic Way of Power' – by the Taoist sage Lao-tzu.
9. The period of mourning for a dead mother was to be increased to three years, even when a father was still alive. Before, only a father had been mourned for that period.
10. All civil servants who had been retired honourably before 674 would not be recalled, or have their previous actions re-examined, and were to be allowed to keep their titles however they had been acquired.

11. The salaries for all officials above the eighth grade who served in the capital were to be raised.
12. All long-serving officials with a good record were to be promoted, even if they had no sponsor to recommend their elevation.

She could have been a modern politician running for office.

These measures were calculated to make Wu popular with the people and the civil service. But Kao-tsung did much to undermine this. In 630, year five Chen Kuan, T'ai-tsung had issued an edict colour-coding clothing across the Empire. Mandarins of the third grade and above were to wear purple. Those of the fourth and fifth grades wore red. The sixth and seventh wore green and the eight and ninth wore blue. Other men of distinction, such as Buddhist and Taoist clerics and eminent scholars, were also allowed to wear purple and wives wore robes of the same colour as their husbands. Under this edict white – the traditional colour of mourning – was prescribed for commoners. But the people did not like the colour of their clothes being imposed on them by statute. They took to wearing colourful underwear, commonly short tunics or chemises in vivid hues. Some would strip off their white outer garments and parade around their villages in this underwear. When the Emperor got to hear about this in 674 he issued an edict ordering everyone to wear underwear in the same colour as their outer garments.

Kao-tsung was particular about dress. When the Chinese version of the burnoose, which covered a woman completely, began to go out of style, the Emperor believed that this signalled a serious decline in public decency and in 663, year three Lung Shuo, and 671, year two Hsien Heng, he issued edicts trying to revive the garment. But no mere man can dictate fashion and by 705, when Wu Chao died, the burnoose had disappeared completely. Instead women had taken to wearing curtained hats that merely covered the face with a veil of gauze. The more adventurous even went out with their face uncovered, which Kao-tsung found positively obscene.

Although Wu was a Buddhist, the Empress Wu's twelve points were aimed to cultivate the support of Taoists directly and Confucianists by cutting back the building of Buddhist temples and monasteries. The twelve points were incorporated in an edict and initialled by the

Emperor, though there was no doubt who the real author was. A general amnesty was declared. Then the following year, Wu cut taxes again, ending all levies that had been raised to fund the Korean war.

However, although Wu Chao has been lauded by Marxist historians, the peasantry suffered under her rule. Aristocrats, mandarins, military governors, merchants, and army officers began establishing huge estates, undermining the 'equal fields' system of agriculture and depriving the peasants of their land. But, as these people were powerless, their fate did not concern her.

The greatest challenge to the Empress Wu's power came from her own son the Crown Prince Li Hung. He was twenty-four in 675 when Kao-tsung suffered another attack of paralysis and dizziness. He proposed making Wu Chao regent, but the Vice President of the Secretariat Hao Ch'un-chün was against it, saying, 'The Son of Heaven manages the external and the Empress the internal – this is the way of heaven.' Other courtiers pointed out that Li Hung was very able and could be regent himself. He had carried out much of the government's business from Ch'ang-an while the Emperor and Empress were away in Luoyang. He was of age, humane, filial, and serious, and could soon be expected to rule in his own right. There was then a falling-out between mother and son. Li Hung discovered that the two daughters of the Pure Concubine, Kao An and I Yang, had been confined to their apartments for the twenty years since the death of their mother on Wu Chao's orders. They were now past thirty and unmarried. Li Hung took pity on them and petitioned the Emperor for their release. Kao-tsung could hardly refuse. Wu Chao took her revenge by finding the two women army officers of low rank to marry, effectively humiliating them. But the Empress Wu was still furious. When Li Hung visited his mother at the summer palace in the imperial park outside Luoyang on the twenty-second day of the fourth month, Yi-hai, year two Shang Yuan – 25 May 675 – he mysteriously died. It was thought at the time that he had been poisoned by the Empress Wu or on her orders. After he was dead, Kao-tsung said that he had only been prevented by illness from abdicating in Li Hung's favour and he gave his son the posthumous name Hsiao-ching huang-ti – 'Filial and Reverent Emperor' – as if he had actually been Emperor.

The Pure Concubine Hsiao's son, Li Su-chieh, had had some influence over his father, but the Empress Wu had forced him into exile in 666 after it had been alleged that he had some contagious disease. The rising official Chang Chien-chih petitioned for his return. The Scholars of the Northern Gate intercepted the petition. Li Su-chieh was accused of offering bribes and was despatched to an even more remote place of exile under guard. Li Shang-chin, another son of Kao-tsung's by a minor consort, was exiled to the wilds of Hunan on trumped-up charges.

Closer to home was Kao-tsung's young aunt the Princess Ch'ang Lo, who was much loved by her nephew and seems to have had some influence over the Emperor. She was a danger on another front. Her daughter, Lady Zhao, was married to Wu Chao's eldest surviving son, Li Che, Prince of Ying. The Empress Wu had the unfortunate young woman imprisoned in quarters where she had to do her own cooking. After a while, her jailers noticed that there was no smoke coming from the chimney. Entering her cell, they found she had been dead for some time. Princess Ch'ang-lo and her husband were then exiled and all communication between her and the Emperor was banned.

Li Hsien, probably the son of Wu's sister Lady Ho-lan, took over as Crown Prince on 1 July 675, the last day of the fifth month, Bing-zi, year two Shang Yuan. He was twenty-one and was seen as a capable successor, who already had sons of his own. He was also interested in Buddhism and scholarship. Wu Chao herself had supervised his education, writing letters of instruction and reprimand and even allowing the appointment of four men known to be hostile to her as his counsellors. The year after he was made Crown Prince, he presented a famous commentary to the throne. However, his position was precarious. He was a favourite of the Emperor and, hence, a threat to Wu Chao.

The Empress had two more sons, known to be her own – nineteen-year-old Li Che and, her favourite, thirteen-year-old Li Tan, who, against convention, she had kept in court with her. There was also her beloved daughter the Princess Tai-ping. In 677, year two Yi Feng, when she was around thirteen, the King of Tibet was suing for peace and offered to marry her. But Wu Chao did not want to despatch her daughter to a land that the Chinese considered barely civilized. To avoid offending the Tibetans with a direct refusal, the Empress Wu had part of the palace remodelled as a convent and the Princess Tai-ping formally became a Taoist nun – and thus ineligible for marriage. She had nominally been enrolled as a nun at the age of six, when her grandmother died. Her enrolment was said to have been done in atonement for her mother who had reneged on her vows. Although Wu Chao was a Buddhist and had been a nun in a Buddhist monastery, it was important politically for her to embrace Taoism, which, since the toppling of the Sui, had resumed its position as the state religion. Whereas Buddhism has an exclusively male pantheon, Taoism absorbed cults of some antiquity that were devoted to the worship of female deities such as Hsi-wang Mu, Queen Mother of the West. Its most prominent tradition, the Shang-ching school of Mao-shan, traced itself back to a female founder – a 'Mysterous and Marvellous Jade Woman' named Hsüan-miao yü-nü, a being of supernatural dimensions which were also endowed on her children.

However, the convent life did not suit Princess Tai-ping. One day, when she was of marriageable age, she came to sing and dance before her parents dressed in the ceremonial costume of an officer, including purple robe, jewelled belts and a turban on her head. The Emperor asked why she was dressed that way, since she was not a soldier. Would the outfit do for his son-in-law then? Tai-ping asked. Her parents took the hint and on the twenty-second day of the seventh month, Wu-zi, year one of K'ai Yao – 11 August 681 – she was married to an officer of the guards named Hsüeh Shao – son of Princess Chengyang, the daughter of Emperor T'ai-tsung and Empress Wen-te – in a lavish ceremony held at night. The reign name K'ai Yao means 'To Open and Dazzle'. The wedding was marred by the fact that, during a great torchlit procession, the trees along the route caught fire. By this time, Li Hsien had already fallen from grace.

The Crown Prince had surrounded himself with an experienced band of advisors and, when the Emperor fell ill again in 679, Li Hsien stepped in and gained great praise for his administrative competence. Rumours then began to circulate that he was not the Empress Wu's son at all, but that of her sister Lady Ho-lan, who had entered the imperial harem in the 640s. This story was impossible to counter, since Li Hung had been born one year before Li Hsien and Li Che one year after. And the same year Li Hsien was born the Empress Wu had given birth to the daughter she had smothered.

Li Hsien was fond of wine and sex and he had a relationship with one of the Empress's household slaves, a boy named Chao Tao-sheng, giving him both money and silks. He was admonished for this and the Empress Wu got her Scholars of the Northern Gate to write the *Shao-yang cheng-fan* – 'Model of Government for an Heir Apparent' – and the *Hsiao-tzu chuan* – 'Biographies of Filial Sons' – directly criticizing him.

At the time, the Empress Wu had a new magician and sorcerer named Ming Ch'ung-yen, who had also found favour with the Emperor. He pointed out that Li Che looked like Kao-tsung and his younger brother Li Tan also resembled a former ruler, but Li Hsien did not have the physiognomy of an Emperor. Ming Ch'ung-yen was killed on the road by bandits who were never caught. The Empress Wu suspected that Li Hsien was behind the murder. Formal complaints were laid and a high-ranking commission was set up to investigate. Wu Chao's slave and Li Hsien's lover Chao Tao-sheng was arrested and confessed that Li Hsien had ordered Ming Ch'ung-yen's death. Investigators then found a large cache of arms and armour in the Crown Prince's stables and came to the conclusion that Li Hsien was planning a coup.

The Emperor did not believe this and sought to pardon him. The public did not believe the accusation either, so the arms and armour were burnt very publicly at the Bridge of the Ford of Heaven in Luoyang so that both the populace and officials could see the evidence of his guilt. Li Hsien was then demoted to the rank of commoner and imprisoned. Later, he was banished to Szechwan, where, after a few years exile, he was forced to commit suicide at Wu Chao's behest. Several of his advisors were also banished, along with two more royal princes, Li Wei, Prince of Chiang, and Li Ming, Prince of Ts'ao, the son of Lady Yang, former Princess of Chi. Both were allowed to return to court sometime later, but their authority had been fatally undermined.

When Li Ming was banished again three year later, false accusations were laid against him by the district governor seeking to curry favour with the Empress Wu. She then ordered Li Ming to commit suicide. Later, the story goes, the governor was asleep one night when an assassin entered his house, decapitated him and fled with his head. Sometime after that, in a fresh purge, Wu Chao had Li Ming's sons executed. When government officials were confiscating their property, which was forfeit to the state, they found the governor's skull. It had his name inscribed on it, and was lacquered and had been turned into a chamber pot. Sadly the official histories do not support this colourful tale, merely saying that the governor committed suicide after being dismissed by the Emperor Kao-tsung following Li Ming's death.

With Li Hsien out of the way, Wu Chao's next son Li Che became Crown Prince on the twenty-third day of the eight month, Ji-mao, year one Yung Lung – 'Forever Prosper' – 24 September 680. He had only held two minor posts and had little experience of government. Consequently he was no direct threat to the power of the Empress Wu. However, as Crown Prince, he was still a focus of political manoeuvring. Ho Ch'u-chün, who had opposed Wu Chao being appointed regent in 675, was to be his tutor – an appointment that brought with it evident perils. The Emperor then took the unusual step of making Li Che's son, Li Ch'ung-jun, Huang t'ai-sun – 'Heir Apparent Grandson'. It was thought that this was an expression of Kao-tsung's fear that his son might be deprived of his throne by Wu Chao.

Kao-tsung fell ill again in 681. Li Che acted as regent while he underwent medical treatment. The Empress Wu was happy to have him as a figurehead, since the government was unpopular at that time. The border incursions that had stopped the *feng-shan* sacrifices that Wu Chao had planned for the five holy mountains in 676 and 679 and new palace-building had emptied the imperial coffers. A new round of taxation sought to remedy this, but a drought and a famine sent prices soaring. Efforts to tame the economy by cutting the minting of new coinage – already in short supply – proved disastrous and the imperial family were reduced to selling off the horse manure from the imperial stables. Although this was highly profitable, bringing in twenty million coppers in the year 681, year one K'ai Yao, alone, Empress Wu stopped it on the grounds that 'later ages will call the T'ang sellers of horse manure'. She also banned, on similar grounds, the superintendent of the Forbidden Park north of Ch'ang-an from selling fruit and vegetables grown there.

The following year – 682 or year one Yung Jun – China was hit by a plague of locusts and an epidemic, along with fresh droughts and floods, causing famine in the two capitals. Corpses lined the streets and people resorted to cannibalism to survive. Traditionally the Emperor took personal responsibility for such calamities, since he alone was supposed to intercede between his people on earth and the workings of heaven. When locusts arrived in Ch'ang-an in 628, year two Chen Kuan, Kao-tsung's father T'ai-tsung seized a grasshopper in the Forbidden Park.

'Mankind depends on grain for life,' he declared. 'If the people have committed sins, I am solely accountable for them. You should devour me only, and not harm the people.'

With that, T'ai-tsung devoured the locust.

And later the Emperor Hsüan-tsung, the grandson of Wu Chao, exposed himself naked for three days to the sun during a drought while praying to the gods in an attempt to elicit their sympathy.

But Kao-tsung was not up to such gestures. He distracted himself by sending an expedition up the Yangtze to search for a rare species of bamboo. Although it was plain by 683 that the Emperor was on his last legs, the Empress Wu still planned further *feng-shan* sacrifices the following year to set the seal on his reign. They too had to be cancelled. Kao-tsung was now in no condition even to see his ministers and many suspected he was already dead. However, in the eleventh month of 683 he held one last audience at the Bridge of the Ford of Heaven.

On the fourth day of the twelfth month – 27 December 683 – Kao-tsung declared a general amnesty and changed the reign name to Hung-tao, which means 'Make the Great Tao'. He decreed that no less than three Taoist monasteries should be set up in each superior prefecture, two in each middle prefecture and one in each inferior prefecture. He wanted to ride to the Tse-tien Men – the great south gate of the Palace City – to proclaim the amnesty there but found he was too weak to mount his horse. Instead the people of Luoyang were summoned to the Hall of Audience in the palace to hear the proclamation. Afterwards, he was too frail to be moved. That night he was attended by P'ei Yen, who held a senior post in the Department of State Affairs, the Secretariat and the Chancellery, and gave him his last will. The Crown Prince, Kao-tsung said, should ascend the throne 'in front of his coffin' – that is, before he was buried. He alone should settle the important affairs of state and only 'when matters of defence and administration cannot be decided, the course of action recommended by the Celestial Empress shall be adopted'. Then Kao-tsung died. He was fifty-five. His widow Wu Chao gave him the posthumous name T'ien-huang ta-ti, the title of Lao-tzu in his divine aspect. According to precedent, Wu Chao, now fifty-eight, was to go into an honourable retirement. But the Dowager Empress Wu had other plans.

CHAPTER EIGHT
THE REGENT UNBOUND

THE DOWAGER EMPRESS took no notice of the wishes of the late Celestial Emperor. Instead of allowing the new Emperor to take the throne before the old one was in his grave, she delayed the coronation for a week.

Little is known of Li Che before he came to throne. As the Emperor's seventh son – the third by Wu Chao – he was not expected to succeed. He was also unsuited for the task. He had already shown weakness in the face of his mother when he had allowed her to put his first wife, the daughter of Princess Ch'ang-lo, in prison, where she died. Like his father, Li Che had a penchant for strong women. His second wife was a member of the powerful and extensive Wei clan from the north-west, centred on Kuan-chung. She gave him a son and a daughter. While Kao-tsung was alive, he had named the son Li Ch'ung-jun, 'Heir Apparent Grandson'. This was tantamount to a death sentence and the boy was executed in 701.

The court officials liked Li Che, who ascended the throne as Chung-tsung, since the succession gave them a chance to shrug off the power of the Dowager Empress Wu. But one of his first acts in office was to appoint his father-in-law, Wei Hsüan-chen, First Minister. This was a violation of the protocol concerning the family of the consort. Wei Hsüan-chen had been made a prefect when Li Che had become Crown Prince and that was the highest rank he should have been allowed. Chung-tsung also sought to raise the son of this wet nurse – a man said not to be of 'the clear stream' – to the fifth rank. He had already ennobled the wet nurse herself because it was she, not his mother, who had raised him. Wu Chao had deliberately avoided raising up any of her clan in such a fashion and, in her eyes, these actions made Chung-tsung unfit to rule.

The President of the Chancellery P'ei Yen had been an ally of Li Che when he had been regent. But now he saw his authority being challenged by Wei Hsüan-chen and, worse, the Empress Wei. She was a headstrong woman – her clan, the Wei, had produced both consorts and First Ministers earlier in the dynasty. P'ei Yen was particularly put out because Wei Hsüan-chen had achieved his position by patronage, whereas P'ei Yen had entered government service through the examination system and worked his way up. He turned for support to the Dowager Empress Wu and thwarted Chung-tsung at every turn. Kao-tsung's will had said that, 'when matters of defence and administration cannot be decided, the course of action recommended by the Celestial Empress shall be adopted'. P'ei Yen took a contrary position on every issue, ensuring that every decision had to be referred to the Dowager Empress. But the Empress Wei persisted and, out of frustration, Chung-tsung threatened to replace P'ei Yen as President of the chancellery with Wei Hsüan-chen alongside his position as First Minister. This would make him the most powerful man in the Empire. P'ei demurred.

'What is to stop Us handing the whole of the Empire to him?' asked Chung-tsung in pique. 'So why should I not make him President of the chancellery? Of what concern to Us is your opinion?'

P'ei Yen was stunned by this rebuke and immediately reported it to the Dowager Empress Wu. The following day, the Empress assembled the whole court in the Ch'ien Yüan Hall, one of the main audience halls inside the south gate of the Palace City. She accused her son of treasonous intent and calmly read out a Decree of Deposition.

'What is my crime?' Chung-tsung protested.

'You intended to give the Empire away to your father-in-law?' said the Dowager Empress. 'Is that not a crime?'

Then the Yü-lin Guard, led by P'ei Yen and Scholar of the Northern Gate Liu Wei-chih, dragged Chung-tsung from the throne. Although traditionally numbering just one hundred men, the Yü-lin Guards determined every palace coup in the early T'ang period. As they were Li retainers, it was all the more surprising that they backed the Dowager Empress Wu and P'ei Yen against the legitimate Li descendent on the throne. They would be rewarded. Under the Empress Wu, the Yü-Li Guard would be greatly expanded until it was ten thousand strong.

There was a precedent for Wu Chao's move. During the Han dynasty, the Dowager Empress Lü had seized power from her son Hui-ti, but that does not seem to have been mentioned at the time. Instead, Wu Chao argued that the throne risked being usurped by the Wei and that she had acted to save the T'ang dynasty. The ambitious politicians that surrounded her were easily convinced out of self-interest.

Chung-tsung was demoted back to his princely rank and imprisoned. The following day, 27 February 684 – the fourth day of the second lunar month, Xin-you, year one Wen Ming – 'Enlightened Civilization' – Wu's twenty-two-year-old son Li Tan was proclaimed Emperor under his temple name Jui-tsung.

Historians such as the Sung Neo-Confucian Chu Hsi, who wrote the standard work *T'ung-chien kang-mu* – 'Fundamental Elements of the Comprehensive Mirror' – believed that this deposition was illegal and recognized Chung-tsung as the true Emperor until his death in 710. Certainly Jui-tsung was nothing more than Wu Chao's puppet – he was a reluctant ruler even when he later came to power in his own right. The Empress Wu merely claimed that she was his mouthpiece: as he had a speech impediment he could not talk. In the *Comprehensive Mirror*, Chu Hsi took a more forthright view: 'Political affairs were decided by the Dowager Empress. She had Jui-tsung installed in a detached palace and he had no chance to participate.'

Indeed, Wu now made no pretence to rule as regent. She no longer hid behind a curtain in the audience chamber as she had when Kao-tsung had been alive. She faced her audience in full imperial regalia. There were, in fact, fourteen sets of imperial regalia for different ceremonial occasions – audiences on the first day of the lunar month or New Moon, audiences on the fifteenth day of the lunar month or Full Moon, passing legal judgements, feasting officials, funerals, memorial services at tombs, hunting, worshipping the gods of the grain and soil, worshipping heaven, sacrificing to former rulers, giving offerings to the gods of the mountains and sea, and, most importantly, enthronements. The stitching of imperial ceremonial robes was said to be so fine that you could not see the seams. They were embroidered with pictures of holy mountains, dragons and other imperial symbols. These robes would be like a modern dressing gown with voluminous sleeves that hung well below the knee. The right lapel would be crossed over the left and the robe was closed with a leather belt fastened with jade hooks. A ceremonial sword, decorated with jade and gold, would hang from the belt, along with silk pouches for carrying seals and jade girdle pendants. The outfit would be completed with silk slippers with upturned toes and a mortarboard held in place by a chin strap with strings of pearls hanging down front and back. These ceremonial robes and other official attire were designed by a court artist, who also provided paintings for fans, parasols and palanquins – the oriental version of a sedan chair carried on the shoulders of two or more men.

Jui-tsung did not get to wear this fancy attire and was not present when the affairs of state were discussed. Shut away in his palace, he was, to all intents and purposes, a prisoner. However, his wife Lady Liu was named Empress and his five-year-old son became Crown Prince. But this position was undermined when Wu Chao raised her nephew Wu Ch'eng-ssu to the rank of First Minister and named him *Huang-ssu* or 'Emperor Expectant'. She used him to undertake sensitive and confidential business and, as President of the Board of Rites, he headed the party that sought to make her Emperor in her own right.

Plainly this was Wu Chao's ambition and she solicited the help of the heavens. In 684, year one Wen Ming, the Hsüan-nü or 'Mysterious Female', consort of the Yellow Emperor, had appeared on a cloud of auspicious colour to confer an elixir upon the Empress. In the ninth month of that year, now carrying the reign name Wu-chen, she declared that the mother of Lao-tzu should not be left without a title; after all Kao-tsung had bestowed a lengthy one on her son. From then on Lao-tzu's mother was to be known as Hsien-t'ien t'ai-hou – 'Great Empress Who Preceded Heaven' – and statues of her were to be placed in Taoist temples, though some sources believe this figure to be a likeness of Wu Chao's own mother, Lady Yang. Prophecies also circulated saying that Wu Chao had the divine support of the Lady Tzu-wei, an important goddess of the fourth-century Mao-shan revelatory tradition.

Wu Chao stopped the endless commuting between Ch'ang-an and Luoyang. Luoyang was named Shen-tu – the 'Sanctified Capital' – and Wu's palace there T'ai-ch'u – the 'Great Beginning'. At least 100,000 households from the seven districts surrounding Ch'ang-an were resettled near Luoyang to boost the city's power.

But Ch'ang-an was too important to be left to its own devices, so Wu Chao tried to persuade Liu Jen-kuan, one of her generals from the war against Korea, to come out of retirement and take over as viceroy there. She compared this to the Emperor Kao Tsu, the founder of the Han dynasty, entrusting the province of Shensi, where Ch'ang-an stands, to one of his most trusted ministers. Liu Jen-kuei refused the position and accused her of acting like Kao Tsu's widow, the cruel and vindicitve Empress Lü. She had ruled as dowager in the second century BC, nine hundred years earlier, in the place not just of her son the Emperor Hui-ti but also of his two sons in an attempt to seize the throne for her own family. As a result, when she died the Lü clan were massacred. The comparison between the Empress Wu and the Empress Lü was often made, but it was said that the Empress Lü was *luan er pu yin* – 'disorderly but not lewd' – while Wu Chao was *yin er pin luan* – 'lewd but not disorderly'.

Wu Chao ignored Liu Jen-kuan's insult, saying that she would bear in mind what he had said as a wise warning. She plied him with flattery and he eventually accepted the post. Despite Confucianism's injunction against the rule of women, like most leading figures in the administration, he recognized that Wu Chao was the person best fitted to rule the country.

With Chung-tsung publicly ousted and Jui-tsung sidelined, the only threat to Wu Chao's authority was Li Hsien, the supposed son of her sister Lady Ho-lan, who was still alive in exile in Szechwan. As a former Crown Prince, he was still a possible focus for revolt. Wu Chao sent an envoy, General Ch'iu Shen-chi, ostensibly to protect him. He moved Li Hsien to a remote town, imprisoned him and harried the prince until he committed suicide. Ch'iu Shen-chi was then blamed for this and demoted. The late Li Hsien's former titles were posthumously returned and he was given a state funeral. Afterwards, Ch'iu Shen-chi's rank was quietly restored.

Tsa-she or 'Acts of Grace' were imperial edicts that pardoned felons and rewarded good service. During the T'ang dynasty they were also used to outline the state of the nation and announce new administrative provisions. Wu Chao issued *tsa-she* with unusual frequency, one on each of the sixteen changes of reign names she made between her assumption of sole power in 684 and her deposition and death in 705.

The first Act of Grace was issued in 684 under the reign name Kuang Che – the third reign name that year, since Kao-tsung, Chung-tsung and Jui-tsung had all had one. It means 'To Glorify the House', ostensibly to commemorate the discovery of some Buddhist relics. The Act of Grace proclaimed the 'measureless virtue of the people', pardoned various types of criminals and gave alms to the aged and relief to the poor and sick. Once again taxes were to be cut. The corresponding cut in expenditure would be made by sacking extraneous female servants from the palace. This demonstrated Wu Chao's commitment to the Confucian virtue of thrift. Soldiers garrisoned on far-flung frontiers were to be allowed home to make sacrifices to their ancestors, demonstrating her filial piety.

Years of internal peace had resulted in rapid population growth. This had brought with it corruption. Censuses found it hard to keep up, providing opportunities for false registration, tax evasion and other malpractices. These were to be stamped out by a new branch of the Censorate who would make snap inspections of the provincial administrations. New prefectures would be created where the population exceeded ten thousand households and new counties formed where they exceeded thirty thousand. In the army, morale was low, so length of service was to be cut, rewards were to be redistributed and those who bought commissions but never turned up for duty were to be punished. These reforms were to be administered by a new intake of Confucian 'men of virtue' into the civil service.

There were to be symbolic changes too. The new regime's banners were to be gold trimmed with violet. Officials were to have new robes and insignia. Posts were to have more aspirational names. Some harked back to the early Chou era, running approximately from 1050 to 600 BC, which Confucians saw as a golden age of peace and prosperity. Under the Han, the usurper Wang Mang had also adopted these so-called Chou-li designations in an attempt to legitimize his short-lived Hsin dynasty when he seized the throne in AD 9. Other names were Taoist in nature. The new Censorate was to be the Su-cheng t'ai or 'Terrace of Circumspect Law'; the Secretariat was to be the Feng-ko or 'Phoenix Terrace' and the Chancellery became the Luan-t'ai or 'Luan Terrace'. The *luan* was a type of phoenix that was supposed to have carried the Han Taoist adept Mei Fu to the land of the immortals, and the appearance of the phoenix had, since ancient times, heralded the arrival of the sage-king. Again Wu Chao had carefully balanced Taoist, Confucian and Buddhist imagery to appeal to a broad swathe of the population.

The Empress Wu made other changes that made her intentions clear. The late Lady of Jung was posthumously named Dowager Empress, making her daughter, by implication, the Emperor. And seven temples were to be dedicated to Wu Chao's ancestors, all of whom would receive appropriate titles. Seven was the number customarily reserved for the imperial family. This move was encouraged by Wu Ch'eng-ssu, since promoting their ancestors to royal rank would also legitimize his claim to succeed Wu Chao, or even, being a man, to depose and replace her. However, P'ei Yen protested at the building of the temples and, like Liu Jen-kuei, compared her to the reviled Empress Lü.

'Your Majesty is the mother of the Empire,' he said, 'and Your great virtue runs the government. But Your Majesty should exercise impartial judgement. Your Majesty should not allow Your ancestors to be promoted to royal rank, in case it is said that You are seeking private advantage. Your Majesty should not risk following the example of the Empress Lü of the Han.'

'The Empress Lü drew her imperial authority from living individuals,' Wu Chao replied, meaning her son Hui-ti and, when he died, her grandsons, whom she had imprisoned. 'Honouring my ancestors concerns the dead. How can the two things be similar?'

'Creeping plants tend to spread,' said the wily P'ei Yen.

Some sources say that Wu Chao took on board what P'ei Yen had said and stopped the elevation of her ancestors. However, there is no indication that she shelved her plans to seize the throne in her own right and her clear intention sparked a rebellion.

It was led by Li Ching-yeh, the grandson of Li Chi, the conqueror of Korea and a key figure in Wu Chao's rise to become Empress. He had followed his grandfather into battle and fought with distinction. However, on his deathbed in 669, year two Tsung Chang, Li Chi was said to have foreseen his grandson's downfall. Inheriting the title Duke of Ying, Li Ching-yeh had enjoyed privileged entry into the civil service and had risen to become a provincial governor, until he was convicted of corruption and sacked early in 684. He was exiled to Yang-chou, along with his brother Li Ching-yu and others involved in their money-making scheme.

At the junction of the Yangtze river and the Grand Canal, Yang-chou was a wealthy commercial centre where ships from Persia, Arabia and South-East Asia unloaded rare perfumes, jewels, drugs, dyes, and other exotic goods. It produced fine furniture, felt hats, bronze mirrors, sugar refined from cane, and boats that fetched five million cash. It was also a haven for the disgraced sons of good families who had no future in imperial service to look forward to. They had nothing to do all day but plan insurrection. By overthrowing the Empress Wu and returning the country to male rule, Li Ching-yeh and his cohorts thought they would make themselves national heroes and all their previous crimes would be forgotten. This charmed circle included the poet and former imperial treasurer Lo Pin-wang, former Grand Secretary of the chancellery T'ang Chih-chi and the former censor Wei Ssu-wen.

The exact aims of the rebels are not clear. The ostensible purpose of the revolt was to free Chung-tsung and put him back on the throne. Later, Chung-tsung said that he had been tempted to lead a rebellion himself at that time, but having seen the country's problems laid out in the Act of Grace of 684 he knew that they could only be solved by a strong and experienced ruler – the one thing he was not. The rebels took as their titular head the dead Li Hsien, Chung-tsung's elder brother, but Li Ching-yeh may merely have borrowed the dead man's name to cloak his own imperial ambitions.

Having been civil servants themselves, the conspirators had good connections in the government. Wei Ssu-wen contacted his former colleague Hsüeh Chung-chang and arranged for him to visit Yang-chou. When Hsüeh Chung-chang arrived the prefect of the city, another conspirator named Wei Ch'ao, told him that the governor of Yang-chou was planning a rebellion. Hsüeh Chung-chang, who was not a disgraced former civil servant but a high official on government business, did his duty and arrested the governor. Then Li Ching-yeh turned up, courtesy of the imperial postal service, posing as a serving officer. He carried with him a forged document appointing him military governor and claimed to have a decree authorizing him to raise troops to put down a supposed rebellion in the remote Kao Chao region of southern Szechwan. Li Ching-yeh demonstrated his authority by having the governor of Yang-chou executed, along with a supporter. He seized the provincial treasury and emptied the prisons, arming the former inmates. Making his co-conspirators the officers in this army of villains, he opened a military headquarters and, within ten days, raised 100,000 men.

As self-styled Grand General of the Restoration, Li Ching-yeh denounced the Empress Wu and issued a manifesto, written by Lo Pin-Wang, a brilliant polemicist, outlining his intentions. It read,

> The woman Wu, who has usurped the throne, is not of noble extraction, but is by nature obdurate and unyielding and, by origin, truly obscure. Formerly she was among the lower ranks of T'ai-tsung's servants, served him with her body, and then made use of an occasion when the Crown Prince [Kao-tsung] was changing his clothes to fornicate with him. When she reached a mature age, she brought disorder to the Crown Prince's palace. Concealing her intimacy with the former Emperor, she sought to become the favourite of the Sovereign. Hiding her mouth behind her sleeve, she skilfully slandered other women and with cunning flattery and perverse talents she deluded the Ruler. She plotted the ruin of the then Empress, usurped her pheasant regalia and entrapped the Emperor into an incestuous relationship.
>
> Then, with the heart of a serpent and the nature of a wolf, she favoured evil flatterers while destroying her good and loyal officials. She murdered her own children, slew her elder sister, butchered her brothers, murdered the Emperor and poisoned her mother. She is hated by the gods and men alike. Neither heaven nor earth can bear her. Yet still she harbours disastrous intentions and plans to steal the sacred regalia of the Ruler. She keeps the beloved son of the Ruler sequestered in a separate palace and has given the most important offices of the state to her own coterie of bandits.

Lo Pin-wang then rehearsed the Confucian objections to women wielding political power and gave numerous historical examples of its perils. He concluded with a personal statement from Li Ching-yeh:

> I, Ching-yeh, am a former minister of the imperial T'ang and the eldest son of a noble family. I received the testament of our former Emperor and I owe a debt of gratitude for the liberal graciousness of our ruling dynasty ... My spirit rises with anger like the wind and the clouds. My will is set

on restoring tranquillity to the altars of soil and grain. The whole world has lost hope and the people of the Empire have put their trust in me. I therefore raise the standard of righteous rebellion to purify the Empire of baleful omens of disaster ...

You, my lords ... some of you have been entrusted with weighty charges by the words of the late Emperor. Others have received his dying commands in the Hall of Audience. His words are still in your ears. How can loyalty have fled from your hearts? The earth covering his tomb is not yet dry and where are his young orphan princes, not yet grown to maturity? We may yet change bad fortune into good fortune, show homage to the dead Emperor and serve his living successor. You should one and all arise and devote yourself to the cause of the Ruler. Do not permit our former Emperor's orders to be brought to nothing ... I ask you to look at the world at the present time. Which house possesses the Empire?

A copy of this diatribe reached the Empress. She read it with interest, then condemned her First Ministers for allowing such a great literary talent as Lo Pin-wang to languish in obscurity in the provinces.

Some of the allegations made against her were false. It is unlikely that she poisoned her mother, who seems to have died of natural causes. Although Wu Chao may have been reluctant to have the Empeor Kao-tsung bled, there is no suggestion that she killed him either. Lo Pin-wang may have mistaken the murder of her sister for the murder of her niece Ho-lan Kuo-ch'u, since they had the same surname. And the exile of her brothers on Wu Chao's orders may have led to their deaths, but it could not be said that she actually murdered them. However, many of the accusations were true and would have won the sympathy of the populace at large as well as many at court. Indeed it was the house of Wu that possessed the Empire, not the house of Li. But Wu Chao was not the least perturbed at the accusations. She was now fifty-nine and had spent her entire life in court outsmarting those who conspired against her.

The rebellion met with some initial success. The governor of Ch'u Chou defected to Li Ching-yeh, bringing three sub-prefectures in northern Kiangsu with him. Only the small hill town of Hsiu I on the shores of Lake Hung-tse held out. The Empress Wu quickly rewarded the leader of the town's defence and his brother with high military ranks. She then announced an amnesty for the peoples of Yang-chou and Ch'u Chou who had been dragooned into helping the rebels. A price was put on the heads of Li Ching-yeh and his followers, and Li Hsiao-i, Duke of Liang, was sent with an army of three hundred thousand to put down the rebellion.

Li Ching-yeh's response was to find a man who looked like the former Crown Prince Li Hsien and parade him around his camp. The prince, he maintained, was not dead but was leading the fight against female misrule. This might have proved a rather embarrassing ploy if the rebellion had succeeded and Chung-tsung had been returned to the throne.

Like his cousin Wu Ch'eng-ssu, Wu San-ssu was now a favourite of the Empress Wu. He warned her that the senior T'ang princes were not behind her and urged her to execute Kao-tsung's uncle Li Yüan-chia, Prince of Han, and Li Ling-k'uei, Prince of Lu. When Wu consulted her First Ministers, they refused to speak, fearing the consequences whichever way things turned out. Only P'ei Yen spoke up against executing them, earning Wu Chao's displeasure. But then, P'ei Yen was already compromised. He was the uncle of the unwitting dupe in the conspiracy, Hsüeh Chung-cheng.

It is said that Lo Pin-wang tried to persuade P'ei Yen to join the rebellion by composing a ballad for children to sing in the capital. It went, 'One bit of fire, two bits of fire, the boy in red sits on the throne.' The character 'P'ei' is composed of part of the word *fei* – 'red' – and the word *yi* – 'clothes' – and two characters of the word *huo* – 'fire' – make up the word *yen* – 'flame'.

Though he was out of favour with the Empress Wu, P'ei Yen had nothing to gain by siding with the rebels, for he had helped in the deposition of Chung-tsung. So now he had to set his own course. Learning that the Empress Wu was to visit the Cave Buddhas at Lung-men – the 'Dragon Gate' – outside Luoyang, a religious site she sponsored, he planned to seize the opportunity to capture her outside the city, imprison her and restore Jui-tsung to the throne, thus securing his position. However, the heavens intervened. Heavy rain caused Wu Chao to cancel the trip and P'ei Yen lost his opportunity.

By this time, Li Ching-yeh's rebellion had spread through the eastern province of Kiangsu and the Empress Wu called a council meeting to discuss its suppression. P'ei Yen used the opportunity to urge Wu Chao to retire in favour of Jiu-tsung. This, he argued, would restore male rule by the house of Li and undermine the rebellion politically.

'The Son of Heaven is now of age, yet he does not govern,' he said. 'That is why a man of no account can raise a following. If the Dowager Empress were to hand the government over to the Emperor, the opposition would be pacified, even if no force was used against the rebels.'

But none of the other ministers was prepared to speak up in his support. Instead a censor quickly stepped in to condemn him.

'P'ei Yen has been entrusted with the highest authority in the land and it is his duty to protect the interests of the Emperor,' he said. 'Yet when he is told of a rebellion he does not move to suppress it. On top of that, he urges the Dowager Empress to give up government. There are some dark forces at work in all this.'

P'ei Yen was immediately arrested and handed over to the censor for further investigation. When his house was searched a secret message was discovered among his documents, but no one could decode it. It read simply '*ching e*', which means 'blue goose'. Then Wu Chao dissected the two characters. Put together another way, they meant, 'The twelfth month, I do it myself.' This was taken to mean that P'ei Yen intended to take the throne for himself, though historians suspect that the whole thing might well have been created by Wu Chao's henchmen to frame P'ei Yen.

With dissent close to home, Wu Chao sought the views of Liu Jen-kuei, the viceroy of Ch'ang-an. Like P'ei Yen, he had accused her of acting like Empress Lü, so she could not be sure of his loyalty and sent a courier with a despatch enquiring his position. When Liu Jen-kuei had read the despatch, he asked the courier for the news from Luoyang. The man told him of the arrest of P'ei Yen, boasting that he had known about P'ei Yen's plot at Lung-men. Liu Jen-kuei then sent the courier back to Luoyang with a message for the Dowager Empress Wu. When she opened it, she found it read simply, 'The bearer of this despatch knew that P'ei Yen was plotting against you, but did not report it.' Wu Chao had the courier strangled. She was now assured of Liu Jen-kuei's loyalty.

Wu Chao now knew about the Lung-men plot, but the Censorate did not. The tribunal that examined P'ei Yen were convinced of his innocence. The Vice President of the Secretariat came to Wu and said, 'P'ei Yen is a great statesman who is loyal to the dynasty and has served the throne with all his heart. He deserves good treatment by the state. All the Empire knows that. Your humble servant assures you that P'ei Yen is no traitor.'

'I have proof that P'ei Yen plotted treason,' said the Empress Wu. 'Only you on the investigating tribunal do not know it.'

'If P'ei Yen is a traitor, then we are also traitors,' said the Vice President of the Secretariat, offering his own life instead of P'ei Yen's.

'I know that P'ei Yen is a traitor and you are not,' said Wu Chao.

Despite clear evidence of his treason, P'ei Yen was not without his followers. When he was arrested, General Ch'eng Wu-ting, known as the 'Terror of the Turks' for his actions along the frontier, sent a memorandum defending him. This angered the Empress Wu. Ch'eng Wu-ting's opinion could not be lightly dismissed, since he had proved his loyalty to her while commanding the Yü-lin Guard when Chung-tsung was deposed. But this very fact put him close to P'ei Yen. It was soon alleged that he was a long-time friend of the rebel general T'ang Chih-chi and other conspirators in Yang-chou. Then it was said that he was a secret supporter of Li Ching-yeh and had been party to the Lung-men plot. The Empress Wu insisted that she could not afford any hint of disloyalty among her generals and Ch'eng Wu-ting was beheaded in front of his own troops, who were so intimidated they offered no protest. The Turks were delighted when they heard the news and celebrated Ch'eng Wu-ting's death with a feast. They even erected a temple to their old adversary and sacrificed in it whenever they set out to attack the Chinese.

Other supporters urged P'ei Yen to put up a reasoned defence. He refused, saying, 'When a First Minister is put in prison, reason is of no help' – implying that he was the innocent victim of political persecution. But he had been behind the Lung-men plot and he could hardly have argued that, by trying to restore Jui-tsung to the throne, he was being loyal to the Emperor when he had already connived at the deposition of Chung-tsung.

P'ei Yen suffered a degrading public execution on 30 November 684 – the fifteenth day of the tenth month, Ji-si, year one Kuang Che. His supporters were demoted and exiled to the provinces. The Dowager

Empress Wu then had P'ei Yen's grandfather's tomb desecrated and his family stripped of all honours and titles. However, his sixteen-year-old nephew would not give up without a fight. He demanded an audience. Wu Chao granted one.

'Your uncle plotted against me,' she said. 'What else is there left to say?'

'I have some advice to give Your Majesty,' he said. He told her that she was a wife of the Li family and she should devote herself to its interests, to give up meddling in government for her own ends and promote the interest of her children instead. He also insisted that his uncle was a loyal subject, falsely accused. And he charged her with contriving his downfall.

'I am afraid for Your Majesty,' he said. 'Your Highness should immediately restore the rightful heir and retire to a peaceful old age in the Inner Palace. Then the dynasty will be saved. Otherwise, there will be revolution and the imperial family will be lost.'

'How dare you speak to me like that,' cried Wu Chao and ordered the boy to be dragged from the Hall of Audience. But he put up fierce resistance. Three times they tried to haul him from her presence, but he continued shouting, 'Only by doing what I say will you be saved.' As he could not be removed, the Dowager Empress, outraged, ordered him beaten severely, there and then.

Li Ching-yeh's rebellion might have caused splits in court, but the rebels were equally divided. Wei Ssu-wen, who was now Li Ching-yeh's chief of staff, advised him to march on Luoyang and free the Emperor. As soon it was clear that Li Ching-yeh planned to restore the Son of Heaven to his rightful place, the men of Shantung and Honan, the provinces they had to pass through on the way, would rally to his cause. With this huge following, he could take over the Empire. But other advisors urged Li Ching-yeh first to go north to the province of Ho-pei, where the finest fighting men were to be found and where the people were the most resentful of the rule of the Dowager Empress.

Hsüeh Chung-chang, who had thrown his lot in with the rebels by then, suggested instead that they move south and take the southern cities of Chen Chiang and Ch'ang Chou as a base. Then they could occupy the old southern capital of Nanking, giving the rebellion some much-needed legitimacy, and march north from there. This was fiercely resisted by Wei Ssu-wen, who insisted that the taking of Nanking was a trap that would ensure the failure of the rebellion and bring certain death to the conspirators.

The split between Wei Ssu-wen and Hsüeh Chung-chang was political as well as military. Wei Ssu-wen was loyal to the T'ang dynasty and wanted to place its rightful heir Chung-tsung on the throne. Hsüeh Chung-chang sought to pacify China under his counterfeit Li Hsien and then found a new dynasty, using Nanking as the imperial capital during the transition period.

Hearing of the dissent in the court in Luoyang, Li Ching-yeh came to believe, with Hsüeh Chung-chang, that the T'ang dynasty was finished. The short-lived dynasties of the past had been replaced by generals who had fought ostensibly to restore a rightful heir to the throne, then made themselves regent and finally put their own family on the throne. So Li Ching-yeh moved his main force south across the Yangtze and besieged Chen Chiang. The city was nearly relieved when the governor of Tan Yang, forty-eight li, or sixteen miles, to the south, attacked. The rebels beat off his forces and he was slain in battle. Nevertheless, the city held out for nearly a month. This gave the Korean war veteran General Hei-Ch'ih Ch'ang-chih time to move south and take command of Wu Chao's troops in the T'ang Empire's vast southern province of Kiangnan. The ultimate T'ang loyalist, Hei-Ch'ih Ch'ang-chih had also led successful campaigns against the Tibetans and the Turks, though he was, himself, a Korean from Pai-chi. His name means 'Black Teeth Always' – the Black Teeth were a leading noble clan in Korea.

To protect his rear as he moved south, Li Ching-yeh sent his brother, Li Ching-yu, and the former prefect of Yang-chou, Wei Ch'ai, northwards to hold the strategic approaches to Yang-chou on either side of Lake Hung-tse, two hundred and twenty-seven li, or seventy-five miles, to the north-east. Li Ching-yu occupied Huai Yin on the Grand Canal and Wei Ch'ao held the isolated hill of Tu Liang Shan, seventy-six li, or twenty-five miles to the south-east of the loyalist town Hsiu I.

When three hundred thousand men of the Imperial Army under Li Hsio-i arrived, Wei Ssu-wen despaired. The rebel troops were now divided and, having failed to make any significant advance on Luoyang, they had no more men than the original one hundred thousand they had amassed in the first few days of the rebellion. Li Ching-yeh had no choice but to cancel the advance on Nanking and turn back. Now the rebel forces were on the defensive. He crossed back over the Yangtze and occupied the city of Kao Yu seventy-six li or twenty-five miles to the north of Yang-chou, where the Grand Canal touched Lake Kao Yu.

The Imperial Army attacked Huai Yin, but were beaten off by the rebels. Li Hsiao-i was a cautious general, fearful of what would happen to him if he were defeated. He withdrew and set up camp, awaiting the arrival of Hei-Ch'ih Ch'ang-chih from the south. However, he was accompanied by a censor named Wei Yüan-chung who had experience of the Tibetan war.

'What is at stake here, General, is the fate of the Empire,' Wei Yüan-chung pointed out. 'The Empire has been at peace for many years. News of this rebellion came as a shock and the people want to hear that it has been suppressed. If the Imperial Army stays where it is and makes no move, they will lose hope. And if the court sends another general to take over and you are charged with dilatory conduct, what will you be able to say in your defence?'

The question, coming from a censor attached to the army, amounted to a threat and Li Hsiao-i ordered an advance. This time he attacked Wei Ch'ao on Tu Liang Shan. One of Wei Ch'ao's frontline commanders was slain and he had to rush reinforcements forward to hold the line.

Again Li Hsiao-i withdrew again to consider what to do. Most of his generals considered that Wei Ch'ao was in a strong position. If attacked, he would fight to the death, considerably weakening the imperial forces. Instead, they should contain him, allowing the main force to bypass him, attack Li Ching-yeh at Kao Yu and march on Yang-chou.

Others disagreed. The amount of troops needed to contain Wei Ch'ao adequately would substantially weaken the main force for the attack on Li Ching-yeh. And if they left too few men, they risked Wei Ch'ao breaking out and attacking them from the rear.

Wei Yüan-chung put forward a third point of view. They should attack Li Ching-yu at Huai Yin on the other side of Lake Hung-tse first. Li Ching-yu was no military man. He was a ne'er-do-well who knew nothing of soldiering. It stood to reason that the best of the rebel troops were with Li Ching-yeh's main force at Kao Yu. They had assembled from every region that had rebelled. The inferior forces at Huan Yin could be routed easily, then Li Hsiao-i's men could march on Kao Yu with a victory under their belt. It made sense to attack the weaker force before the stronger one.

The majority of Hsiao-i's officers were against Wei Yüan-chung's plan, pointing out that, if Li Ching-yu held out, his brother would come to his aid and the Imperial Army would be caught between two forces. They said that the rebels' northern outposts at Tu Lian Shan and Huan Yin could be ignored. Once the main force under Li Ching-yeh was defeated, Wei Ch'ao and Li Ching-yu would offer no further resistance.

Ever cautious, Li Hsiao-i looked for the best way of avoiding defeat rather than achieving victory. He attacked Wei Ch'ao on Tu Liang Shan again. Wei Yüan-chung was proved partially right. The best of the rebel forces were with Li Ching-yeh at Kao Yu. Wei Ch'ao barely put up a fight and withdrew from Tu Liang Shan at night. Then the Imperial Army marched on Huan Yu. Li Ching-yu fled, offering no serious resistance. The way was now open to Kao Yu.

This was going to be more of a fight. Li Ching-yeh had set up a defensive position along the banks of the Hsia Ah, a river that connected the Grand Canal to Lake Kao Yu. The Imperial Army attacked at night with a force of five thousand men. But Li Ching-yeh had posted his best men along the river. The attackers were forced back. More than half their number were lost, many drowned as they tried to escape. The general in command was captured. At first he was mistaken for Li Hsiao-I, but when he volunteered his name he said, 'The Imperial Army is upon you. You will be beaten before the day is over. When I am dead, my family will be honoured; yours will be exterminated.' In reply, the rebels beheaded him.

Further attempts to shake Li Ching-yeh from his defensive positions failed. The imperial generals began to think that the rebels' position was too strong to take and Li Hsiao-i suggested falling back to Tien Ch'ang, seventy-six li, or twenty-five miles, to the west. But Wei Yüan-chung urged him to stay. He had noticed the flocks of crows circling over Li Ching-yeh's camp, and deduced that many of his men had been killed.

Wei Yüan-chung had also noticed a dense bank of reeds along the shore Li Ching-yeh was defending and that the wind was blowing from the north.

'The rebels are defeated,' he cried. 'The reeds are dry; the wind is right. We will win if we set them on fire.'

By this time, Li Ching-yeh thought that he had seen off the Imperial Army. Convinced that they would not attack again that day, he withdrew his elite troops from the riverbank to rest them before marching them south to meet Hei-Ch'ih Ch'ang-chih's army, leaving the Hsia Ah river in the hands of second-line troops.

With the reeds on fire, the entire Imperial Army crossed the creek under the cover of flames and smoke. The rebel troops posted there were scorched and blinded. The line broke and the crack troops at the rear could do nothing to stem the rout. In a matter of minutes, the rebel army was crushed. More than seven thousand lay dead on the battlefield. More drowned in the creek and canal as they tried to escape. Li Ching-yeh, Lo Pin-wang and T'ang Chih-ch'i rode off to Yang-chou, where they burnt their papers and collected their families. They planned to take a ship from Chen Chiang and flee to Korea. But when they reached the estuary the wind turned against them. They hid out in the hills until one of the junior officers, in the hope of saving his own life, murdered Li Ching-yeh and twenty-four of his party. He presented their heads to the Imperial Army on 27 February 685 – the sixteenth day of the first month, Ren-shen, year one Ch'ui Kung. Li Ching-yeh's family were exterminated and their tombs – including that of the great Li Chi – were destroyed. Wei Ssu-wen and T'ang Chih-ch'i were captured and beheaded. In another version of the story Li Ching-yeh and Li Po-wang escaped with their lives and became Buddhist monks. In any case, the revolt had been suppressed in little more three months and affected only the small region around Yang Chou and Chen Chiang.

Wu Chao had crushed a rebellion and thwarted a palace coup. Now she would consolidate her power. She called an audience of the entire court and berated them for their incompetence and disloyalty.

'We did not blame the Empire for this. You know that, don't you?' she said. 'We assisted the late Emperor for thirty years and wore Ourselves out with the cares of the Empire. Your ranks, titles and prosperity all come from what We give you, and the peace and tranquillity of the Empire is the result of Our care. When the late Emperor died, he bequeathed his power to Us. We took it not for Ourself, but rather because We loved you. However, among the leaders of this uprising are generals and First Ministers. Why are they so opposed to Us? Among them there was a statesman who had received the will from the late Emperor, yet P'ei Yen was insubordinate and treacherous. There was the offspring of a great general who became a rebel – Li Ching-yeh. And there was a general who showed great skill in war – Ch'eng Wu-t'ing. These three men were looked up to and tried to harm Us, but We were able to destroy them. If any of you believe that you are more able than these three men, then make your move straight away. If not, reform your hearts and serve Us with respect, or become the laughing stock of the entire Empire.'

Those listening took this to heart. Now that there was no one left to oppose her, Wu could rule untrammelled.

CHAPTER NINE

THE PHOENIX ARISES

IN 685, year one Ch'ui Kung, Liu Jen-kuei, viceroy of Ch'ang-an, died. He was the last of the leading figures of the regime to owe his allegiance to T'ai-tsung. Now Wu Chao could start the moves that would make the dynasty her own. First she exiled Chung-tsung, who had been held in prison in Luoyang since he had been stripped of power. He was sent to Fang-chou in Hupei with his pregnant wife and did not return to the capital until 698, year one Shen Lung. There he lived in relative freedom with his family. But Fang-chou was surrounded by hills and was easily guarded.

At this time the President of the Board of Rites was a relative of Li Ching-yeh who had saved his own head by denouncing the rebels. He came up with a suitable quotation from the classical *Shu Ching*, or 'Official History' written in the fourth century BC or before, which helped Wu Chao's bid for ultimate power. It read, 'They let fall altogether their robes and governed the Empire.' This was supposed to convey how effortlessly those who had been chosen by heaven to rule took power – it was as easy as letting your robe fall. It could also be seen as being particularly apt in Wu Chao's case, since she had achieved power by letting fall her robe for T'ai-tsung and Kao-tsung. The quotation was published throughout the Empire and the reign name was changed to Ch'ui Kung – 'Let Fall Altogether', the opening words of the quote – for the next four years. Other prophecies and predictions were circulated, giving the impression that Wu Chao's right to power was written in the heavens.

Now a widow, the Empress Wu had taken a lover named Feng Hsiao-pao. This means 'Little Precious'. He was a lowly peddler, an 'unlicensed seller of sedge, herbs and cosmetics' – essentially a dealer in drugs and aphrodisiacs. Powders and potions were widely used to improve love-making in medieval China. Sulphur was used as an astringent to tighten the vagina. A red powder that was a mixture of cinnamon, mustard, pepper and ginger was applied to the male glans. This was designed to make the head of the penis and the mucus membrane of the walls of the vagina swell, increasing stimulation, and opium pills were used to prolong an erection. A poem ran,

> Take only a speck of it; once it comes on you
> Run like the wind to the bedchamber.
> The first encounter will leave you invigorated;
> The second will make you stronger than before.
> If twelve beauties, dressed in scarlet, were waiting for you,
> You would be able to have them all, any way you wished.
> All night long, your weapon would stand on end.
> You would find new strength in your limbs and belly;
> Your testicles would constantly be refreshed and your penis invigorated.
> If you take a grain or so each time,
> Your weapon would be merciless,
> Your manhood would be rigid.
> At the first planting, the seed would germinate.
> You can have ten women in one night
> And feel no slackening of your vital powers.
> Older women will furrow their brow.
> Younger ones will be exhausted.
> When you are satisfied and want to stop
> Take a mouthful of cold water.
> Withdraw your weapon;
> You will not be harmed.

Herbs were used if there were problems in gaining an erection in the first place. One recipe ran,

> If, upon rubbing and toying with it, the prickle will not stand at point, thy mistress must take dried aromatic herbs – such as are scattered upon corpses – a couple of handkerchiefs and a gugglet of water. Wash the prickle, as if it were a dead body, then shroud it with herbs and lament the untimely fate of such a young and vigorous yard; for such must ward

away the Evil Eye, which has ensorcelled thy member. Verily, thy penis is buried so that it may soon experience resurrection.

And there were ways of enlarging the penis. For some reason, they often involved butchering a dog. This recipe is typical:

Take three fen of prime *jou ch'ung jung* [a herb] and two fen of *hai taso* [a special seaweed] and grind them into a powder. Find a white dog born in the first moon of any year. Mix the secretions of its liver into the powder to make a paste. Apply this to your jade stem three times. The next day at dawn, draw water from the well and wash the paste off. Your jade stem will definitely have grown three inches.

Arriving in Luoyang in the mid-680s, Feng Hsiao-pao had first become the lover of a maidservant of the Princess Ch'ien-chin, Kao-tsu's eighteenth daughter – a T'ang and in fear of her life. Princess Ch'ien-chin sought to ingratiate herself with the Dowager Empress Wu by introducing Feng Hsiao-pao to her via the good offices of Wu Chao's daughter, Princess Tai-ping. He was, it was said, *fei-ch'ang ts'ai-yung* – a man of 'unusual abilities'. Plainly he demonstrated these to the Empress when he was summoned to an audience. It is clear that they became lovers almost immediately and, soon after, he was given unrestricted entry to the palace. Although the official histories are discreet about their relationship, it caused a scandal at the time. In imperial China, it was obligatory for functionaries allowed regular access to the palace to be eunuchs. One of the courtiers pointed out that, during T'ai-tsung's reign, when a musician had been employed to teach Wu Chao and the other ladies of the court music, he had first been castrated. Wu Chao declined to follow precedent. Instead Feng Hsiao-pao was give the surname Hsüeh and adopted into the family of the Princess Tai-ping. Her husband Hsüeh Shao had been forced to adopt the newly renamed Hsüeh Huai-i, not as his son, but as his uncle. This may have led Hsüeh Shao into, rashly, backing the forthcoming princes' rebellion.

Hsüeh Huai-i became a Buddhist priest so that he could serve in the palace chapel. That way, he and Wu Chao could spend a lot of time alone together without outraging protocol. Then Wu Chao installed him as abbot in the White Horse Monastery in the west of the capital, which she had spent a great deal of money having restored. This was the oldest repository of Buddhist scripture and ancient law in China. The shrine there had been founded by pilgrims who had brought the first of the Buddhist scriptures from India on a white horse. But Hsüeh Huai-i filled the monastery with his mates, a bunch of drunken ruffians who, on his orders, went about beating up Taoist priests. Hsüeh Huai-i mocked the Taoist clerics' long hair and would have his followers shave their heads. In the palace he was given the pick of the horses in the stables and had eunuchs to attend him. Even Wu Chao's two nephews, Wu Ch'eng-ssu and Wu San-ssu, waited on him. No one dared criticize him after a censor who had repeatedly called attention to his behaviour was beaten within an inch of his life.

The monk also insulted the President of the Chancellery, one of the government's highest officials. Entering the palace one day, Hsüeh Huai-i brushed passed him without a word. When the President of the Chancellery's servant took the matter into his own hands and slapped Hsüeh Huai-i, he complained to the Empress, but she knew better than to side with a boorish lover against an important statesman and told Hsüeh Huai-i to use the north gate to the palace in future. That way he would not risk running into any more government dignitaries.

Hsüeh Huai-i was useful to her though, even outside the bedroom. The histories do not record how he came about his education, but Hsüeh Huai-i was a skilled architect and oversaw the building of the Empress's longed-for *Ming-t'ang*, or Hall of Illumination. The Scholars of the Northern Gate had been employed to come up with designs for the *Ming-t'ang*, ignoring more conservative scholars who insisted that it should be a modest structure in the suburbs. For maximum effect, Wu Chao wanted a huge building in the centre of the capital, conveniently near the palace. Construction began in 688, year four Ch'ui Kung, on the site of one of old audience halls, just inside the south gate of the palace. A huge work force was assembled. Massive beams had to be hewn in distant forests and dragged by teams of up to a thousand men to Luoyang.

With a height of two hundred and ninety-four feet, the *Ming-t'ang* was the first of the tall structures built in the reign of the Empress Wu. It was a huge three-storey pagoda with a base area of three hundred square feet. While the lower two floors were rectangular, the third storey was round. The walls of the ground floor were decorated with depictions of the four seasons – with the winter along the north wall and summer along the south. The second storey showed the twelve hours of the Chinese day and the third storey showed the twenty-four solar periods of the Chinese year. The roof was supported by nine great iron pillars shaped like dragons. These carried huge beams that acted as trusses and took the weight. At the apex of the roof, crowning the huge edifice, was a ten-foot iron phoenix, covered in gold. Wu Chao had now taken the phoenix as her personal symbol.

To the north, Hsüeh Huai-i built a small annex called the *T'ien-t'ang* – 'The Heaven'. Though it had five storeys, chroniclers say it was 'slightly less huge, beautiful and awe-inspiring'. After it was first built, it was blown down by a gale, so the Empress had Hsüeh Huai-i rebuild it. Ten thousand workmen were employed to haul fresh wood from distant Kuangtung.

The two buildings were completed at the end of 688 and on 24 December – the twenty-third day of the eleventh month, Wu-wu – they were opened with a great feast. Even then the Chinese had a vast cuisine, employing most of the ingredients and spices still in use – pork, lamb, duck, fish, crab, oysters, squid, jellyfish, seaweed, fermented soya, garlic, ginger, cardamom, pepper, vinegar, pickles, cinnamon, ginseng, pine kernels, rice, bamboo shoots, lychees, oranges, mandarins, tangerines, peaches, kumquats, bananas, dates, figs, hazel nuts, pistachios, and puffers called 'river piglets' – the poisonous fish now eaten raw in Japan. The seafood was brought from the coast by relays of runners covering one hundred and eighty to three thousand li, or sixty to one hundred miles, a day. Added to that were exotic items such as marmots, sea otters, snow pheasants, flying cockroaches, bamboo rats the size of dogs that fed on the roots of bamboo, Bactrian camels (particularly their humps), soups made from turtles' shells or the heads of macaque monkeys, green peacock jerky, mice stuffed with honey and eaten alive at table, frogs dropped live into boiling taro, live shrimps served with vegetables and thick sauces, python hash flavoured with vinegar, salted hornet larvae served with a sauce made from ants' eggs, citron carved into the shapes of flowers and birds, bears (their paws were considered a delicacy), and elephants slain with a poisoned arrow (whose trunks were particularly savoured). Some dishes were served in a form we would now recognize as dimsum. Generally beef was avoided, since cattle were needed to pull ploughs and both Buddhist and Taoists shunned strong-smelling vegetables such as garlic, onions, scallions, leeks, and coriander, though Confucians indulged. Honoured guests were plied with silks, brocades and other gifts.

After the feast the people of Luoyang and those people who had managed to travel from remoter regions were allowed to look around the building. This was Wu Chao's one concession to those whose taxes had paid for the *Ming-t'ang*. During the building of the *Ming-t'ang* and the *T'ien-t'ang*, it was said that Hsüeh Huai-i spent money 'like sand'. But Wu Chao authorized anything he asked for, regardless of the expense. Appalled by the spiralling costs, a censor pointed out that, by tradition, a *Ming-t'ang* was supposed to be a simple thatched hut. Wu Chao's was covered in gold and jewels and decked out like a 'temporary nirvana'. The *T'ien-t'ang* even housed a huge gilded Buddha, which was two hundred feet tall, so large it was said that twenty or thirty men could stand on his outstretched finger. The censor was studiously ignored and a grateful Empress Wu rewarded Hsüeh Huai-i with the rank of general and the title of duke. From then on, all Wu Chao's great ceremonies were held in the *Ming-t'ang* and it became known as the Palace of the Ten Thousand Divine Appearances.

Wu Chao began building a new party of supporters to help her take the throne. She sought out men of talent who were outside the educated and privileged classes, and gave them titles and ranks, so key positions were packed with men who owed everything to her. Those who did not come up to scratch or who wavered in their loyalty were sacked or executed.

This policy alienated those who had traditionally held power, so she developed a system to detect and suppress further conspiracies. Anyone with any information about a plot against the throne was to report to a local official who would give them the salary of an official of the fifth grade and provide them with transport to the capital. They were to use the horses from the relay stations of China's 'pony express' to reach Luoyang as quickly as possible. Food and lodging for an official of the fifth grade were laid on along the way. The day the informant arrived at the capital, they would be given an audience with the Empress, and lavishly honoured, entertained and fed at government expense to encourage others to follow their example. Officials were not to delay or dissuade informers, no matter how lowly their status. Any official who did not send an informer to the capital was charged with the same crime the informer was volunteering information about.

As a result, everyone in the country was terrified that they would be informed on. They offered no opinion that might appear in any way critical and there was no open discussion. Careless talk cost lives. A number of soldiers were eating in an inn at the capital when one of them remarked that as the new Emperor Jiu-tsung was powerless it was much less profitable working for him than it had been working for his predecessor Chung-tsung. One of those present left the table and went to inform the police. The soldiers had not even finished eating when the police arrived and arrested them all. The man deemed to have criticized the government was beheaded. The rest were strangled, and the informer promoted.

Regular informers were given government jobs and a networks of these spies were soon turned into an effective secret police force. Those within it sought more and more power. One informer, originally a seller of cakes, was given the rank of general and was sent out around the country to imprison conspirators. But that was not enough for him. He wanted to be a censor. When the Dowager Empress pointed out that he was unsuited for the job, since he could neither read nor write, he said, 'Neither can leopards, but they are feared none the less.' The man impressed Wu Chao with his devotion to duty. He refused the standard reward of the possessions of those he helped condemn, saying that he did not want to sully himself with the property of traitors. For him, seeing traitors topple was its own reward.

To make this secret police force more efficient, a spy school was set up under Lai Chün-ch'en and Chou Hsing, two officials in the Board of Justice and Censorate whose biographies appear in the dynastic history under the special category 'Evil'. They used forgery, torture and underhand methods outlined in the handbook *Lo-chih ching* – 'Classic of Entrapment' – to ensnare suspects. Those they arrested were denied food and sleep. They were interrogated night after night and when they dozed off manure was hurled into their cells. Others were confined in underground pits. If no confession was forthcoming, they would be hung up by their hair or suspended upside down with a rock tied to their head. Prisoners would have vinegar poured in their nostrils, their ears filled with mud and slivers of bamboo jammed under their fingernails. There was worse. A small cage was fitted over the victim's head. Then wedges were driven down the sides, cracking the skull until the brains oozed out.

Lai Chün-ch'en and Chou Hsing gave the new and ever more fiendish tortures they developed poetic names. The devices were paraded before those freshly arrested, who quickly confessed all. Lai Chün-ch'en and Chou Hsing's torture methods were so effective that those who suffered at their hands were willing to implicate anyone they were asked about, so it was possible to remove anyone a whiff of suspicion had attached to – or anyone the secret police did not like. Sometimes Wu Chao's henchmen simply executed first and made up the charges afterwards.

Although this brutality often suited Wu Chao, she was careful not to let others use it to their advantage. When one of Governor Pei's subordinates wanted to remove his boss, he cut up one of the governor's memorandums and pasted it back together so that it seemed to contain seditious remarks. The governor was arrested. He admitted that the handwriting was his, but denied writing the treasonous document. Three investigations failed to resolve the matter. But Wu Chao was confident of Pei's loyalty and sent a fourth investigator. He examined the document in sunlight and spotted the joins. Wu Chao then summoned Pei's accuser and, in front of him, dropped the document into a bowl of water. The paste dissolved and the pieces came apart. The man confessed and was executed.

The rebellion and conspiracy of 684 had left the Empress Wu wary of plots hatched against her and believed Lai Chün-ch'en and Chou Hsing when they constantly unearthed a wealth of fresh plots. No one could be allowed to slip through their grasp. When they heard that an amnesty was about to be proclaimed, they killed their prisoners, so that no one could reveal what went on in their torture chambers. This ruthless system served its purpose and when it had done its job Wu Chao liquidated the torturers as readily as she had their victims. While it lasted, the secret police force performed one essential task. This was to crush all opposition to her becoming Emperor in her own right. This, she believed, would come from the traditional aristocracy whom she mercilessly persecuted.

The headquarters of the secret police was located within Li Ching-men – the 'Beautiful View Gate' – though different characters with the same tone and sound render the name as the 'Gate of Legal Finality'. Those who worked there boasted that no one who entered their head-quarters came out alive. This was not quite true. Wei Yüan-chung, the censor who had advised Li Hsiao-i during the crushing of the Li Ching-yeh revolt, was arrested and taken there. Condemned, he was kneeling on the execution ground waiting to be beheaded when the news came through that the Dowager Empress had commuted his sentence to exile. When he showed no sign of relief, he was asked why he was still kneel-ing there. He replied that he was not sure that the news was true, since no one had shown him the decree yet.

Such sangfroid was not unusual. Years later, two British officers witnessed the beheading of three Chinese in Canton,

> where it is of such daily occurrence, and is thought so little of, that in one corner of the execution ground some scores of heads – without any exag-geration – may always be seen piled in all stages of preservation or cor-ruption. But there it was done in such a business-like, informal way, and the Chinamen seemed to be so little affected by their approaching fate – actually laughing and talking till the moment when, as they knelt down, their tails were pulled forward and the short, heavy sword took their heads off one by one – that we looked upon it in quite a different light ... nor experienced any of the disagreeable sensations.

The former marshal of the household of the Crown Prince did not fare so well. A woman servant accused him of plotting rebellion and he was left to the tender mercies of Chou Hsing. Nevertheless, he was given a trial and acquitted. However, Wu Chao disliked the marshal's grandfather, the general and statesman Hao Ch'u-chun, who had opposed her becoming regent when Kao-tsung was first struck down with paralysis, so the judges were deposed and exiled and the marshal found himself on his way to the execution ground. But he would not go quietly. On the way, he denounced the Dowager Empress to the crowds in the streets. When the guards tried to stop him speaking out, he grabbed some faggots from a hawker's cart and beat them off. Eventually the executioner had to despatch him in the street. For the rest of Wu Chao's reign, the condemned had a wood ball stuffed in their mouth before being taken to the execution ground.

Despite the machinations of the secret police, the Empress Wu was not completely deaf to justice. She allowed Hsü Yu-kung, the Assistant of the Supreme Court of Justice, to argue cases for clemency before her. He had the reputation of being a merciful man. When he was a provincial judge, he had never once sentenced a man to flogging. It was said that if you met Lai Chün-ch'en, you were sure of death; if you met Hsü Yu-kung, you were sure of life. He argued the case of hundreds of men before Wu Chao in the Hall of Audience and saved many lives. She admired his courage and trusted his judgement.

In 686, year two Ch'ui Kung, perhaps to meliorate the rigours of the secret police, the Empress Wu had a bronze urn set up in the Hall of Audience. It had four side openings. A note could be slipped into these to be read later when the urn was opened. The first slot was marked 'Delayed Favour'. This was for people who wanted to recommend themselves for office or had schemes to improve agriculture or the people's welfare. The next was called 'Invited Rebuke' and was for criticisms of the government. The third was 'Redress of Grievances', where people could complain of injustice or oppression. And the fourth was marked 'Penetration of the Abstruse', which was for omens, prophecies and the reporting of secret plots.

The inventor of the urn was the son of one of Wu Chao's censors. Although it was ostensibly set up to advertise the Empress's concern for the welfare of the people, it quickly became a repository for anonymous accusations. One of these concerned the inventor of the urn, who was accused of supplying arms to the Li Ching-yeh rebels and who soon became a victim of his own ingenuity.

With Chung-tsung safely in exile, Wu Chao had to deal with Jui-tsung, who was still, nominally, Emperor. She employed the simple device of issuing a decree restoring the full powers of sovereignty to him. But Jui-tsung was not stupid. According to the *Comprehensive Mirror*, he 'knew the Dowager Empress was not sincere'. He realized that if he seized the opportunity and accepted power, his mother would find some other, possibly lethal, way to thwart him. As several members of the family had already lost their lives by crossing Wu Chao, he declined the offer and the Empress Wu continued to exercise power with no constitutional opposition.

With the heirs to the throne so palpably weak, there was a chance that a powerful figure from the collateral family of Li could make a bid for the throne. One suitable candidate was Li Hsiao-i, the general who had crushed the Li Ching-yeh revolt. To bolster his own position, the Emperor Expectant Wu Ch'eng-ssu moved against him, accusing him of claiming that portents foretold his ascension to the throne. But as Li Hsiao-i had given good service to the Empress Wu, his life was spared and he was exiled to the south, where he died soon after.

Jui-tsung, himself, was not without his supporters. One of them was Liu Wei-chih, who had been one of the Scholars of the Northern Gate and, at the age of fifty-seven, had risen to become Vice President of the Secretariat. He had been a principal Wu loyalist who had participated in the deposition of Chung-tsung, but now he was growing disillusioned. He told a colleague, in confidence, 'The Dowager Empress has deposed a stupid ruler and raised up a clever one, so why is regency still necessary? Wouldn't it be better to restore the government to the Emperor and calm the hearts of the people?'

The colleague reported the remark to Wu Chao, who was furious. She rebuked the ingratitude of 'one whom We have given employment'. Liu Wei-chih was accused of having improper relations with the concubines of the late Hsü Ching-tsung and taking bribes from a provincial governor. When an official of lower rank was sent to arrest him, Liu Wei-chih demanded to see the decree.

'This is not a decree,' he said when shown it. 'It has not passed through the Secretariat.' The Secretariat was, after all, his own department.

After Liu Wei-chih had been arrested, Jui-tsung wrote to the Empress on his behalf. Although his friends were optimistic, Liu Wei-chih realized that, as he had advocated the restoration of power to Jui-tsung, Jui-tsung's intervention meant his certain death. Empress Wu was merciful and ordered him to commit suicide.

As she prepared to take the throne, Wu Chao constantly looked around for beneficent portents. Late in 686, year two Ch'ui Kung, an earthquake in Hsin Feng threw up a new mountain peak. For Wu Chao this had to be a good omen and she ordered the peak to be called, in the Emperor's name, Ch'ing Shan – 'Lucky Mountain'. However, some saw things differently. An earthquake was usually thought to indicate that the balance between the yin and the yang in the natural environment was disturbed. The Emperor, with his unique position between heaven and earth, was supposed to maintain that balance. It was plain, for those who could see it, that the balance was disturbed by the yin of a woman nearing the throne which, as the seat of power, was exclusively yang. An official wrote to the Emperor to point this out:

> When the weather is disturbed, there is an unusual cold or heat. When a man's health is not good, he gets diseases. When the condition of the earth is disturbed, bumps and hills appear. Now that Your Majesty has placed a woman in the seat of the male, contrary to the order of nature, the spirits of the earth are curbed and frustrated and the mountains change their shape. This is a portent. Your Majesty may regard this as a lucky mountain, but I, Your servant, see it as an ill-omen.

When Wu read this, she was angry and the official was sent into exile in the south.

Other auspicious omens attended Wu Chao's reign. A three-legged chicken was born in 684. There was an unseasonal snowfall in 693 and the footprint of the Buddha was seen in 701. However, one had to be careful reporting these portents. Although Wu Chao was adept at sorcery herself, like other T'ang rulers she found it necessary to outlaw magic.

Some signs that Wu Chao was about to ascend to the throne were manufactured. By 688, year four Ch'ui Kung, the Wu ancestral temple in Luoyang had been completed. It was equal in size to the Li ancestral temple of the imperial family in Ch'ang-an. Wu Chao also appeared leading lavish ceremonies, costing millions of cash, and frequently evoked the splendour of the Chou dynasty that ruled China for nearly a thousand years in what was seen as a golden age. The greatest of these spectacles was the veneration of the *pao-t'u* in 689.

Wu Ch'eng-ssu was also looking for portents that would give the change of dynasty the air of divine sanction, as he stood to benefit if the Wu family took over. In the seventh month, Jia-yin, of 688, he claimed to have found a white stone – the *pao-t'u* – in the Lo river. It had on it the inscription, 'A Sage Mother shall come to rule mankind; and her imperium will bring eternal prosperity.'

This had echoes of the Wang Mang usurpation during the Han dynasty. Wang Mang was the nephew of the Dowager Empress Wang. Her son, the Emperor Ch'eng, showed little interest in governing and the country was run by a series of regents, all brothers and cousins of the Dowager Empress. When the fourth of them resigned in 8 BC, Wang Mang became regent. The following year, Ch'eng died without children and the throne was inherited by his nephew Ai. As Ai was not of the Wang clan, Wang Mang fell out of favour and retired to live on his estates. But when the Emperor Ai died without issue in AD 1, the imperial seals were left with his homosexual lover. The Dowager Empress Wang seized the moment. She rushed to the imperial palace, grabbed the seals and threw Ai's lover in jail, where he soon killed himself. Wang Mang was recalled from the country to act as regent to the next in line, the eleven-year-old Emperor P'ing. Wang Mang soon installed his own daughter as Empress beside P'ing. However, in AD 6, when he was just fourteen, P'ing suddenly died. This was somewhat inconvenient for Wang Mang, though his enemies accused him of poisoning P'ing. The problem of the succession was solved by Wang Mang himself, who picked the youngest of the fifty possible candidates. The infant was not officially enthroned, but installed as 'Young Prince' while Wang Mang became 'Acting Emperor'. He began a propaganda campaign to show that the Han had run their course and that heaven had mandated a new dynasty. This culminated in the discovery of a white stone with red writing on it that proclaimed that Wang Mang should become Emperor. He was enthroned in AD 9, proclaiming the new Hsin dynasty. Like Wu, he modelled his court and its ritual on the Chou. However, during his short reign the Yellow River changed course causing widespread disruption. Displaced peasants banned together in a group known as the Red Eyebrows, which eventually became strong enough to defeat Wang Mang's armies. Forced from the imperial palace, he was killed on the Terrace Bathed by Water in AD 23 and the Han dynasty was restored.

All sources agree that the discovery of Wu's white stone was fabricated by Wu Ch'eng-ssu. It was deliberately contrived to mirror the story of the Emperor Fu Hsi who found the tortoise with the trigrams that form the basis of Chinese characters on its back in the Lo river. How much Wu Chao knew about the deception is not known, but she went along with it when the *pao-t'u* – 'Precious Design' – was presented to the Empress as a talisman with great solemnity. To give thanks, on 12 January 689 – the thirteenth day of the twelfth month, Ji-wei, year one Tsai Shou – she led the entire court, including the Emperor Jui-tsung and his son the Crown Prince Li Hsien, to the Altar of Heaven. There all the treasures of the Empire were displayed, along with gifts from the rulers of distant lands. Among all the insignia of Empire, she proclaimed the Lo river sacred. Fishing in it was banned and she took the title of Sage Mother Sovereign Divine. The word 'Sovereign' – *huang* – was well chosen, since it applied to both sexes. Wu Chang was now just one step away from calling herself Emperor.

She then began planning a huge ceremony to venerate the stone and change the reign name to 'Eternal Prosperity' – Yung Ch'ang – in accordance with the prophecy inscribed on the *pao-t'u*. This was to be held in her new *Ming-t'ang*, giving it a proper inauguration. She decreed that all important persons in the Empire, without exception, must turn up at Luoyang for the festivities. This, of course, included many members of the collateral Li family who had previously been scattered to provincial prefectures. For them it was not a welcome invitation. If the dynasty was to be changed, they plainly stood in the way. The remaining T'ang princes feared that Wu Chao would have them killed, or at the very least degraded and exiled. They had no choice but to rebel.

The moving spirit was Li Chuan, Duke of Huang, the uncle of Jui-tsung, who was currently the prefect of T'ung-chou in Szechwan. As the son of Li Yüan-chia, Prince of Han, he was one of the surviving grandsons of the Emperor Kao-tsu. He wrote a cryptic letter to Li Chen, Prince of Yüeh, who was the brother-in-law of Wu Chao and was now governor of the city of Yü-chou, near Luoyang, in the province of Anhui, along with other potential conspirators. It read, 'My wife's [literally "her indoors"] illness is growing worse and must soon be remedied. If it is allowed to continue until the coming winter it is to be feared that it will prove fatal.' One source says that it was Li Yüan-chia, not his son Li Chuan, who sent the letter.

Li Chuan then issued a forged decree, ostensibly coming from Jui-tsung, calling on the T'ang princes to raise troops and come and rescue him. This was sent out to the T'ang princes, who were spread widely across the country. The son of Li Chen, Li Ch'ung, Prince of Lang Yeh, was then the governor of Po-chou in the northern province of Ho-pei, where the men were particularly warlike. He issued another decree stating the true purpose of the levy – to prevent the Dowager Empress destroying the imperial family and replacing it with the Wu dynasty. Even though Wu Chao was thought to be particularly unpopular in that area, Li Ch'ung only managed to raise five thousand men. Li Ch'ung also sent out messages to other T'ang princes, including his father, urging them to raise troops and march on Luoyang. The second decree had undermined the spurious legitimacy of the first and the response was half-hearted, but Li Ch'ung had no choice but to go ahead.

On 16 September 688 – the fourteenth day of the eight month, Yi-mao, year four Ch'ui Kung – he marched on Chi Nan, the capital of Shantung province. Hearing of this, Wu Chao mobilized the Imperial Army and despatched the famous general Ch'iu Shen-chi to put down the revolt. But all that was required was a little local resistance. On the way to Chi Nan, Li Ch'ung had to take the small town of Wu Shui, just forty-five li, or fifteen miles, from his base at Liao Ch'eng, and cross the Yellow River. Wu Shui's district magistrate called on neighbouring towns for help. One sent seventeen hundred men, who met Li Ch'ung's column on the road. Outnumbered, the loyalist forces pulled back to Wu Shui. Li Ch'ung then attacked the town. His plan was simple. He would send in carts of burning grass to burn down the gates, then use the smoke as cover as he stormed the defences. However, the wind changed, blowing the smoke and flames back on his own men.

The rebels were demoralized by this setback and his officers cooled towards the whole enterprise. To stiffen morale, Li Ch'ung decided to make an example of one of his officers and had him beheaded. The rest of his men were so shocked by this action that they disbanded. With only his household retainers around him, Li Ch'ung headed back to Liao Ch'eng, arriving there on 22 September, the twenty-fourth of Yi-mao. Seeing the Prince return without his army, the guards knew that the rebellion had failed. Their only course now was to ingratiate themselves with the powers that be, so they slew him at the gates. But their ploy did not work. When Ch'iu Shen-chi arrived outside Liao Ch'eng with the Imperial Army, Li Ch'ung's officials came out to submit to him wearing mourning clothes as a sign of penitence. Ch-iu Shen-chi rejected this gesture and put them and their families to death, killing a thousand.

With Li Ch'ung in open revolt, his father Li Chen now had no choice but to raise the flag of rebellion in Anhui. But before he had time to raise an army he heard that his son was dead. Li Chen was on the verge of surrender when he heard that his followers had taken two towns in the region. So when the Imperial Army turned up he had no choice but to resist. However, his officers and men had no stomach for the fight. As soon as they engaged the enemy, they turned and fled. Li Chen fled back to Yü-chou and slammed the gates. When the Imperial Army arrived outside, an officer called up to Li Chen on the wall, 'Prince, why are you sitting up there waiting for death?'

With no ready answer to this question, Li Chen committed suicide, along with his daughter and son-in-law.

The princes' revolt marked the end of internal resistance to Wu Chao, though she exacted a fearful revenge. Over the next two years, the name of the Li clan was changed to Hui – Chinese for 'viper' – and they were systematically wiped out. Twelve of the collateral families were exterminated, with the adults executed and the younger children exiled to the far south. Kao-tsung's beloved aunt Grand Princess Ch'ang-lo was to suffer in this persecution, along with Li Yüan-chia, Prince of Han, and the conqueror of the Turks in Kao-tsung's reign, Li Yüan-k'uei, Prince of Huo, who was T'ai-tsung's half-brother. Ch'ang-lo, the mother of Lady Zhao, the wife of Wu Chao's third son Li Che, later Emperor Chung-tsung, was an active supporter of the rebellion. When she saw the men falter, she sent a message to them, urging them not to be cowards. She and her husband acted with Li Chen, and paid the price.

The two sons of the former Crown Prince Li Hsien were killed and the two surviving sons of Kao-tsung not born to Wu Chao were accused of conspiracy and ordered to appear in the capital. Li Shang-chin committed suicide, while the Pure Concubine's son Li Su-chieh set out on the doleful journey. On the way, he passed a funeral. Pointing out the weeping mourners to his guards, he said, 'To die of disease. If only one could achieve that, there would be nothing to weep about.' When he reached the Lung-men his guards strangled him. Orders were given that both men's families were to be wiped out, though in both cases a young son was hidden. Years later they reappeared and received their fathers' honours when changing times had returned them to favour.

Thanks to the secret police, other heads rolled. Chou Hsing built a case against the veteran general and T'ang loyalist Hei-Ch'ih Ch'ang-chih. Charged with treason, he was arrested and hanged himself in prison. Wu Chao's son-in-law Hsüeh Shao was accused of supplying arms to Li Ch'ung and then slaying a fellow officer to hide his guilt. As he was the husband of Wu Chao's beloved daughter Princess Tai-ping, lenience was shown. Instead of the humiliation of public execution, he was left to starve to death in his cell.

An accusation did not always prove fatal. Even in the reign of terror following the princes' revolt, Hsü Yu-kung could sometimes work his magic. An official who had lent money to Li Ch'ung was accused of conspiring with the prince and the chief torturer Lai Chün-ch'en set about investigating the case, but an amnesty was declared and the man escaped with a sentence of exile. Wei Yüan-chung, the censor who had escaped death after the Li Ching-yeh rebellion, then produced correspondence between the accused and Li Ch'ung showing that the man was not a mere accessory but an active participant in the rebellion. So Wu Chao sentenced him to death. In front of a hushed court, Hsü Yu-kung argued his case.

He said that the amnesty applied to all those who were involved in the rebellion of Li Chen, Prince of Yüeh, and he quoted the *Official History*, which said, 'Slay the chief leader.' According to the law the one who first conceived the rebellion was the 'chief rebel' and the 'chief rebel' in this case had been put to death. Before the amnesty, the official had been accused of being an accessory and thus had his sentence commuted. But now he was being charged with being a 'chief rebel'. It was, essentially, he said, a case of double jeopardy.

'This is to turn life into death,' said Hsü Yu-kung. 'It would have been better not to have had an amnesty: if you grant life and then take it away it would be better not to have lived. The court should not proceed in this manner.'

Wu Chao grew frustrated at the legal niceties Hsü Yu-kung had teased out.

'Who are these "chiefs" and "leaders"?' she cried.

'A "chief rebel" is a commander of the rebel forces,' said Hsü Yu-kung patiently. 'A "leader" is one of those who first conceived the plot.'

'But isn't this man both a "chief" and a "leader"?' said Wu Chao.

'The "chief" and "leader" was Li Chen, Prince Yüeh,' said Hsü Yu-kung. 'He has already been executed. Now this man is being accused, not of being an accessory, but as a leader.'

Wu Chao grudgingly ordered that the case be reconsidered and the man escaped with his life.

Justice found another champion in the person of Ti Jen-chieh, an official who had been sent to Yü-chou after the princes' revolt. He wrote to Wu Chao saying that, along with the former followers of Li Chen, innocent people were being indiscriminately charged with rebellion and were being persecuted. If he objected to this publicly, he said, he himself would be accused. But if he did nothing, he would be allowing the Dowager Empress's reputation to be sullied with these injustices committed in her name. Wu Chao responded by ordering the release of hundreds of those accused, and many sentenced to death had their sentences commuted to exile. This annoyed the military governor of the Yü-chou, who asked Ti Jen-chieh what business of his it was to interfere. Ti Jen-chieh replied that the previous mischief had been caused by one rebel, Li Chen, who was now dead. But he had been replaced by a thousand others – the governor's own soldiers, who slew, executed and banished people, and robbed them of their worldly goods. They were doing ten times the harm of Li Chen and were, therefore, ten thousand times as bad. The military governor was outraged at the accusation and laid trumped-up charges against Ti Jen-chieh. But Wu Chao dismissed them and the military governor was transferred to another province. Soon after, Ti Jen-chieh was summoned to Luoyang and had a distinguished career in the government.

Some openly protested against the secret police's reign of terror. One prominent critic was Ch'en Tzu-ang. In 689, he wrote to Wu Chao, saying, 'Your Majesty is human and merciful ... but you have appointed a deceitful and evil group of officials, who are reckless and in competition with one another. With angry looks of suspicion, they report the existence of clandestine plots. One man is accused and a hundred fill the prisons ... Some say that for every man Your Majesty loves, there are a hundred You harm. This Empire gasps and no one knows a place of rest.'

But the terror was useful to Wu Chao. It distracted people's attention from the fact that she, a woman, was running the country against all the tenets of Confucianism. Besides, most people were unaffected by the terror, since it was restricted in its scope. Almost all its victims were officials of the the fifth grade or above. It effectively removed aristocrats who opposed her from the government. Their sons were refused honours, titles and privilege; their families were exiled or enslaved and their property was confiscated by the state. In one purge alone in 697, year one Wan Sui T'ung T'ien – 'Ten Thousand Years to Reach Heaven' – known as the conspiracy of Liu Ssu-li, thirty-six landowners were disposed of and over a thousand of their relatives and friends were sent into exile – sometime later to be massacred there. This let more able men, who had risen through Wu Chao's reformed examination system, replace them. Consequently, the terror was popular in many quarters and the fear the terror engendered also prevented ministers attempting to get power over her.

But Wu Chao could be generous as well as cruel. She gave one of her ministers a set of expensive silk gauze bed curtains after visiting his house and seeing that he slept behind ones made of cheap silk. But he could not get used to them. After a sleepless night, he begged Wu Chao to allow him to return to his own cheap curtains, explaining that when he was young a diviner who read faces told him not to be extravagant.

Although Wu Chao was still technically only regent, in 688, year four Ch'ui Kung, she celebrated the *feng-shan* sacrifices on Sung-shan, as she had planned with Kao-tsung in 676. She did it again in 696 and built a residence there, which she visited in 700 and 701.

On the Chinese New Year, 27 January 689, Wu held a ceremony in the *Ming-t'ang*. This time she wore the imperial robes of the ancient Chou, known as the dragon costume, and carried a jade sceptre called a *kuei*, which was the ancestral symbol of authority. Following hard on the heels of the thanksgiving for the *pao-t'u* this was the most lavish ceremony of the T'ang era. During the sacrifices, the nominal Emperor Jui-tsung acted as first assistant, his sacrifices following hers. The second assistant was Crown Prince Li Hsien. The first sacrifice was for Shang-ti, the supreme deity of heaven. The second was to Kao-tsu, T'ai-tsung and Kao-tsung, founders of the T'ang dynasty. Next came a sacrifice to Wu Chao's father Wu Shih-ho. It was clear that he was being honoured as the founder of a new dynasty and he was posthumously renamed *T'ai-huang*, which means 'Great Emperor of the Past'. Five generations of Wu ancestors were raised to the rank of prince. Wu Ch'eng-ssu became President of the Chancellery, one of the most important posts in the government. His successor would be Wu Yu-uning, the grandson of Wu Shih-huo's brother. The reign name was changed to Tsai Chu, which means 'To Record the Beginning'.

Further steps were made toward usurpation. Emphasizing the comparison between herself and the legendary Emperor Fu Hsi, who invented writing, Wu Chao created twelve new characters – substituting new simplified forms for such common words as 'day' and 'month'. Scholars have discovered new characters appeared around that time for 'heaven', 'earth', 'sun', 'moon', 'year', 'beginning', 'country', 'minister', 'life', 'upright', 'man', 'proof', 'luminous', 'sage' and 'give'. Chillingly, the new character for 'moon' was a swastika in a circle and a swastika alone was used around that time to mean 'ten thousand'.

In the edict enacting this, Wu Chao pointed out that the old characters had become so complicated that even scholars could not understand them. She also invented a new character for her own name Chao. The top half was the *ming* cipher showing the sun and moon together. This means 'bright'. Below was the *kung* showing the void, the air or the sky. The character suggests ever-lasting, all-encompassing brilliance, since the sun shines during the day, the moon during the night and their light fills the entire sky. This symbol, she said, 'would make all men submit to Us and facilitate good government' – and with the sun and moon together it united the yin and yang. Others have suggested that Ming-kung was the name she was given as a Buddhist nun, since it has a distinctly Zen sound. The name change also avoided inconvenience, since *chao* – meaning 'shine' – is a common word in Chinese and the name of the monarch became taboo when they ascended the throne. The punishment for using the name of a reigning Emperor was three years' penal servitude.

In the same edict, Wu Chao reintroduced the Chou calendar. Religion was also on her side. During Wu Chao's lifetime, Buddhism had became a major force in Chinese life and she endorsed it because it empowered women. In 689, Lao-tze, the founder of Taoism and legendary forefather of the T'ang, was stripped of the honorific given him in 666. And Confucian classics that formerly had to be studied for written examinations were eased from the curriculum. Wu Chao herself took charge of the examination system, which now admitted officials of all nine ranks – previously aristocrats inherited the privilege to obtain government positions without passing the examinations. In Luoyang, Wu Chao would demonstrate publicly the role examinations were to have in her dynasty when she examined candidates herself in the palace, questioning a number for several days before sending them away because none of them met the required standard. She also squeezed out personal favouritism by having a slip of paper pasted over the candidates' name on written papers, so that the examiners would not know whose paper they were marking.

Wu Chao favoured literary ability over political ability and added a poetry examination in 681, year one K'ai You. When examinations were due, candidates swarmed to government offices with poems and other examples of their writing in the hope of preferment. Young men of all ranks were eager to become mandarins. As well as getting the weekend off – that is, one day every ten days – most positions were not very time-consuming. Civil servants also got three days off for a family 'capping' ceremony, when a boy entered manhood, nine days for the marriage of a son or daughter, a lesser period for other marriages in the family and fifteen days off every three years to visit their parents, or thirty days if they lived more than five hundred li, or one hundred and sixty-seven miles, away. High officials also got fifteen days off in the fifth lunar month as a 'farming holiday' and another fifteen days off in the ninth lunar month as a 'holiday for the bestowal of robes'.

Once a man acquired a post, he was assessed annually by his superior, who rated him in four categories: diligence, impartiality, virtue, and righteousness, and integrity and prudence. Then he was assessed on his actual performance, according to twenty-seven criteria, including his own selection of subordinates.

At the time, the Mahameghan strand of Buddhism that originated in Sri Lanka was popular in China. This predicted that, in the last period of law or dharma, Yama, the Indian god of death, would send Maitreya, a new enlightened one, who would forgo entry into nirvana and descend to earth as the universal monarch, cleanse the corrupt and confused world and usher in a golden age. This belief had been around for three centuries and was now widespread in China. However, recent events had raised its profile in the public mind. In 677, year two Yi Feng, a mysterious aura had appeared in the sky near the capital and a great cache of Buddhist relics were found beneath it. The Kuang-chai Temple was founded there. Then in 683, year one Hung Tao, more relics were said to have been found under another strange Buddha light in Sui-chou. This was dismissed as a hoax, but the perpetrator rose up in rebellion in the name of Maitreya and had taken over two *hsien* − counties − before being suppressed.

The Empress Wu's monastic lover Hsüeh Huai-i and seven fellow monks seized on the *Mahamegha* or 'Great Cloud' which foretold the return of the Maitreya. In a commentary, they asserted that the Maitreya − 'the Compassionate One' − would be reborn as a woman and that the long-awaited reincarnation was, in fact, the Empress Wu, who had come 'like a mother to rule over the ten thousand countries and educate myriads of men as her own children'. This commentary was presented to the throne in mid-August 690, the seventh month, Wu-yin, year one T'ien Ch'ang.

Fragments of this commentary survive and scholars note that it was prepared by monks who were extremely knowledgeable. Hsüeh Huai-i, they imply, served as only the instigator of this ruse. He and the seven other monks were rewarded with red copes, instead of the standard black ones, and the silver belt ornaments of fourth-rank officials, and other Great Cloud monks were given posts in the government.

One surviving fragment of the commentary reads,

The Buddha then praised the goodness of [the queen] Ching-kuang [Pure Light] who had been ashamed, and went to fulfil the prophecy of the [great goddess] Devi that she should rule over the land in the body of a woman. This woman is the one who is called Shen-mu shen-huang

[Empress Wu]. How do we prove it? We prove it by the omen of the *Cheng-ming ching* which says, 'The Venerable One has said to Maitreya that when the Bhagavat [great lord] is reborn he shall eliminate all evil. If there are arrogant and recalcitrant men, I will send the young Devi with rods of gold to punish them ... East of the river one meets the Luminous Head and the King of the Brilliant Law ... The Venerable One wanted Maitreya to build for him a City of Transformation with a pillar of white silver above and an inscription for the myriad generations below. The Devi will put on heavenly robes, hang gold bells on the pillar, and summon Buddha's disciples to enter the city.' It is clear from this that Maitreya is the Empress.

The commentary goes on to argue that Maitreya – 'the Compassionate One' – must be a woman because the *Vimalakirti-sutra* says that 'the merciful or compassionate mind is that of a woman or daughter'. The omen talks of the punishment of 'arrogant and recalcitrant men'. This meant the Empress Wu's destruction of all those who rebelled against her. The 'Luminous Head and King of Brilliant Law' east of the river comes from the *I Ching* or *Book of Changes* where it says, 'The Emperor comes from Chen. Chen is in the east.' Wu Chao came from Chen and ruled over the Empire. Where she lived in the Sanctified City, Luoyang, lay to the east of the river. The City of Transformation, the commentary continues, was the *Ming-t'ang* and the pillar of silver was its central column. This, apparently, had a long inscription on it which was the 'inscription for myriad generations'. The commentary also maintained that the Devi putting on 'heavenly robes' referred to the dragon costume Wu wore for the ceremony on 27 January 689.

The commentary went on to quote more from the *Great Cloud Sutra*, which said,

The Luminous King and Sage Lord will both be in the City of Transformation and on top of the tower and will beat the golden drum to proclaim the message to all disciples. It will immediately reach all those who believe this law even if they are ten thousand miles away. But those unconnected to the law will hear nothing even if they are in the next room.

The commentary maintained that the beating of the golden drum meant the great ceremony held in the *Ming-t'ang*. Those who believe this law heard it 'even if they are ten thousand miles away' because news of the ceremony was carried across China by courier. 'The "deafness of those in the next room",' the commentary said, 'meant that, if among those myriad regions the Empress rears as a woman rears her children, there are some who cause disorder, they will surely be destroyed, and the cunning and vicious will ruin themselves. The *Ho-t'u* says, "All those who are evil become good as, if they rebel, they destroy themselves." '

Ho-t'u literally means 'the River Diagram' and is said to have appeared on the back of the mythical dragon-horse that appeared out of the Yellow River and was acquired by the legendary sage-king Fu Hsi. It was developed into the *bagua*, or the eight trigrams of the *I Ching*. As a book of prophecy, it had a wide circulation during the Han dynasty, but was later banned because some of its verses were used subversively. The commentary went on to explain who these deaf people 'in the next room' might be:

> Because the *Ming-t'ang* was raised and sacrifice was to be offered to the Three Sages [the first three T'ang Emperors], officials from all over the Empire as well as the imperial family were gathered at the Sanctified Captial for the grand ceremony. Then all those members of the Hui [Li] clan rebelled and reaped defeat and destruction. Those who survived were pardoned and exiled to distant regions where they did not hear of the ceremony. This provides proof of the deafness of those in the next room.

The commentary went on to quote the *Sutra* again, saying, 'She will obtain one quarter of the realm of Cakravartin' – the legendary universal monarch – 'whose chariot wheels roll everywhere without hindrance.' And the commentary pointed out, 'Now the Empress has united the Empire and rules south to Jambudvipa' – the southernmost of the four Buddhist kingdoms but probably meaning eastern China here – 'this is already one-quarter of the domain of Cakravartin.'

The commentary interpreted the *Sutra* to mean that under the rule of Wu Chao there would be no more rebellions or wars. Everyone within the Empire would be totally loyal and the 'four foreign peoples' would submit to her. 'They will have many sons and grandsons, and the years will be without scarcity and everyone will be happy without sickness or other misfortunes.' This was because 'a Buddha transformed, came down from on high and stroked her head'.

Many other sources are quoted to show that, after the first three T'ang Emperors, China would be ruled by a woman who had 'brought all states to submission and her power is without equal'. Her Sanctified Capital would be Luoyang, where she would remain motionless while the world turned around her. At the same time 'she will enlighten and reside in the four continents and reach the eight extremities all at once' and 'for a thousand years the ancestral temple will remain unmoved'. Wu Chao, it said, 'will govern the world and make the foundations laid by the first three T'ang Emperors prosper for ever'. All this chimed with the times, since the belief was widespread that the world was the last period of the dharma, Maitreya was on her way and the new golden age was imminent.

As a 'guardian of the true law' Wu Chao vowed to build 840,000 stupas to house holy relics throughout the world. The *Sutra* also said, 'She will teach and convert all the places she rules, and men and women, young and old with observe the *Pancaveramani*' – the five commandments of Buddhism that prohibit killing, lying, stealing, adultery, and intoxication. She would also 'destroy the heterodox and the various perverse doctrines'. The text also made repeated use of the various names and titles Wu Chao had used throughout her life and the reign names that had been adopted since she became Empress. There was even mention of 'a unicorn born with two horns and for generations the people did not know it'. This is a reference to Wu Chao's mother Lady Yang: *yang* means 'poplar', but sounds like another character transliterated in English as *yang* which means 'sheep' – that is, a unicorn with two horns. And the Chinese for 'people' is *shih-min* – Shih-min was T'ai-tsung's original personal name.

There had been four female rulers in China before who had taken power as dowager Empresses or Empress consorts. But they were not the Maitreya because, in the hexagram representing a king, only the fifth line was a broken or female line. The previous Empresses had ruled in a man's name, maintaining the unbroken male line, while Wu Chao, the fifth, would reign under her own name as a woman.

'From the Han period to that of the Empress Wu, there have been various female rulers who were served and accepted, but they were called dowager Empresses and did not conform to the *Sutra* 's prophecy,' said the commentary. 'Only our Holy Mother Empress fits the prophecy exactly and this is why the *Sutra* says that the female ruler of Jambudvipa will erect precious stupas everywhere and benefit the work of Buddha.'

There were other signs. In the city of Ping-chou, near the tomb of her father, there was a well, known as the Well of Wu, that had long since dried up. However, from the end of the Sui dynasty it began to fill again. Nor was the prediction made by the Grand Astrologer forty years before forgotten – that the T'ang dynasty would fall and be replaced by a woman Emperor named Martial Prince, or Wu-wang.

The commentary also pointed out that that year harvests were abundant throughout the Empire – usually good harvests were regional, other places suffering drought or famine at the same time. 'The powerful bandits are all thwarted' – meaning the various rebels – and there would be 'great accumulation in the eight month, wisdom and brilliance will reach everywhere, stop war and bring prosperity'. Wu Chao was set to usurp the throne in the eighth month, Ji-mao. Then the 'female ruler, standing straight, raises high the T'ang' – Wu Chao's contradictory claim to the throne was that she would continue the tradition of the T'ang. 'Evil men are driven from power. A dragon comes to stand guard, purifying all within the four seas and standardizing the eight directions.'

The commentary not only evoked the traditions of Buddhism to justify Wu Chao taking the throne; it also tapped into the myths of *mofa* – or the 'Latter Days of the Law' – that were spreading at that time. It was now thought to have been over fifteen hundred years since Buddha had attained enlightenment and that the world was now falling into a state of religious decay. The Li clan were the *devadatta* or demons that plagued the world at that time and had to be destroyed to purify the world. This also justified the murder of P'ei Yen and the former Crown Prince Li Hsien. The commentary also made it plain that, with Maitreya back on earth, the churches ought to confine themselves to spiritual matters, allowing the universal monarch temporal jurisdiction by relating the parable of the King of Jambudvipa who destroyed errant priests. That said, the *Sutra* concluded,

> Harvests will be bountiful, joy without limit. The people will flourish, free of desolation, illness, worry, fear and disaster ... The rulers of the neighbouring lands will all come to offer allegiance ... At that time all her

subjects will give allegiance to this woman as the successor to the imperial throne. Once she has taken the Right Way, the world will be awed into submission.

Wu Chao was not going to rule over the old Chinese Empire of the family and its ancestors. She was going to rule over a universal Buddhist Empire under the name Maitreya the Peerless, the Golden Wheel, Sage and Holy Emperor – all titles she would take during her reign. She herself would be worshipped. She even donated her dressing room to a Buddhist monastery as a shrine. This started a trend. Men and women of high standing donated cartloads of cash and silk as an act of repentance. The monasteries became enormously wealthy. One monk set up what he called the 'Inexhaustible Treasury', whose assets were said to be so great that it was impossible to spend the interest.

While Wu Chao promoted Buddhism to promote herself, she also reined it in. As it was the official state religion, taking precedence over Taoism, the church and its clergy were put under the control of the Board of Rites that had long exercised similar control over the Taoist religion, and in 685, year one Ch'ui Kung, special censors were assigned to oversee the activities of Buddhist monks in Luoyang.

Although Wu Chao still attempted to maintain a certain balance between Buddhism, Taoism and Confucianism in her public pronouncements to keep as much of the populace as possible under her sway, state funds were poured disproportionately into Buddhism. Vast numbers of Great Cloud temples were founded – or existing temples redesignated – as the repository for the *Sutra* and the commentary that justified Wu deification. In every prefecture over a thousand monks were specially ordained to go forth and chant the *Sutra* and explain its meaning to the faithful. Meanwhile the monks who had composed the commentary were ennobled as dukes and given the insignia of high-ranking officials.

New images of the Buddha were erected at the Lung-men and in the capital, and Hsüeh Huai-i staged 'no barriers' rites in front of the gilded Buddha in the *T'ien-t'ang*. At these, people of all social classes met and were plied with money. According to one source, at each rite ten thousand strings of cash were given away. Another talks of ten cartloads of cash being deposited among the crowd, causing them to fight to get it and several to be trampled to death in the stampede. It was also said that Hsüeh Huai-i conducted bloodthirsty and orgiastic rites there.

It was only towards the end of her reign that Wu Chao found the financial burden too much for the exchequer. In 700 she proposed a new tax to pay for these excesses. This was dropped when Ti Jen-chieh pointed out that the Buddhist temples and monasteries of the day already looked like imperial palaces. The wealth of the church was a burden on the people, he said. Its priests were mere parasites who produced nothing but extorted money from the populace through sales of relics and *Sutras*. Buddhism was supposed to be a compassionate religion, he said. It was not supposed to impose an extra burden on the backs of the people.

Although it could be argued that Wu Chao used Buddhism for her own ends, she seems to have been sincere in her religion and occasionally urged on others religious frugality. She frequently banned fishing and the butchering of meat. In fact, for the eight years from 692 to 700, it was against the law to take the life of a sensate being to eat its flesh. The penalties for offences involving temples or monasteries were the same as those against imperial property. Wu Chao supported the translation of the scriptures and called eminent monks to give lectures, sometimes acting as an assistant. An accomplished religious scholar, she took an interest in the doctrinal debates of the day. Fa-tsang, the founder of the Hua-yen sect, was called to head the T'ai-yüan temple founded to commemorate Wu Chao's mother. Wu Chao called him Hsein-shou – 'Sage Head' – and honoured him with this holiest form of ordination. They were close companions until her death. Fa-tsang served at the T'ai-yüan temple alongside the great translator Divakara. Together they decided that a new translation of the vast *Avatamsaka Gandavyuha*, or *Hua-yen Sutra*, was needed. To accomplish this task, Wu Chao summoned the great scholar Siksananda from Khotan in Central Asia, which had been conquered by the T'ang. He brought his own copy of the *Avatamsaka Gandavyuha* with him and took charge of the project. All eighty volumes were finished in 699, year two Sheng Li – 'Sacred Era'. Wu Chao herself was said to have helped with the editing and wrote the preface for the final work. It was, naturally, full of references to the Great Cloud prophecies.

Around that time Wu Chao invited the northern and southern patriarchs, Shen-hsiu and Hui-neng, to the capital. Hui-neng could not make it owing to ill health, but when Shen-hsiu arrived at the palace Wu Chao received him on her knees. As a result he was lionized in Luoyang. And in a new catalogue of the *Tipitaka* – or 'Triple Basket', the full canon of southern Buddhism – the compiler Ming-ch'üan called her the 'long-awaited universal ruler who would bring salvation to all'.

As Buddhism now played a vital role in the accomplishment of her political aims, Wu Chao eventually brought it completely under the control of the state. The Bureau of National Sacrifice controlled ordination and clerical appointments, as well as designating services and prayers for state occasions. The conduct of Buddhist priests was now subject to secular law. Though no one wanted to return to the confrontation between church and state that had humiliated Kao-tsung, Wu Chao did issue three edicts imposing discipline on monks and priests. Two were designed to reduce the friction between Buddhists and Taoist priests. The third banned the showing of inappropriate emotion at the death of a fellow monk and the burying of relics. Anyone caught doing so would be reduced to the ranks of the laity. Despite being under government, the church remained corrupt and continued to ignore its obligation of charity to the poor. Priesthoods were sold. Clerics falsely registered and the church was involved in large-scale property scams.

With the heavens – or at least the Buddhist church – behind her, Wu Chao was now ready to take the throne in her own right. In September 690, three petitions arrived in Luoyang requesting Wu Chao to found a new dynasty. One of them contained the names of sixty thousand imperial officials, priests and monks, both Buddhist and Taoist, commoners and foreigners. Seeing which way the wind was blowing, Jui-tsung asked for the Wu surname to be bestowed on him. The move was backed by the whole court.

It was customary for future Emperors to turn down invitations to take the throne, at first, in a display of modesty. Wu Chao did so. But then there was a reported sighting of a phoenix, heralding the arrival of a sage-king. Then a flock of red birds appeared in the Hall of Audience. This was reminiscent of the red bird of the first Chou Emperor. Wu Chao had already decided to name her new dynasty Chou. It was thought that this was because her father had been posthumously created Duke of Chou. She had consciously been aping the splendour of the thousand-year

Chou dynasty for some time and she now claimed the celebrated Duke Wu of Chou, a legendary sage, as her first ancestor, just as the Li had claimed Lao-tzu. His name, of course, was Wu-wang and he was the 'Martial Prince' who overthrew the Shang and established the Chou dynasty. With the appearance of the red birds it was clear that the will of heaven could no longer be denied.

CHAPTER TEN

THE HOLY AND DIVINE EMPEROR

ON 21 SEPTEMBER 690 – the tenth day of the eighth month, Ji-mao – Wu Chao proclaimed an amnesty from the tower of the Tse-tien Gate and announced the change of dynasty from T'ang to Chou. Jui-tsung abdicated to become Emperor Expectant. His son was demoted from Crown Prince to Imperial Grandson and Wu took the throne as Shen-sheng huang-ti – Holy and Divine Emperor, the first and, until now, only woman Emperor of China. She was now the Daughter of Heaven.

She chose as her first reign name T'ien-shou – 'Heaven Bestowed'. This was a reference to the white stone and the Lo-river prophecy. Her parents became Non-Pareil Imperial Majesty and Empress Dowager. The yellow banners of the T'ang were replaced with red ones and 'Wu' replaced 'T'ang' in place names throughout the Empire. Otherwise, court dress, ceremonial and official titles, and office names remained much the same after the change of dynasty, since Chou styles had already been adopted.

Wu Ch'eng-ssu now became Prince of Wei and Wu San-ssu Prince of Liang, and the other twenty-one surviving members of the Wu clan were given princely rank. Other Wu supporters were promoted and given titles. The censor who had arranged the petition asking Wu Chao to become Emperor was promoted through the ranks so quickly that he wore the different colour robes of four different ranks – blue, green, red and purple – in a single year. In court he was known as the Official of the Four Seasons.

The change of dynasty from T'ang to Chou was to be celebrated by another monumental building, the *T'ien Shu* or 'Pivot of Heaven'. It was a stele one hundred and five feet high that stood outside the Tuan Men – the south gate of the Imperial City – directly in front of the Bridge of the Ford of Heaven in the middle of Luoyang. Its iron base, one hundred and seventy feet in diameter, provided a plinth for huge bronze dragons to sit on. These supported the twelve-foot-wide octagonal pillar whose faces were five feet across. They were decorated with reliefs showing other fabulous beasts. It was topped by a canopy thirty feet around and ten feet high, made to look like clouds. Four twelve-foot dragons stood on it, holding a ten-foot-diameter ball of copper. The castings were designed by Wu Chao's youngest nephew Wu San-ssu and crafted by Mao P'o-lo, using over a thousand kilograms of iron and copper. The names of all tributary chieftains and imperial officials who owed allegiance to Wu Chao were carved on the pillar, along with an inscription written by Wu Chao herself: 'The Celestial Pillar commemorating the ten thousand virtues of the Great Chou dynasty.'

She also began the massive task of walling the city and continued building temples, monuments and public works with the aim of making Luoyang a worthy rival to Ch'ang-an.

After taking the imperial throne, Wu Chao believed that she was still surrounded by enemies. Due to pay a visit to the Shanglin Park, she sensed danger. She wrote later, 'On the eighth day of the twelfth lunar month, the second year of the T'ian-shou reign [4 January 692], some officials intended to deceive me into visiting the Shanglin Park by announcing that the flowers were already in bloom there. In fact, they were planning a conspiracy. I agreed to their invitation but soon after suspected their scheme. So I sent a messenger to read this proclamation.'

It read,

> Tomorrow morning I will make an outing to Shanglin Park,
> With urgent haste I inform the spring:
> Flowers must open their petals overnight,
> Don't wait for the morning wind to blow.

'The next morning the Shanglin Park was suddenly filled with blossom,' she said. 'The officials all sighed with relief over this unusual phenomenon.'

This is often quoted as evidence of Wu Chao's early attempts to create an image as the all-powerful Emperor, though it was written well after the establishment of the Chou dynasty. She was so powerful, she proclaimed, that even the flowers obeyed her. In fact, once she was Emperor, there was little opposition. Even the official history of the T'ang dynasty was none too critical of her rule. It said, 'Reward and punishment came from her alone and she did not borrow the authority of her ministers. She usurped above, but governed well below and so could rule the Empire.'

In the first six years of her reign, China prospered. It then suffered a downturn after the country was defeated by the Tibetans. The economy revived under Ti Jen-chieh, but flagged later under the corruption brought in by the Chang brothers.

Like Roman Emperors, Wu Chao ruled by providing bread and circuses. She used the tax money flooding in during this initial period of prosperity to fund Grand Carnivals in which the populace took to the streets and ate and drank too much. There were sideshows, street performers and parades that featured huge floats called 'mountain carts', built like gigantic wagons and hung with silk, or 'drought boats', made from bamboo and wood. These were accompanied by carts drawn by bullocks dressed in tiger-skins, carrying musicians brought in from hundreds of miles away. Entertainments included slim young girls who could hang by their chins from poles, Taoists who would climb barefoot up a ladder of swords and an armless beggar who could juggle brushes with his feet and reproduce the finest calligraphy. Two wrestling teams headed by sumo-sized grapplers named Peng and Gao put on a show equal to anything on the World Wrestling Entertainment stage today. At one contest Peng grabbed a live suckling pig and gnawed the flesh from its head and neck, then released it squealing into the crowd. Not to be outdone, Gao ate a live cat tail first, consuming its rear end, intestines and belly while the creature screeched and scratched. At this point Peng conceded.

Medieval Chinese carnivals had a tradition of gruesome magic acts. An Indian cut off his tongue, showed the stump, handed round the severed portion, then put it back in his mouth and rejoined it to the stump. And a Buddhist monk pulled out his intestines and washed them, then returned them to his belly cavity. Kao-tsung had tried to ban these grisly performances in 656, year one Hsien Ch'ang. But they soon reappeared. In 670, year one Hsien Heng, a magician appeared who could suspend a jug of water from a rope, then cut the rope, but the jug would not fall.

More horribly, he would put the jug in a locked room and, after a while, spectators would be allowed into the room to find the magician's dismembered body in the jug, floating in his own blood. Then, after the spectators had been ushered out, he reassembled himself and appeared outside in one piece once more. He had a sideline selling fortunes, but was reported, arrested and sentenced to death. Predicting the future in medieval China was against the law – as it was in medieval England – since prophesying the death of the monarch constituted treason. He was seen marching to the execution ground without the slightest apprehension, perhaps believing that judicial decapitation was also reversible.

What is now called the 'Indian Rope Trick' was performed regularly. The tale is told of a prisoner escaping this way. He climbed to the top of a two-hundred-foot rope, then flew off like a bird. But the worst of the T'ang magic acts was called 'Penetrating the Horse's Belly'. The details are recorded in a Japanese scroll. The illusion was that a man crawls through a horse's entrails, by having one performer climb into a horse's anus and then another emerge from its mouth. One can only hope, for the horse's sake, that the performers were small children or midgets. On a more tasteful level, carnivals also featured dancing horses and hedgehogs, mechanical toys, and bands of performing spiders that, following musical cues, would form up in various formations.

Wu Chao staged more of these fiestas than any other Emperor – seventeen in her fifteen-year reign. They lasted three, five, seven or even nine days, always an odd number. And they were staged quite randomly on top of the ten regular festivals that occurred throughout the year and the celebration of imperial birthdays, births, deaths, and marriages.

Six months after coming to the throne in her own right, Wu Chao issued an imperial edict that formally gave Buddhist monks and nuns precedence over the Taoist clergy. She had done this, she said, because 'Buddhism opened the way for changing the mandate of heaven' – that is, changing the dynasty. However, she did not forget the Confucianists. In the ten-day period when she founded the Great Cloud temples she bestowed a new title on Confucius and she did the same for his principal disciples later in her reign. She modestly refused any further titles herself and demurred when, in 691, year two T'ien Shou, it was suggested that she perform the *feng-shan* sacrifices on Mount Sung in Ho-nan. Just a year into her reign, it was too soon. However, she did perform the *feng-shan* sacrifices to heaven and earth in a southern suburb of Luoyang in 695, year one T'ien Tse, celebrating the event with a year-long tax break throughout the Empire. A skilled politician, she certainly knew how to keep the people on her side with financial handouts while, simultaneously, bolstering her authority.

Once the Chou dynasty had been securely established, Wu Chao had little more need of her secret police. But Chou Hsing and Lai Chün-ch'en did not see that times had changed and they continued in their old ways. They tried to remove the advocate Hsü Yu-kung, who had repeatedly thwarted them. When he failed to win an acquittal for a provincial governor, Chou Hsing accused Hsü Yu-kung of being an accomplice of the condemned man and charged him with conspiracy. Wu Chao heard the case, but refused to condemn Hsü Yu-kung to death. However, she did remove him from office. A short time later she recalled him and appointed him to the Censorate. Hsü Yu-kung refused the appointment. Falling to the ground with tears in his eyes, he said, 'The deer on the hills and in the forest are constantly hunted for their flesh. If Your Majesty makes me an officer of the law, I would not assist those who try to pervert Your Majesty's laws and, consequently, I would be done to death.'

Wu Chao trusted the judgement of Hsü Yu-kung and began to accept that excesses had been committed in her name. Nevertheless she insisted that be become a censor. The news of his promotion was greeted with joy throughout China. Wu Chao then moved against Chou Hsing and Lai Chün-ch'en. General Ch'iu Shen-chi, who had been instrumental in the suppression of the princes' revolt and the suicide of the former Crown Prince Li Hsien, had recently fallen victim to their predations. Chou Hsing was accused of being a confederate of the executed general and Wu Chao ordered Lai Chün-ch'en to investigate.

Lai Chün-ch'en invited his old friend and colleague to dinner without telling him about the charges. Over the meal Lai Chün-ch'en complained to Chou Hsing that too many of those accused of serious crimes refused to confess – which is hardly surprising, since they were, for the most part, innocent. He asked Chou Hsing whether he could come up with a new torture device that would guarantee a prisoner would admit any charges levelled against them. Chou Hsing was flattered and said that it was really a very simple matter. What Lai Chün-ch'en should do was boil a large cauldron of water and show this to the prisoner, saying that if he did not confess he would be hurled into it. Lai Chün-ch'en agreed that this was an excellent idea and he ordered that a cauldron be prepared while the two friends continued eating. When dinner was over and the cauldron was boiling nicely, Lai Chü-ch'en said, 'My brother, I have evidence against you. Please step into the cauldron.'

Chou Hsing was right. The device worked. He immediately confessed everything Lai Chün-ch'en put to him.

'Please step into the cauldron' – qing jun ru weng – has become a Chinese idiom for luring a victim into a trap and is sometimes used as the title for the Chinese translation of Shakespeare's Measure for Measure.

Despite his confession, Wu spared Chou Hsing's life, banishing him to the southern province of Kuangtung. But during his time in the secret police Chou Hsing had ruined the lives of thousands of people and earned himself a great many enemies. Wu Chao, herself, found him guilty of hundreds of miscarriages of justice. On his way south, he was waylaid by the family of one of his many victims and killed. To appease public opinion, Wu Chao had other secret policemen executed, but Lai Chün-ch'en held on, since he still enjoyed the support of the Wu clan thanks to the efficient job he had done in exterminating the Li after the princes' revolt.

Wu Ch'en-ssu was angling to become Crown Prince and a petition, instigated by a minister named Chang Chia-fu and signed by several hundred people, was presented on his behalf. Wu Chao referred the matter to her ministers. Perhaps realizing that she was not very keen on elevating Wu Ch'en-ssu, they pointed out that she had already named her son Jui-tsung as her successor. That being the case, the matter should never have been raised, since the Emperor's decision in these matters should not be questioned. Two ministers even asked for those who had organized the petition to be prosecuted for sedition. The Wu clan fought back and, with the help of Lai Chün-ch'en, had the two ministers prosecuted for conspiracy and executed.

As Wu Ch'en-ssu could not himself raise the matter of the succession, he employed Wang Ch'ing-chih as an agent to forward his cause at court. But when he was granted an audience Wu Chao was adamant.

'My son is the Imperial Heir,' she said. 'Why should I have him deposed?'

'The spirits do not consort with those of another kind,' Wang Ch'ing-chih replied. 'And men do not respect those of another clan. A Wu now holds the Empire. How can a Li be Your Majesty's successor?'

Wu Chao was furious with Wang Ch'ing-chih, since Jui-tsung had already had the good sense to change his name to Wu, and she ordered Wang Ch'ing-chih from her presence. Wang Ch'ing-chih promptly fell to the ground, weeping and begging her forgiveness. To get rid of him, she gave him a pass to the palace.

Meanwhile Wu Chang-ssu sought to move against T'ang loyalists in the government who might oppose his elevation. He accused Ti Jen-chieh, the censor Wei Yüan-chung and five other T'ang officials of conspiracy and got Lai Chün-ch'en to arrest them. Wu Chao had given Lai Chün-ch'en a decree saying that all those who admitted their guilt at their first interrogation would be spared. Unwilling to die over a palace intrigue, Ti Jen-chieh promptly confessed.

'Following the Chou revolution, everything is being changed,' he said. 'The old T'ang officials are in fear of their lives, so we joined in a conspiracy.'

But Wei Yüan-chung was made of sterner stuff. He refused to break even under torture.

'If you want my head, cut it off,' he told Lai Chün-ch'en. 'Why bother with a confession?'

After making his own confession, Ti Jen-chieh was allowed a certain amount of freedom. His guards even thought that, as he was to be spared, he might even rise to power again, and asked favours of him. Ti Jen-chieh's only reply was to curse and beat his head against a pillar. Unsettled by this reaction, the guards withdrew. This allowed Ti Jen-chieh time to write a letter to his son on the silk lining of his coat, explaining that he had been forced to confess even though he was not guilty. When the guards returned, Ti Jen-chieh remarked that it was warm in jail and asked them to take his coat home for him to have the thick winter lining removed.

Keen to ingratiate themselves with Ti Jen-chieh, they did so. When the lining was being removed Ti Jen-chieh's son found his father's message and petitioned Wu Chao for an audience. After reading the letter on the silk lining, Wu Chao summoned Lai Chün-ch'en, who said that the letter could not be genuine, since the prisoners had not been stripped of their clothes and Ti Jen-chieh still had his coat. When Wu Chao sent an official to check out his story, Lai Chün-ch'en had Ti Jen-chieh dressed up in a borrowed coat. The official, not daring to hang around the prison too long, made no further enquiries and Lai Chün-ch'en, thinking he had got away with it, sent to the court forged statements from Ti Jen-chieh and the others admitting their guilt and petitioning for the sentence of death.

In the meantime, the ten-year-old nephew of another of Lai Chün-ch'en's victims, who had been sold as a slave to the Department of Agriculture when his family was destroyed, managed to get an audience with Wu Chao. When she asked why he had come, he replied, 'My father is dead and my family is no more because Lai Chün-chen and his henchmen have twisted Your Majesty's laws. If You Majesty does not believe that, please send Your most loyal and trusted ministers to Lai Chün-ch'en as if he were a traitor. If he is not, Lai Chün-ch'en will certainly make him one.'

Perhaps the Grand Astrologer was right forty years before when he predicted that after Wu Chao came to the throne she would mellow with age. She did not have the boy beaten as she had the nephew of P'ei Yen. Instead she took on board what he had said. She called for ministers whom she trusted. They were Ti Jen-chieh, Wei Yüan-chung and the other T'ang officials who had been charged with conspiracy.

When Ti Jen-chieh was brought before her, she asked him why he had confessed to conspiracy. He replied that, if he had not, he would have died.

'So why then did you petition for a death sentence?' she asked, showing him the statement forged by Lai Chün-ch'en.

Ti Jen-chieh was able to demonstrate that it was a fake and all seven were spared. Despite their acquittal, Wu Chao had to save face, so the seven were demoted and sent to the provinces.

Although Lai Chün-ch'en had now shown himself to be a liability, Wu Chao was not ready to move against him, since he still had the backing of Wu Ch'eng-ssu. However, her nephew's star was already on the wane when it was demonstrated that Wu Ch'eng-ssu was using his position to further his own interests. A court official had a beautiful maidservant called Bewitching Damsel, who was also renowned for her singing and dancing. Wu Ch'eng-ssu asked to borrow her on the pretext that she was to teach his consorts how to apply make-up. Instead he took her as his concubine and refused to return her. Her master, lamenting the loss of such a beautiful and talented woman, sent her a poem. After reading it, she threw herself in a well and drowned. When her body was recovered, the poem was found in her sash. Wu Ch'eng-ssu was so angry that he paid an informant to lodge false charges against the official, who was then beheaded. Such behaviour did not go unnoticed by Wu Chao.

However, the Wu clan were not yet done for. Wang Ch'ing-chih still had his palace pass and returned to the Hall of Audience to press Wu Ch'eng-ssu's case. Wu Chao grew annoyed by his persistence and ordered Li Chao-te, the Vice President of the Secretariat, to have him flogged. Li Chao-te was another T'ang loyalist and he had Wang Ch'ing-chih flogged to death at the gate outside the Hall of Audience. Wu Chao refused to listen to complaints about the harshness of this punishment. She trusted Li Chao-te and listened to his advice on the matter of the succession.

'The Celestial Emperor [Kao-tsung] was Your Majesty's husband and the Imperial Heir is Your Majesty's son,' he said. 'From Your Majesty have come sons and grandsons that can inherit the Empire down the generations. Why make a nephew heir? Has anyone ever heard of a nephew making sacrifices to an aunt in an ancestral temple? Besides, Your Majesty received the Empire in trust from the late Celestial Emperor. If Your Majesty hands it over to Wu Ch'eng-ssu, the late Celestial Emperor will see all his sacrifices wasted.'

Wu Chao was convinced by Li Chao-te's line of argument, but she kept her decision to herself, fearing that if she came down on one side or the other in the matter – for the Wu or for the Li – she would provoke fresh conspiracies among the clan that had lost out. Li Chao-te was such a trusted advisor, he was even allowed to mock the white stone from the Lo river which foretold she would become Emperor. On one occasion Wu Chao said that she venerated the *pao-t'u* because of its 'loyal heart' and Li Chao-te said, 'I suppose, then, that all other stones have disloyal hearts.' Wu Chao joined in the general laughter.

Despite the setbacks, Wu Ch'eng-ssu was still confident that he would inherit the throne. He was still First Minister and had long been Wu Chao's favourite. But Li Chao-te was against him and sowed the seeds of suspicion in Wu Chao's mind. Li Chao-te pointed out that she had been responsible for the downfall and death of Wu Ch'eng-ssu's father and the hardship meted out to the rest of his family. Although Wu Ch'eng-ssu now enjoyed power and position thanks to her, he might well harbour a grudge against her and Li Chao-te warned against giving him too much power. At first Wu Chao would not listen. She had long treated Wu Ch'eng-ssu as a trusted confident. But Li Chao-te was insistent.

'A nephew is not as close to an aunt as a son is to a father, and yet there have still been parricides,' he said. 'How much more likely is it for a nephew to move against an aunt than a son against his mother.'

He pointed out that, as First Minister and a prince, Wu Ch'eng-ssu had powers comparable to her own and he said, 'I fear that Your Majesty may not long possess the throne.'

Wu Chao did not have to be told twice. She moved swiftly and, on the fifteenth day of the seventh month of year one of Ch'ang Shou – 1 September 692 – Wu Ch'eng-ssu and his cousin Wu Yu-ning were moved out of the government and given honorary posts outside the administration.

That year Wu Chao was seventy by Chinese reckoning and appeared heavily made up at public appearances. She was, it was said, so 'skilled with cosmetics ... she concealed her age, and even her closest attendants could not tell', and her fine features still retained some of the beauty of her youth. It was also said that she grew two new teeth that year, demonstrating her perennial vitality – hence the change of reign name to Ch'ang Shou, which means 'Long Life'.

On New Year's Day, year two Ch'ang Shou – 11 February 693 – Wu Chao staged another ceremony at the *Ming-t'ang*. She decorated the walls with brand new works of art, probably bronzes, and nine hundred performers sang and danced to music and choreography provided by Wu Chao herself. This time, despite being edged from power, Wu Ch'eng-ssu was first assistant at the sacrifices, and Wu San-ssu was second assistant.

Jui-tsung was nowhere to be seen. It seemed to all the world that the Wu were still in the ascendancy and that Wu Ch'eng-ssu was still in the running to be Wu Chao's successor. The Princess Ch'ien Chin, who had introduced Hsüeh Huai-i to Wu Chao, remained in high favour and was granted the surname Wu. Her son was married to the daughter of Wu Ch'eng-ssu. However, when Jui-tsung was finally replaced as Emperor Expectant, it was by his elder brother Chung-tsung, after he too adopted the Wu surname. No Crown Prince was named and, despite the struggle between the Li and Wu clans, the succession never left the hands of the Li. Nevertheless Wu Ch'eng-ssu was furious at being sacked from the government. He blamed Li Chao-te for this and denounced him to the Holy and Divine Emperor. She refused to listen.

'Since I employed Li Chao-te, I can sleep at night,' she said. 'He has saved me a great deal of work.'

Li Chao-te was a gifted administrator and had taken some of the weight off the shoulders of Wu Chao, who had been overburdened since the instigation of the secret police. She had had to sit in judgement on countless treason and sedition cases. This had been necessary during the run-up to the change in dynasty. But now Chou rule was secure and she no longer feared a secret backlash by the supporters of the T'ang. Meanwhile, thousands of good generals and imperial officials had been disposed of, along with their family members. This was bleeding the administration of talent and making her unpopular with those she depended on for support.

Since the acquittal of Ti Jen-chieh, the power of the secret police had been in decline. Now was the time for Wu Chao to rid herself of them. She asked a censor to review the outstanding cases. Among them he found over eight hundred and fifty that were based on false accusations and he proposed prosecuting the perjured informers in these cases to the full extent of the law. This would have sounded the death knell for the secret police, who responded by accusing him of conspiracy. To save face for the system she had instigated, Wu Chao had the censor banished. Soon after, she had him recalled and reinstated. This was a signal for all those in court who had previously held their tongues for fear of prosecution to speak out. One of the censors took the opportunity to point out that the Ch'in dynasty had lost the Empire after holding on too long to the harsh laws they had needed to conquer it, whereas the Han dynasty had held on to power by relaxing the laws once they were sure the dynasty was secure. Wu Chao found much merit in this argument.

However, relaxing the laws allowed criticism of the regime. One critic point out that, as the Holy and Divine Emperor had rooted out the old T'ang hierarchy, she had brought a lot of new, lower-class blood into the government. Men who mended broken pottery had become ministers; sawyers of wood had become censors, the detractor said. It was as if putrid dumplings had been fried, so that they looked delicious, but, in truth, they were rotten inside and fit only to deceive the Holy and Divine Emperor. The new officials who were his target took offence. They had the offender arrested and asked to have him flogged in the Hall of Audience. But Wu Chao rejected their plea and pointed out, 'If you gentlemen are not really rotten inside, flogging him will only make you look ridiculous.' She then ordered the man to be freed.

Again Wu Chao showed her good sense in government. Nothing could be more harmful to a ruler than to look ridiculous. By then she had even won the admiration of the dynastic historians.

'Although the Empress promoted many of humble origin to gain the hearts of the people, if they proved inefficient she quickly punished or dismissed them,' wrote one. 'The power of reward or punishment she maintained in her own hand and government came from her alone. She was astute, and quick and sure when making a decision. Consequently, all the brave and distinguished of the era were happy to serve under her and sought out opportunities to do so.'

However, it was a time of ill-omen. Wu Chao had trained a cat to live peacefully in a cage with some parrots. It was not much of a trick, since all she needed to do was keep the cat so stuffed with food that it had no reason to attack the parrots and no appetite for anything but sleep. One day, she wanted to show off her remarkable achievement and displayed the cage in the Hall of Audience and passed it around the officials, who all claimed to be duly impressed. However, the cat had either grown hungry or had been unsettled by this unusual attention and attacked, killed and ate one of the parrots. The courtiers could hardly stifle their chuckles, though Wu Chao was greatly put out. This incident showed that Wu Chao had got over her fear of cats. Or perhaps, remembering the

Pure Concubine's dying curse, she could only abide them if they were caged. And maybe the Pure Concubine Hsiao, reincarnated as promised as a cat, had taken the first instalment of her revenge by humiliating Wu Chao before the whole court. 'Parrot' in Chinese is *ying wu*. As Wu was her family name, Wu Chao might have been trying to show that the Wu and the Li could live together. If so, she conspicuously – and portentously – failed. Looked at another way, for the normally supine cat to kill and eat a pigeon could be seen simply as a harbinger of war.

Between 690 and 694, year one T'ien Shou and year one Yen Tsai – 'Prolong the Year' – there had been a series of border incursions by more than three hundred and fifty thousand Tibetans in the west and by the Turks in the north. In 692, year one Ch'ang Shou, it was decided to teach the Tibetans a lesson and two experienced generals, Wang Hsiao-chieh, who had once been a prisoner of the Tibetans and knew their strengths and weaknesses, and T'ang Hsiu-ching, were sent west to recover the 'Four Garrisons' lost to Tibet in 678, year three Yi Feng. These Four Garrisons were the four Central Asian oases of Chiu Tzu, Yü Tien, Su Lei and Sui She – or Kucha, Khotan, Kashgar and Karashahr in Turkish – in the west of modern Sinkiang province. The two generals crushed the Tibetan army and set up a protectorate on the frontier to act as a buffer zone. But later, under the first reign name of 695, Cheng Sheng – 'To Bear Sacred Witness' – the Tibetans caught Wang Hsiao-chieh far from the frontier and defeated the entire Imperial Army. Wang Hsiao-chieh himself escaped and was demoted, then sent to deal with the Khotan the following year.

The whole of China lay at the Tibetans' feet, but the Tibetan King – or Tsuan P'u, whose name was probably Chinu-shihnung – knew that he did not have the manpower to occupy the whole of the Chinese Empire, so he sued for peace. Again he proposed a marriage alliance, but insisted on holding on to the Four Garrisons. They provided vital foodstuffs for Tibet, but they were far from China and of no use to the Chinese if a state of peace existed between the two nations. Wu Chao agreed, since it appeared to her that the Tsuan P'u's regime faced considerable internal opposition and the Tibetans were soon to be embroiled in a civil war. She was right. In 698, year one Shen Lung, the Tsuan P'u moved against the family of the Lün, or Prime Minister, who was so powerful that his armies controlled state affairs and threatened the young king. In the ensuing massacre more than two thousand of the Lün's faction were killed. The Tibetans' best general sought asylum in China, and Tibet posed no further threat during Wu Chao's reign.

When it came to repelling the Turks along China's northern border, Hsüeh Huai-i's star was still rising. In 693, year two Ch'ang Shou, he had presented Wu Chao with a second sutra called *Pao-yü ching* or 'Precious Rain', reconfirming her mystical status. Wu Chao appointed her lover commander-in-chief and sent him to fight the Turks. He was accompanied by Li Chao-te and the experienced general Li To-tso, who had served with distinction in the Tibetan wars. In the face of the Imperial Army, the Turks fell back. Hsüeh Huai-i erected a monument to his bloodless victories and rode back to court in triumph.

On the tenth day of the first month of year one of T'ien Tse Wan Sui – 30 January 695, Hsüeh Huai-i staged another of his strange ceremonies at the *T'ien-t'ang*. It was called the 'Rising from the Earth'. A pit fifty feet deep was dug in the floor of the *T'ien-t'ang*. It was decked out like a hall and filled with images of the Buddha. These were then raised mechanically. In the midst of the ceremony, Hsüeh Huai-i seemed to fall into religious reverie, slashing his leg. He said that the blood from this wound was used to paint an image of the Buddha, two hundred feet long – though the blood, in fact, seems to have come from an ox slaughtered for the purpose. This image of the Great Buddha was set up on the Tien-tsin Bridge, or 'Bridge of the Ford of Heaven', in the middle of Luoyang and another festival was held there. Wu Chao took this amiss. In his arrogance, Hsüeh Huai-i's risked upstaging the Holy and Divine Emperor herself.

Hsüeh Huai-i began to hold court at the White Horse Monastery and seldom bothered to visit the palace. The rest of the Buddhist clergy began to follow his arrogant example. They took over land and occupied private houses without the owners' consent, resisting any attempt to evict them. As Hsüeh Huai-i was now a rare visitor to the imperial bedchamber, one of the censors realized that this was the time to move against him and petitioned to investigate his conduct on the grounds that there were rumours that Hsüeh Huai-i and his cabal in the White Horse Monastery were plotting against Wu Chao. She granted her permission for the investigation to go ahead and ordered Hsüeh Huai-i to appear before the tribunal.

Hsüeh Huai-i did as he was told, but, in a typical display of arrogance, he rode his horse into the courtroom, then dismounted and took a seat on the bench. When it became clear that the object of the hearing was to investigate his own conduct, Hsüeh Huai-i got back on his horse and rode off. The censor reported this to Wu Chao, who dismissed it as the monk's habitual eccentricity. The censor was told to ignore this affront. However, shrewd as ever, Wu Chao gave him permission to move against Hsüeh Huai-i's followers in the White Horse Monastery and they were banished to the pestilential frontier regions. Hsüeh Huai-i then sought revenge and eventually got the censor dismissed.

As Hsüeh Huai-i was not paying Wu Chao the attention a lover should, she began to encourage other favourites. One was her imperial physician Shen Nan-mou, who, it is said, coached her in the art of the bedchamber and concocted aphrodisiacs and other sexual recipes for her. Wu Chao also formed a liaison with a Buddhist mother-superior who said she could see into the future. She also claimed to be able to live on a single grain of rice a day. But at night she secretly feasted with a bevy of beautiful novices. These women also entertained the young men of Luoyang and the nunnery was more of a brothel than a convent.

Hsüeh Huai-i grew jealous of Wu Chao's other favourites and sought revenge by burning down her precious *Ming-t'ang*. In other accounts, it was Wu Chao's physician who set fire to the *Ming-t'ang* to discredit Hsüeh Huai-i, assuming that he would take the blame. The blaze could be seen right across the city. The *T'ien-t'ang* caught fire and the gilded Buddha was destroyed. The Great Buddha painted in blood was also torn to shreds in the wind. A devout Buddhist, Wu Chao was greatly distressed by the destruction of these Buddhas. But accusing her unpopular lover of arson would have involved loss of face, so she claimed that the fire had been caused accidentally by servants burning hemp and commissioned him to rebuild the *Ming-t'ang*, the *T'ien-t'ang* and the Buddha, though he remained under grave suspicion. Despite the huge expense of rebuilding these edifices – which again drew the criticism of the censors – the Chinese people paid the money necessary in taxes with scarcely a grumble, even though the reign of terror and the secret police were a thing of the past. This bears testimony to how wealthy China was under

Wu Chao. The new *Ming-t'ang* was renamed the Tung Tien Palace – the 'Palace to Reach Heaven'.

Seeking to exploit the fact that her rival Hsüeh Huai-i was now in disfavour, the clairvoyant mother-superior turned up at the palace to express her condolences. But Wu Chao gave her short shrift. She said, 'If you can foretell the future, why didn't you tell me that the *Ming-t'ang* would burn down?'

The mother-superior was exiled to the frontier and her novices fled before the true nature of their calling was revealed. However, when Wu Chao discovered what had really been going on in the convent, she pardoned the mother-superior and the novices and ordered them to return to the capital. She then had them arrested and they were punished by being made palace slaves.

After the burning of the *Ming-t'ang* Wu Chao had little time for Hsüeh Huai-i and, in year one Chen Sheng – early 695 – she decided to rid herself of him. She got her daughter Princess Tai-ping to select some of the sturdier palace women. They were to lure him into a chamber, then overpower him and tie him up. In one version of the story, they then strangled him under the direction of Princess Tai-ping's nurse. In another, he was handed over to First Minister Wu Yu-uning – a distant cousin of Wu Chao, though under the Chinese system of kinship he was considered her nephew – who had him tied to a tree and beaten to death by the palace guard. Whatever his fate, his body was returned to the White Horse Monastery on a cart, where he was cremated and the ashes placed in a stupa.

Wu Chao also tired of her physician. As a replacement, her daughter Princess Tai-ping offered her one of her own lovers as a consort. Other studs were sought. Although Wu Chao was now in her seventies, she made love to her young consorts regularly. Frequently, it was said, the sound of 'eight horses rolling in wet mud' emanated from her bedchamber. This was the source of great amusement in the palace. To mask the sound Wu Chao had musicians play outside her bedchamber. This was the origin of a unique kind of music called *tai ko* that developed from these bedroom concerts.

Later, during the restored T'ang dynasty, the courtier Chang Mu wrote *Secret Chronicles of Kung Ho Chien*. The Kung Ho Chien was an office established by Wu Chao to organize her lovers, like the office of *nü-shih* under her male counterparts. The book has been lost, though some fragments survive. In one, Chang Mu recorded a conversation between the Minister of the Army Tsui Shih and his lover Shang-kuan Wan-erh. She was the granddaughter of the statesman Shang-kuan I, who fell from power after accusing Wu Chao of sorcery. Sent to the palace as a slave, she had risen to become Wu Chao's secretary and confidante. Tsui Shih asked Shang-kuan Wan-erh how Wu Chao chose her lovers and Shang-kuan Wan-erh replied that the Empress rejected any whose jade stalk was 'all skin and sinew'.

She went on: 'Considering the parts of the human body, the tongue has no skin, so it is able to relish all the tastes, while the heels have thick skin, as they touch only the lowly ground. A woman's cinnabar grotto is lined with a delicate membrane. So is the best part of a man's jade stalk. Thus the most tender parts touch during copulation. The protruding ridge of jade stalk sensitizes the rubbing and massaging of parts. When the jade stalk is in repose, it is a hidden bud; when it expands, it is an exposed eggplant, pleasure reigns, as if all the fecund essences of heaven and earth were being turned into rich wine. But if the skin of the jade stalk is too thick, it acts like a suit of armour. This deadens the pleasure while the jade stalk advances and retreats.' Clearly the women of the palace were very open about their sexual needs.

When the new *Ming-t'ang* was finished in 696, year one Cheng Sheng, it was somewhat smaller than the original, though, to save face, the official record maintained that the dimensions were the same. However, the new one was topped by a phoenix twenty feet high – twice the height of the original. It was blown down by a high wind and replaced by a huge copper ball held up by a band of dragons. The new *Ming-t'ang* was renamed T'ung T'ien Kung – the 'Palace that Reaches Heaven'. However, the taller of the two original buildings, the *T'ien-t'ang*, was not rebuilt.

With Wu Chao now growing old, the problem of the succession became more pressing. She had placed the tablets of her own Wu ancestors in the Temple of the Imperial Ancestors, as the T'ang Ancestral Temple had been renamed. Only three Emperors were venerated there – Kao-tsu, T'ai-tsung and Kao-tsung. Earlier T'ang ancestors no longer received sacrifices. This downgrading of the Li put Jui-tsung, who had been imprisoned in the palace for ten years, in an even more ambiguous position. As Emperor Expectant, he was the Imperial Heir, not the formal Crown Prince. Though he had been adopted into the Wu family, he was a Li by birth. And his right to succeed as a Li was open to question, since he had an older brother.

By marriage and adoption, Wu Chao had sought to bind the Wu and Li clans together. After the death of Princess Tai-ping's first husband, Wu Chao married her to Wu Yu-chi, brother of Wu Yu-ning and grandson of the elder brother of Wu Chao's father Wu Shih-huo. Some sources say that Wu Chao even arranged for the death of Wu Yu-chi's first wife to make this possible. One of Wu Ch'eng-ssu's sons was married to the daughter of Chung-tsung, who, in his long exile in the provinces, with his family had not yet been honoured with the surname Wu, nor had his four sons. But Li Shou-li, the surviving son of the former Crown Prince Li Hsien, had taken the Wu name, as had the six sons of Jui-tsung.

Despite all Wu Chao's efforts, Jui-tsung remained an object of hatred for the Wu clan, since he stood in the way of their imperial ambitions. And he was no more popular with the Li, since his elder brother Chung-tsung had been deposed in his favour. The T'ang claim to the throne through Chung-tsung was further imperilled by the fact that, of his four sons and eight daughters, only one son had been born to him by his wife, the ambitious Lady Wei. Jui-tsung had six sons and nine daughters. But two of his sons were in the running for the succession – the former Crown Prince, now Imperial Grandson, born to him by his wife Lady Liu and Li Lung-chi, born to his concubine of the first rank, the Te or Virtuous Concubine, who went on to become Emperor Hsüan-tsung.

Tragedy had befallen the family of the Imperial Heir Jui-tsung in 693, year one Ch'ang Shou, further weakening his position. A slave girl took a fancy to him, but was rebuffed. In her embarrassment, she appears to have become a willing tool of Lai Chün-ch'en and the Wu clan. Out of jealousy, she accused Lady Liu and the Virtuous Concubine, Lady Tou, mother of the future Emperor Hsüan-tsung, of sorcery. The allegation was not investigated, but when the two women went to the palace for the New Year ceremony in 693 they never came out again. It was assumed that Wu Chao had had them killed but no one knew what happened to their bodies.

Jui-tsung was both distraught at the murder of two women he loved and fearful for his life. But when he visited his mother he remained calm and made no mention of his two missing consorts. The slave girl then denounced Jui-tsung as a traitor, saying that he was the centre of a restoration plot. But a friend came forward to testify that the slave girl was motivated by malice and she was executed.

The parents of Lady Tou had also been charged with sorcery, but the advocate Hsü Yu-kung, now censor, stepped in to save them. He ordered the proceedings to be suspended and informed Wu Chao that the accused were innocent. Once again, he was accused of being part of the plot himself. This charge could hardly have been made to stick against a man of his standing. However, Wu Chao summoned him to an audience and accused him of releasing too many accused people.

'Releasing the accused may be a small fault in me,' Hsü Yu-kung replied. 'But it is a great virtue in Your Majesty.'

Wu Chao was going through a particularly cruel phase. That year she had a First Minister beaten to death in the Hall of Audience for amassing brocade, a fabric that was the sole prerogative of the Emperor. Two officials who had been visiting Jui-tsung privately, further spawning accusations that he was conspiring to return to the throne, were publicly executed by the excruciatingly brutal method of being sawn in half. Further visits by ministers or nobles were prohibited.

The terrible execution of sawing people in half was not confined to China. It was also used by the Romans, particularly in the suppression of the Christians. St Fausta was sawn in half lengthways, using the cleft of her vulva as a starting groove. The idea was to inflict the maximum pain, so the saw blade avoided cutting through the heart and reached the head last. However, the Chinese usually cut people in half widthways with a butcher's knife, severing them at the waist and leaving them conscious to bleed to death.

The brutal Lai Chün-ch'en was given the task of investigating the charges against Jui-tsung. Members of his household were shown the instruments of torture and began to confess anything required of them. However, Jui-tsung was saved by a retainer named An Chin-chang, who, while being interrogated by Lai Chün-ch'en, cried out, 'If you do not believe me cut out my heart and you will see that the Imperial Heir is innocent.' With that he grabbed a knife attempted to do just that to prove his loyalty to his master. In the struggle, he cut open his stomach. His entrails fell out and he collapsed in a pool of blood.

An Chin-chang's courage in defence of his master impressed Wu Chao, who relented. She sent her own physician to tend the man. The physician pushed the man's intestines back into his abdomen and sewed up the cut with a white mulberry bark thread. A medicated plaster covered the wound and, after a fortnight, An Chin-chang recovered. Wu Chao then summoned him and said, 'My son, who cannot show his own heart, has brought you to this state.'

An Chin-chang lived for another decade, dying eventually of old age. However, Wu Chao ordered Lai Chün-ch'en to drop all charges against Jui-tsung and his household. The *Comprehensive Mirror* says, 'From this time on, Jui-tsung was safe.'

But the excesses of Lai Chün-ch'en and his henchmen were far from over. An informer reported that a rebellion was being planned in the southern provinces of Kuangsi and Kuangtung, where thousands of exiles had been sent, including junior members of the imperial family. Wu Chao sent an acolyte of Lai Chün-ch'en's named Wan Kuo-chun to investigate. When he reached Canton, he herded all the exiles together and produced a forged decree ordering them all to commit suicide. There were cries of despair and disbelief. Fearing that his authority would be challenged, Wan Kuo-chun called his guards and drove the assembled exiles into a creek where more than three hundred drowned. Wan Kuo-chun returned to court and proclaimed that he had discovered widespread evidence of a conspiracy but had nipped the incipient rebellion in the bud, whereupon he was promoted by Wu Chao for his services.

She sent five more investigators to the south to root out conspiracy. They were all lieutenants of Lai Chün-ch'en and were give the rank of acting censor for the task. Seeing the reward Wan Kuo-chun had received for his massacre, they had only one fear – that they would kill too few. When they arrived at Ling-nan, the chief investigator killed seven hundred. His first assistant had killed five hundred and the other three had killed over one hundred each when a halt was called to the purge after provincial officials had reported back what was going on. Wu Chao was appalled when she heard of the indiscriminate killing. Many of the victims had had no connection with the Li clan or any attempt to unseat Wu Chao from the throne. Survivors were freed and they and their families were allowed to return home. Wao Kuo-chun and Lai Chün-ch'eng's other acolytes soon perished. In an attempt to save their own lives, some informed on others, who also perished. The popular story circulated that they had been haunted by the ghosts of their victims and driven to suicide by vengeful spectres.

Lai Chün-ch'eng was accused of bribery, demoted and sent to a post in the provinces. This was a blow to the supporters of Wu Ch'eng-ssu. But at the same time their greatest adversary, Li Chao-te, who had made many enemies in court, fell from grace. Wu Chao took infinite care to balance rival factions in her court. If a Wu supporter such as Lai Chün-ch'eng was ousted so was a T'ang loyalist like Li Chao-te.

Despite the excesses of the secret police, not all conspiracies against Wu Chao were fabricated. A provincial official named Liu Ssu-li was told by a fortune-teller that he was destined for greatness and in 697, year one of Wan Sui T'ung T'ien – 'Confer the Title of Heaven for Ten Thousand Years' – he attempted to muster support in court. This came to the attention of the superintendent of the *Ming-t'ang*, Chi Hsiu, a man said to be over seven feet tall.

Chi Hsiu was a supporter of the Wu. Years before, his father, a provincial governor, had been charged with corruption and to save the family from ruin Chi Hsiu had devised a plan to save him. He had two very attractive younger sisters and offered them to Wu Ch'eng-ssu, a well-known lecher, as his concubines. But after the two girls joined his harem Wu Ch'eng-ssu found them miserable and depressed. Eventually he asked them what the matter was and they explained, at Chi Hsiu's prompting, that they were unhappy because their father faced a sentence of death. Sad concubines were no good to Chi Hsiu, so he petitioned on behalf of their father and secured him a pardon.

With his two sisters now concubines of Wu Ch'eng-ssu, Chi Hsiu rose rapidly in government service. And when he heard of Liu Ssu-li's conspiracy, as a favour to the Wu, he reported it not to Wu Chao but to Lai Chün-ch'en, who seized the opportunity to regain the ear of the

Holy and Divine Emperor. Any accusation of treason was fast-tracked through the palace and she would have heard about Lai Chün-ch'en's allegation straight away. But she was unwilling to recall Lai Chün-ch'en immediately, so she put the investigation of the Liu Ssu-li conspiracy in the hands of the Prince of Ho Nei, Wu I-tsung, the grandson of her uncle, the older brother of her father.

Wu I-tsung was also devoted to the advancement of the Wu clan. He promised Liu Ssu-li that he would spare his life, provided he incriminated the opponents of the Wu clan. Many of the highest officials in court were arrested and executed, and thirty-six families were ruined. In all, a thousand people suffered death or exile. With the entire anti-Wu faction removed, Wu I-tsung went back on his word and, to cover his tracks, Liu Ssu-li was executed anyway.

Although it was Lai Chün-ch'en who had first brought the plot to Wu's attention, he had yet to receive any reward, or even be recalled to Luoyang. He needed a fresh accusation to reach the ear of Wu Chao, so he accused his informant Chi Hsiu of disloyalty. After all, Chi Hsiu had reported the conspiracy to Lai Chün-ch'en, not to the Holy and Divine Emperor Wu as he should have. But Chi Hsiu was closer to the throne than Lai Chün-ch'en and in a better position to play court politics. He secured an audience with Wu Chao and pointed out the fact that he had been the first to denounce the conspiracy. Consequently, he was promoted. But, to balance this, Wu Chao reinstated Lai Chün-ch'en as chief of police. Furthermore Li Chao-te was allowed to return to court.

Being returned to power seems to have turned Lai Chün-ch'en's head. He began invading men's homes to make free with their wives and concubines. Those who complained were denounced and imprisoned, then Lai Chün-ch'en used a forged mandate to take possession of their womenfolk. This alienated not just his old adversaries, the supporters of the Li, but also those who supported the Wu. Fearing that those ranged against him might prove too strong, Lai Chün-ch'en took the extreme course of accusing Jui-tsung, Chung-tsung, the Princess Tai-ping and all the Wu princes of forming one grand conspiracy against the throne. Lai Chün-ch'en had at last overreached himself. Led by the Princess Tai-ping, Wu Chao's favourite, the entire court turned against Lai Chün-ch'en and denounced him. He was arrested and imprisoned. After a summary hearing, his judges found him guilty and passed a unanimous sentence of death. But Wu Chao hesitated for three days.

While riding in the Imperial Park with Chi Hsiu, Wu Chao asked him what the talk in court was. He said that her courtiers were puzzled by the delay in putting Lai Chün-ch'en to death, since people feared he might escape. Wu Chao said that Lai Chün-ch'en had done many good services for the throne and she had to think the matter over. But, as an informant of Lai Chün-ch'en, Chi Hsiu knew the crimes of his master all too well. He explained how Lai Chün-ch'en had misused his position to rid himself of his enemies and amass a huge private fortune.

The Holy and Divine Emperor Wu then confirmed the sentence on Lai Chün-ch'en, but insisted that, to be even-handed, Li Chao-te face execution the same day. This dismayed the populace because Li Chao-te was respected and widely liked. But there was rejoicing at the demise of Lai Chün-ch'en. His headless corpse was trampled by the mob until nothing remained but slime.

Wu Chao was shocked by the crowd's evident hatred of Lai Chün-ch'en, but exploited the moment by issuing a decree detailing all his crimes and blaming him for all the persecutions that had taken place in her name. His family were stripped of their property and disgraced. Wu Chao now proclaimed all persecutions to be at an end.

She also used Lai Chün-ch'en's downfall to her advantage in court. She said she had long suspected that Lai Chün-ch'en and Chou Hsing had made many false accusations. But even the Emperor was bound by the law and the proper procedures had been adhered to. When she had suspected that an accusation had been false, she had sent officials to the prisons to investigate. But the prisoners had admitted their guilt and she was obliged to pass sentence. After all there had been some real conspiracies against the throne.

Replying to her statement from the throne, an up-and-coming minister named Yao Yüan-ch'ung said Lai Chün-ch'en and Chou Hsing had made the false accusations to gain power and feather their own nests. The officials sent to investigate were too afraid of being denounced themselves to contradict the accusations and the prisoners confessed to be spared more torture, opting for speedy death by decapitation. However, those who had made the false accusations were now dead and the Holy and Divine Emperor now knew the truth. Yao Yüan-ch'ung was now willing to personally guarantee the loyalty of the court and suffer the penalty for concealing treason if any of her courtiers proved false.

Wu Chao then took the opportunity to chide the court. Her First Ministers, she said, had taken the opportunity to act like tyrants, putting their own interests before hers and those of the nation. She rewarded those who had tried to warn her and pardoned those in exile, including Wei Yüan-chung.

With Lai Chün-ch'en out of the way, those who owed their position to him rushed to obtain Wu Chao's pardon. They confessed to concealing his crimes, but said that, if they had exposed him, they too would have risked being the target of false accusations and, consequently, death. As no further good could come of punishing them, Wu Chao pardoned them all.

Before he died Lai Chün-ch'en had achieved the impossible. He had united the Wu and T'ang factions in court – if only for a moment. Although a one-time ally of Lai Chün-ch'en, by adding his voice to those denouncing him, Wu Ch'eng-ssu had come out of his downfall rather well and his supporters again began manoeuvring to have him named successor. However, external forces were about to decide the succession.

CHAPTER ELEVEN

THE HALL OF MIRRORS

CHINA'S PRESTIGE was at its high-water mark and over one million people from neighbouring countries had asked permission to live in the Empire. These included six hundred and seventy thousand western Turks of the Shih-hsing tribe. At the same time the Khitan tribe who lived beyond the Wall in southern Manchuria rebelled. In 648, year twenty-two Chen Kuan, they had submitted to T'ai-tsung and had been allowed a fair degree of self-government. In return they had proved useful allies. But in 696, year one Cheng Sheng, there had been a famine and the Chinese military governor had refused relief and treated their chieftains as slaves. Within a week the two Khitan rebel leaders, Li Chinchung and Sun Wan-jung – both provincial officials under the Chinese – had tens of thousands of rebels under arms. An army headed by twenty-eight generals was sent against them. At the first battle, the imperial troops were wiped out. The dead filled a mountain valley near modern-day Beijing. The disaster was compounded when captured Chinese seals were used to forge orders that led the relief force into an ambush. Among the dead was the veteran general Wang Hsiao-chieh.

Meanwhile the Turks had a new leader named Mo-ch'o Khan. He was said to be the 'brother of the younger son' of the previous khan, so he was probably illegitimate. He began testing the borders but was easily repelled. Wu Chao considered the Khitan rebels a greater danger and sought an alliance with Mo-ch'o. Fortunately Mo-ch'o was eager to make peace with China. What he wanted in return was the return of the Shih-hsing Turks who had settled inside the Great Wall. He also wanted her to adopt him as a son and for his daughter to marry one of her sons. This would essentially put him and his offspring in line for the throne of China.

While Wu Chao considered his requests, Mo-ch'o raided the Khitan base and carried off their wives. The Holy and Divine Emperor responded by confirming Mo-ch'o's title of Khan and giving him insignia entitling him to the imperial rank of general. At the time of Mo-ch'o's attack, the Khitans were moving south, through the Great Wall, into Ho-pei, where they defeated another imperial army under the command of Wu San-ssu's nephew Wu Yu-i. Wu I-tsung took over command but did little better. He fled when the Khitans attacked Cho Chou, leaving the inhabitants to be slaughtered, and the Khitan army reached as far as Wei-chou, less than six hundred li, or two hundred miles, from Luoyang, before stopping for the winter. There they sought local support by calling for the deposition of Wu Chao and the restoration of Chung-tsung. The Holy and Divine Emperor responded by offering an amnesty and rewards to convicts and private slaves who would enrol in the army. This offer was so extraordinary that one of Wu Chao's officials declared it was 'damaging to the fundamental structure of the state'.

Wu I-tsung insisted that a more appropriate response would be to massacre all the inhabitants of Ho-pei who had submitted to the Khitan, even though they had been forced to do so. This was strongly opposed by the ministers in the assembly hall, who argued that unarmed civilians had done what they did to survive while Wu I-tsung fled with his army in the face of the Khitan. It was he who should be executed, not the inhabitants of Ho-pei. Wu Chao agreed and pardoned the Ho-pei people. However, Wu I-tsung was left unpunished.

Even though the Khitan threatened the capital, the Chinese court had its mind on something closer to home – the sudden rise of the Chang brothers. Chang I-chih and Chang Ch'ang-tsung were, in fact, half brothers, the grandsons of the distinguished minister Chang Hsing-ch'eng. The elder brother, Chang I-chih, had enjoyed privileged entry into the civil service. He was also 'white of complexion, of great beauty and skilled in music and song'. His brother shared these traits and came to the attention of the Princess Tai-ping, who took him as a lover. This is how Chang Ch'ang-tsung came to Wu Chao's attention and, as ever, the Holy and Divine Emperor showed a great interest in his penis. In another surviving fragment of *Secret Chronicles of Kung Ho Chien*, the author Chang Mu recorded a conversation where the Princess Tai-ping described to her mother what she had seen when Chang Ch'ang-tsung took a bath in her house.

'His jade stalk has a full head and a thin root,' she said. 'When it is in repose it droops down and is not long. It is as smooth as a goose egg and its ridge rises a fifth to a sixth of an inch. It is fresh, red, soft and mellow.'

Wu Chao smiled at the thought and asked the Princess Tai-ping if she had tasted it. Tai-ping admitted that she had not, but she had asked one of the ladies-in-waiting to try it out. Wu Chao turned to the lady-in-waiting and asked her about the experience.

'You may tell Her Majesty frankly,' she said. 'Don't be shy about it.'

To cover her blushes, the lady-in-waiting whispered in Wu Chao's ear.

'At the beginning of the encounter, it was like a luscious lychee from the South Seas, usually smooth and tender,' she said. 'Its ridge expanded like an umbrella. After three or four strokes, my flower pistil opened wantonly. My spirit and my soul were borne aloft. What's so good about him was the he did not decide for himself whether to be slow or fast. Tenderly he timed himself to my desire.'

Wu Chao was delighted at the news.

'I have heard that mediocre women of the outside world crave only muscular hardness and do not appreciate tenderness,' she said, 'That is the sexuality of peasant women. The best male organs are handsome, tender and mellow.'

Some texts said that the Chang brothers then rose to power because they became the lovers of both Princess Tai-ping and Wu Chao herself, while others maintained that they were effeminate and had been castrated. It is true that Wu Chao was particularly indulgent towards eunuchs during her reign, perhaps because she had known so many during her time as a concubine. She allowed them to leave the confines of the imperial palace and take mansions in the countryside nearby. Some took 'wives' and adopted uncastrated children of both sexes so that they could bequeath their property and titles to these heirs.

Whether the Chang brothers were eunuchs or not, they became great favourites. Wu Chao showered them with titles and gifts – rich brocades, horses and slaves. She found them diverting company. She enjoyed their effeminate ways as she had always enjoyed the company of women and she came to believe that Chang Ch'ang-tsung was the reincarnation of the Taoist immortal Tzu-chin. As she grew older, Wu Chao had become increasingly interested in immortality.

Whatever the reason for their rise, the Chang brothers became the dominant figures of the court. Even the Wu princes waited outside their mansion and 'contended to hold the bridles of their horses', calling Chang I-chih, the fifth son, *wu-lang* or 'Fifth Young Master', and Chang Ch'ang-tsung, the sixth son, *liu-lang* or 'Sixth Young Master', like retainers addressing the sons of a noble house. One poet of some renown sought to curry favour by carrying Chang Ch'ang-tsung's urine bucket around for him. But it was the devious Chi Hsiu who became their closest ally in court. He had been censor with the army when Wu I-tsung had been in command and had learnt first-hand how unpopular he and the rest of the clan were. With commanders like Wu I-tsung and Wu Yu-i, and the populace against them, it seemed that the Wu stood no chance of taking the throne, so he changed tack and threw in his lot with the Chang.

It was said that Wu Chao reinstalled the mirrors around Kao-tsung's couch for her sex sessions with Chang Ch'ang-tsung. A satirical poem about their encounters reads,

> In the clear spring, in the hall of mirrors,
> Many a secret game is played.
> The reflected images of the jade-like bodies
> Carefully imitate their every movement.
> Mr Six, drunk with victory,
> Smiles at the brilliant void,
> In a pair the Mandarin ducks sport,
> In the green waves.

'Mr Six' is Chang Ch'ang-tsung and the 'brilliant void' refers both to the surface of the mirrors and to Wu Chao's given name, whose new character showed the sun and moon above and the void below.

The affair was studded with extravagant gestures. Although Wu Chao already occupied the Dragon's Couch – the imperial throne made from gold and bronze – Ch'ang-tsung had another throne made for her. It was fashioned from ivory, with sable cushions, coverings of cricket-mosquito felt and mats made from rushes know as dragon whisker and phoenix pinion, and it was adorned with woven rhinoceros horn. The whole thing was enclosed in a tent embellished with jade, pearls, gold, silver, and precious stones.

With the Khitan on the doorstep, the Holy and Divine Emperor seemed far more interested in the gilding of nine ceremonial tripods that had already used up eight hundred and seventy tons of bronze in their casting. But that summer, she sent two more armies two hundred thousand strong to face the Khitan. Despite their undertaking to put Chung-tsung back on the throne of China, few Chinese had rallied to the Khitan. And Mo-ch'o's raid on their base had robbed them, not just of their wives, but of vital supplies. News of the raid demoralized the Khitan forces and the non-Khitan tribesmen in their ranks mutinied as the Chinese forces moved in. Soon the entire Khitan army collapsed and those who escaped the slaughter fled to Tibet.

However, China's alliance with Mo-ch'o began to unravel. Misreading the situation, Yen Chih-wei, the envoy Wu Chao had sent to negotiate with the Turks, had immediately acceded to all of Mo-ch'o's demands. Thousands of Shih-hsing Turks were handed over to him, along with several tons of iron, thousands of agricultural implements, expensive gifts, fifty thousand rolls of silk and forty thousand measures of grain. However, there was one concession that Yen Chih-wei could not make. No Chinese prince of royal blood had ever been married to a barbarian. Instead, Wu Chao sent Wu Yen-hsiu, Prince of Huai Yang, the second son of Wu Ch'eng-ssu. He was not Wu Chao's son but, given the uncertainty of the succession, he was possibly in line for the throne, so if the Khan's daughter married him, she might well have become Empress. But when Wu Yen-hsiu arrived at Mo-ch'o's camp, the Khan was far from pleased.

'I wanted the son of the Li for my daughter,' he said. 'What use is a Wu? The Li family always treated us with favour. It has been wiped out, except for two sons. I will now lead my troops into China to restore them.'

Wu Yen-hsiu was imprisoned and Yen Chih-wei was browbeaten into assisting the Turks. He helped Mo-ch'o compose a letter to Wu Chao which read,

The seed grain you sent me was rotten and will not grow. The gold and silver pieces you gave me are counterfeit. The insignia presented to my envoys was taken away again. The silks you sent were old and rotten. My daughter is the child of the Khan. She should be married to the son of the Emperor. The Wu family are inferior in rank to my own, and you have used trickery to effect this marriage. For all these reasons I have raised troops with the intention of conquering Ho-pei.

In the autumn of 698, year one Sheng Li, Mo-ch'o invaded the already ravaged Ho-pei to the west of the route taken by the Khitan. But Wu Chao was way ahead of him. Five months earlier she had secretly recalled Chung-tsung and his family to Luoyang to keep him out of the hands of Mo-ch'o, who, like the Khitan, might seek to put him back on the throne. At this time, it seems she had no intention of naming him Crown Prince, but with the country at war she could not name Wu Ch'eng-ssu as her successor. He had never been popular and showed no flare for high office. Besides he was ill and in the eighth month of year one of Sheng Li – 698 – he died. Some sources say that this was due to the extinction of his hopes to succeed.

As Wu Ch'eng-ssu's health failed, his cousin Wu San-ssu began to position himself for the succession. But he was not a serious contender. He had no basis for his claim to the throne. He was not even heir to the senior branch of the Wu clan, for Wu Ch'eng-ssu had other sons besides the unfortunate Wu Yen-hsui, who was still in the hands of Mo-ch'o. With China at war, Wu Chao had become dependent on Ti Jen-chieh, now her most trusted advisor, and he was a long-time opponent of the Wu. Besides the Holy and Divine Emperor Wu's mind was already set on another course.

When Chi Hsiu had returned to court after the Khitan campaign, he had told Wu Chao how difficult it had been to raise men for commanders such as Wu I-tsung. She already knew that Wu I-tsung was particularly incompetent as a soldier on all levels. When she had ordered the execution of an official who had defected to the Turkish Khan and had him tied to a post, Wu I-tsung loosed three arrows at him from seven paces and failed to hit him once. There was only one course of action open to her, Chi Hsiu said. That was to make Chung-tsung commander-in-chief. Then men would rally to her cause. Wu Chao was sceptical at first, so Chi Hsiu adopted another ploy. He went to the Chang brothers and told them that many people in court were jealous of them and longed for their blood. They owed their position and fortune, he said, solely to the Holy and Divine Emperor. One day, she would die and everyone would turn on them. They would be ignominiously ousted and die a fearful death – unless they found a new protector. The Chang brothers were anything but tough guys. They were terrified by Chi Hsiu's words and wept. And they begged Chi Hsiu to tell them what to do.

'The Empire has not forgotten the virtue of the T'ang,' he said. 'Everyone still thinks of Chung-tsung, Prince of Lu Ling. The Holy and Divine Emperor has grown old and the succession has not yet been settled. However, the Wu will not succeed. Why don't you seize the opportunity to use your influence to restore her son, Prince of Lu Ling, and make him Crown Prince to satisfy the will of the people. That way you can avoid disaster and continue to enjoy wealth and privilege for many years.'

The Chang brothers then pestered Wu Chao to restore Chung-tsung. But she was not fooled. They were lightweights and would not have come up with such a plan of their own accord. It seemed plain to her that Chi Hsiu had put them up to it. She summoned him to an audience where he confessed it was his doing and, once again, extolled the advantages of making Chung-tsung Crown Prince. She called Ti Jen-chieh to an audience and asked him what he thought about making Chung-tsung Crown Prince once more. With tears in his eyes, Ti Jen-chieh, a long-term T'ang loyalist, urged her to do it. Unbeknown to Ti Jen-chieh she had Chung-tsung concealed behind a curtain. She pulled it back to reveal him with the words, 'Here, I give you back your Crown Prince.' Or, in another version: 'Here, I give you back your ex-Emperor.'

Ti Jen-chien was overjoyed, but he pointed out that it was no good Wu Chao making Chung-tsung Crown Prince in secret. Not only must the Li succession be restored; it must be done publicly.

At this point, Wu Chao assembled three armies numbering four hundred and fifty thousand. Even this was not enough to contain the highly mobile Turkish forces. But when Wu San-ssu conducted a further levy the people balked and only a thousand men were raised. It was then that Wu Chao played her trump card. She sent Chung-tsung out to Lung-men and on the twenty-eighth day of the third month of year one Sheng Li – 13 May 698 – Chung-tsung re-entered Luoyang with due ceremony and in full view of the public. This rallied the people. Jui-tsung was forced to step down as Imperial Heir and was given the title Prince of Hsiang. Chung-tsung was named Crown Prince and commander-in-chief of the army. In a few days, he had raised fifty thousand men.

Ti Jen-chieh was appointed commander in the field and soon set out at the head of a new army one hundred thousand strong. Within a few months he had captured the key city of Ting Chou and slaughtered its defenders. Mo-ch'o fled back over the Great Wall, leaving behind over eighty thousand dead. There, the author of the *Comprehensive Mirror* Ssu-ma Kuang says, 'the barbarians of the north-west all joined him, and great was their contempt for the Middle Kingdom'. This allowed Mo-ch'o to expand his realm to the north. Within a decade, he controlled all of Inner Asia, from the borders of Manchuria to the valley of the river Ili in Kazakhstan.

Mo-ch'o invaded China again in 702, year two Ch'ang-an, but was rapidly seen off by an army nominally headed by Jui-tsung as supreme commander. Soon Mo-ch'o tried to make peace. In the sixth month, Gui-chou, of year three Ch'ang-an – August 703 – he sent an envoy requesting that his daughter should be married to one of the sons of Chung-tsung. Two unmarried princes were paraded before the envoy in the Hall of Audience. The marriage went ahead, but it did not secure peace. However, Mo-ch'o did stay outside the Great Wall and, after another victory at Ming-sha near Tunhuang in 706, year six Shen Lung, he caused no more trouble in China. He was assassinated by a rival in 716, year four K'ai Yuan – 'Open First'.

Only the invasion of China itself had forced Wu Chao to recognize Chung-tsung as her successor. She was still not prepared to hand the Empire back to the T'ang. Along with the title of Crown Prince, Chung-tsung was forced to adopt the surname Wu. He was allowed to occupy the Eastern Palace, the traditional residence of the Crown Prince, and could attend court, but he was given no taste of power and the command of the garrison of Luoyang was given to the cowardly Wu I-tsung, so that the troops there would be in Wu hands.

But when it came to the succession the Wu cause was now lost. This was said to have been revealed to Wu Chao in a dream. She had dreamt that she was playing chess but constantly lost. Ti Jen-chieh interpreted her dream for her, telling her that it was a warning from heaven. To lose at chess was to lose a son – the words for 'chessman' and 'son' are the same in Chinese. In future, she must not flout the rights of her sons. The virtue of T'ai-tsung had not been forgotten. He had fought with great valour for years to win the throne and the right to pass it on to his heirs. Wu Chao held it in trust for her sons and the sons of Kao-tsung and she had talked of giving it away to Wu Ch'eng-ssu and even Wu San-ssu. It was only the return of the rightful heir Chung-tsung that had saved the Empire from the barbarians. For once, Wu Chao listened in silence.

When the Holy and Divine Emperor Wu died 'after a thousand years had passed', as Ti Jen-chieh and the other courtiers put it, no one could now doubt that the T'ang dynasty would be restored. But Wu Chao was now afraid of what would happen to the Wu once a Li sat on the throne again. As the dynastic history said, 'The Empress Dowager feared that after she was dead the Wu would be trampled down by the T'ang and would have no place even to die in.'

So on the seventh day of the second month of year two Sheng Li – 23 March 699 – she assembled her own children Chung-tsung, Jui-tsung and the Princess Tai-ping along with the Wu princes in the *Ming-t'ang* and got them all to swear a solemn oath before heaven and earth that they would live in peace and harmony after her death. This oath was engraved on an iron tablet and deposited in the archives of the dynasty.

For the moment, though, the battle between the Wu and the Li became irrelevant, since the Chang were in ascendance. Dressed in colourful silks and with their faces powdered and rouged, the two brothers played the role of the Emperor's principal concubines as well as wielding considerable influence in court. Other men flitted around the court fully made up in the traditional attire of imperial consorts. As Emperor, Wu Chao had completely reversed the sex roles in court. Now she was drinking in their yang energy while expelling little of her yin. She had used the arts of the bedchamber that she had been taught as a girl of thirteen when she had joined the harem to make herself Empress and seize the throne. Now she used those same arts to keep her in power. For women, as for men, in Chinese philosophy, sex brought with it health and longevity. The more partners you had, the longer you lived and, as her lack of concern over the succession showed, Wu Chao planned to live for ever.

But those around her were all too mortal. The next to fall from grace was Chi Hsiu. She had always admired his frankness. His manoeuvrings had rid her of Lai Chün-ch'eng, who had brought her regime into disrepute, and, by championing Chung-tsung, he had helped her win the war against Mo-ch'o. But one day in 700 he had an argument with the cowardly and brutal Wu I-tsung in her presence about who was responsible for the discovery of the Liu Ssu-li plot. The row became heated. Chi Hsiu was a tall man, whereas Wu I-tsung was short and squat. Chi Hsiu made some personal remarks about Wu I-tsung's stature. Such things were beneath the dignity of the court and Wu Chao took offence.

'To abuse those of Our Name in Our Presence makes us doubt your loyalty,' she told Chi Hsiu.

Soon after, she grew annoyed at a report that he had written. It was full of quotes from the classical histories. Wu Chao was extremely well read and found this patronizing. She summoned him and told him not to tell her things she knew already. And in future his reports should not be so long-winded. It was then that she related the incident concerning the horse when she was a concubine of T'ai-tsung. To reiterate, Wu Chao said, 'T'ai-tsung had a very wild horse no one could break. I was a palace girl and, standing by his side, I said, "I can master him, but I will need three things: a metal whip, an iron mace and a dagger. If the metal whip does not bring him to obedience, I shall use the mace to beat his head, and if that does not work I will use the dagger to cut his throat." T'ai-tsung understood what I meant by that.' And she added, 'Do you? Now do you want me to use the dagger?'

Chi Hsiu understood perfectly. He threw himself to the ground and begged for mercy. It was granted, but he knew his career was on the wane. Having crossed the Wu, he had many powerful enemies in court. When Chi Hsiu's younger brother was caught using his brother's name to meddle in official business, Chi Hsiu himself was accused of sanctioning it and he was dismissed. But his life was spared and he was posted out to the provinces.

Before he left, Chi Hsiu sought one last audience with the Holy and Divine Emperor. He entered weeping and said, 'Today Your faithful servant is leaving court and will never see Your Majesty again. May I speak one word?'

Wu Chao took pity on him for all the good service he had done. She allowed him to speak and did him the rare honour of inviting him to sit. Although he was usually outspoken, this time Chi Hsiu found it best to couch his words in a parable.

'If you mix water and mud, will they stick?' he asked.

'Of course,' said Wu Chao.

'Can one use such a mixture to plaster a wall?' asked Chi Hsiu.

'Indeed,' said Wu.

'But what if one were to take half of this clay and make it into a Buddha, and the other half and make it into a Taoist deity?'

'That would not do,' said Wu.

Chi Hsiu rose from his seat and bowed.

'The imperial family' – the Li – 'and the relations by marriage' – that is, the Wu – 'each have their rightful place,' said Chi Hsiu. 'Heaven is not pleased to see that, while the imperial family has its Crown Prince, the relations by marriage have also been raised to the rank of princes. In doing this, Your Majesty has bred conflict. These two factions can never live in harmony.'

Again Wu Chao took no offence.

'We realized this,' she said. 'But what is done is done. It cannot be helped.'

Chi Hsiu bid her farewell and left court. He died shortly after arriving at his provincial posting.

Despite Chi Hsiu's foreboding, the Empire was, for the moment, secure from both internal and external strife. The Wu could manoeuvre and the T'ang could scheme, but with her unbridled authority Wu Chao was confident that no one would move against her.

Of course, her relationship with the Chang brothers caused a scandal and brought protests form the censors, but Wu Chao did not care. Like other Emperors before her, she was content to spend her last days surrounded by pretty young lovers. She retired to the seclusion of her summer palaces and toyed the days away with her favourites. The excuse was given that the Chang brothers were involved in some literary work on her behalf, but nothing was ever produced. However, court scholars were invited to write poems praising the beauty of Chang Ch'ang-tsung and Chang I-Chih. Courtiers were also paid handsome sums to introduce other pretty young boys to Chang Ch'ang-tsung. Whether these were for the use of the Chang brothers or the Holy and Divine Emperor was a matter for scandalous speculation.

Taoism, because of its special significance to the T'ang, lost ground during the Chou dynasty. However, when the Chang brothers came to court, its fortunes began to revive. The grand compilation of thirteen hundred volumes called the *San-chiao chu-ying* was completed early in the eighth century by twenty-six scholars nominally headed by the Chang brothers. The title meant 'The Pearls and Flowers of the Three Religions' and it was a collection of quotations and passages from Taoist, Buddhist and Confucian classics, showing Wu Chao's continuing awareness that what was needed was a proper balance between the three faiths, though it is unlikely that she ever overcame the Confucian prejudice against her as a woman. The scholastic institute responsible was called the Office of the Reining Crane. This was the Kung Ho Chien, the bureau that organized her male harem. The name 'crane' had been chosen because the crane was a symbol of longevity and it became a talisman for the Chang brothers.

The Chang brothers became extravagant hosts. Roasted meat was very much in favour at the time, so one of them had a giant cage made and filled it with ducks and geese. A large bowl filled with a sauce of the five condiments – sweet, sour, bitter, salt, and pepper – was placed inside and a charcoal fire was lit underneath. As it grew warm the fowl grew thirsty and drank the sauce, marinating them from within. They died from the heat and slowly cooked. Then, when the feathers had been scorched off, the roasted meat would be served to guests. Not to be outdone, the other brother put a donkey in a large oven with a sauce of the five condiments to drink and fed his guests on marinated ass meat.

Banquets were frequently held at court. There could be as many as a thousand guests and, on these occasions, the regular imperial kitchen staff – consisting of eight dieticians, sixteen supervisors and seven cooks, along with their assistants – were supplemented by the ten supervisors, fifteen recorders, and two thousand kitchen staff of the Service of Radiant Emolument, who boasted twenty-three sauce makers, thirty brewers, one-hundred-and-twenty ale servers, twelve makers of soya-bean paste, twelve vinegar makers, eight vegetable picklers, and five refiners of malt sugar. These events took place both indoors and out, by the light of torches, and as many as fifty-eight courses were served. They were followed by elaborate entertainments featuring trained elephants, tightrope walkers, jugglers, wrestling, sword dancers, tug of war, poetry reading, pole acts, boat races between the various departments of state, and the popular game of football, played with a spherical leather ball filled with feathers. More commonly the court was entertained by the musicians and dancers of the Nine Ensembles – two Chinese, one Indian, one Korean, and five from Central Asia. Musicians used zithers and mouth organs, while a troupe from Samarkand had dancing girls who performed the popular Western Spinning Dance, where they rolled across a stage filled with wooden balls which made a noise like thunder. Feasting continued late into the night and sometimes a banquet might go on for several days.

At these feasts, the Holy and Divine Emperor entertained both the Chang brothers and the Wu princes, who did not dare show any enmity in her presence. Together they drank and gambled the night away. Chinese of the T'ang era were particularly fond of drinking games, including Ale Rules, in which a player might have to down forty measures in a single quaff. The Wus and Changs made gentle jokes at each other's expense and that of the officials around them. But mostly, lest they risk the Emperor's displeasure, the Wu princes resorted to outright flattery. Wu San-ssu said that Chang Ch'ang-tsung was the reincarnation of a famous sage, Wang-tzu Chin (Prince Chin). The disinherited son of King Ling of the Eastern Chou dynasty and the ancestor of those with the now commonplace surname Wang, he was said to have ascended to heaven on a crane. Wu Chao thought this was a splendid idea and had a costume made out of crane feathers for Chang Ch'ang-tsung. Decked with feathers and playing the *sheng* or reed pipe, Chang Ch'ang-tsung was winched aloft by a wooden crane. Again, court scholars were invited to write poems in praise of Chang Ch'ang-tsung's beauty. This event scandalized the court.

The elder brothers of the Chang family used their siblings' position as the Emperor's favourites to enrich themselves. One of them was Chang Ch'ang-i, who had secured himself an influential post in Luoyang and took bribes to secure others' advancement. One day he was stopped by a graduate named Hsüeh, who gave him fifty ounces of gold for a government position. When he reached the palace, Chang Ch'ang-i gave the man's papers to the Vice President of the Board of Civil Service and told him to give Hsüeh a job. However, the Vice President mislaid the papers. Chang Ch'ang-i was furious at his incompetence and all he could remember was that the graduate's name was Hsüeh.

'You had better find him and give him a job at once,' Chang Ch'ang-i said.

Unfortunately Hsüeh was a common name in China. When the Vice President checked his registers he found that sixty Hsüehs had applied for appointments. All sixty were given a job.

With the money he garnered from bribery, Chang Ch'ang-i built a beautiful mansion that outshone anything any of the Wu or Li princes had. One night, someone wrote on the gate, 'How many days can a spider's web endure?'

Chang Ch'ang-i had the graffito removed, but the next night it reappeared. Every time he had it scrubbed off it appeared again. Eventually Chang Ch'ang-i left it, but wrote underneath, 'Even one day is enough.'

The Chang brothers were always looking for new government posts they could exploit. Under their influence, Wu Chao was persuaded to install secular officials as head of the Fields of Compassion. This was a charible foundation, tradionally run by Buddhist monks, that provided medicines and treatment to the sick and cared for the aged, orphaned and destitute. The new managers supplied by the Changs wrung money out of the Fields of Compassion and it became a den of thieves. When Wu Chao eventually fell from power, the Fields of Compassion was closed down.

By the year 700 – year one Chiu Shih, 'To Observe for a Long Time' – Wu Chao was seventy-five and was beginning to feel her age. That year, on the sacred mountain Sung-shan, she received a Taoist leader from Hung-chou, named Hu Ch'ao, who was so far out of the mainstream of Taoism that some texts describe him as a Buddhist. She had commissioned him to produce a hugely expensive elixir for her, which would give her everlasting life. It had taken three years to prepare. Wu Chao swigged it down. It made her feel better, but did not fully restore her vitality and prayers were called for. In 1982, a golden tablet was found on Sung mountain commemorating their meeting in 700. The words inscribed on it say that, on her behalf, Hu Ch'ao had begged the gods for forgiveness for the crimes she had committed in her lifetime.

The year 700 was particularly auspicious. A peasant in the south of China was cleaning out his duck pens when he discovered something glinting among their dung. It was gold. Panning the ducks' dung yielded fourteen ounces. Then he followed the ducks to the foot of a mountain where they had been feeding, dug down and unearthed a further twelve thousand eight hundred ounces. This began a gold rush in Guangsi and Guangdong.

Wu Chao spent more and more of her time at her summer palaces to get away from the heat of Luoyang. Her favourite was the San Yang Palace in the Shansi mountains some one hundred and eighty li, or sixty miles, from the capital. On her way there on one occasion, she was stopped by a Tartar monk who begged her to visit a temple nearby because a Buddhist saint had died and was about to be cremated. Wu Chao agreed to go, but Ti Jen-chieh, who was accompanying her, knelt in the road and blocked her path.

'Buddha is a barbarian god, not fit for the Ruler of the Empire to worship,' he said. 'This foreigner wants to take you to his temple so that it will be famous and people from near and far will flock to it. It is not a fit place for Your Majesty to visit. The road is rocky and narrow and it will not be easy to guard.'

Perhaps remembering the time P'ei Yen had plotted to capture her at the Lung-men, Wu Chao turned back, saying, 'I will follow My upright minister's advice.'

Ti Jen-chieh had become the most trusted of her First Ministers. She had no doubts about his loyalty and called him 'Old Statesman' rather than using his given name as was customary. She even allowed him the rare privilege of arguing with her openly in court and she accepted and followed his advice. When he died on the twenty-sixth day of the ninth month, Geng-chen, year one Chiu Shih – 11 November 700 – she wept inconsolably.

'My court is empty now,' she said. After that, when she had a tricky decision to make she would say, 'Why did heaven take my Old Statesman away so soon?'

Though Ti Jen-chieh is long dead, his name lives on in fiction. During the Ming dynasty he was the protagonist of *Di Gong An* – or 'The Strange Cases of Judge Di' – styled after *Bao Gong An* – 'The Strange

Cases of Judge Bao' – based on a real person from the Sung dynasty. In the twentieth century, Dutch sinologist Robert van Gulik translated *Di Gong An* into English, then wrote his own series of Judge Dee novels. French author Frédéric Lenormand has now followed up with his Judge Ti whodunnits.

Thanks to Ti Jen-chieh, Wu Chao had been left with a number of able ministers. He had recommended the reinstatement of Chang Chien-chih, who had acted for the Pure Concubine's son Li Sui-chieh and had been sent into exile when the Scholars of the Northern Gate intercepted his petition. Chang Chien-chih had then quickly risen from the rank of provincial governor to become Vice President of the Board of Justice.

Ti Jen-chieh had also recommended Yao Yüan-ch'ung, who had distinguished himself in the Turkish war, though Wu Chao only gave him a provincial posting. Ching Hui had become a governor and Huan Yen-fan a censor on Ti Jen-chieh's advice and they were considered two of the ablest ministers in the government. When it was noticed that many of the men he recommended came from his own school, Ti Jen-chieh replied that he recommended them in the interest of the state, not for private advantage.

However, when Ti Jen-chieh died, there was no minister of comparable experience to replace him. Wu Chao took no notice of her palace officials, however able, since she did not trust them. As she succumbed to ill-health she relied more and more on the Chang brothers. Their Office of the Reining Crane became the Office of Imperial Attendants, but it quickly degenerated into a den of drinking, gambling – which was technically illegal under the T'ang – and other dissipations. It was widely seen as Wu Chao's harem and she was known to indulge herself regularly with handsome young men. One official wrote to her complaining,

> Your Majesty has already granted intimate favours to Hsüeh Huai-i and to Chang I-chih and Chang Ch'ang-tsung. Surely this should be enough. Recently I heard that a head of the Servants of the Imperial Apartments, called Liu Mu, himself claimed that his son Liang-pin was white and pure, beautiful in beard and eyebrow. The chief administrator of the Gate Guard of the Left, Hou Hsiang, said that his virility and staying power surpassed that of Hsüeh Huai-i, and unassisted he wanted to recommend himself as fit for membership in the Office of Imperial Attendants.

The official was, as usual, rewarded for his plain speaking. However, rumours concerning Wu Chao and the Changs led to another tragedy in the Li family. The Crown Prince Chung-tsung had a son called Li Ch'ung-jun. His mother was Lady Wei, who had briefly been Empress Wei during Chung-tsung's first reign, and Li Ch'ung-jun had been recognized as Imperial Grandson when Chung-tsung had first been Crown Prince. When his father had been deposed and exiled, Li Ch'ung-jun had been reduced to the rank of a commoner. But, although his father had been made Crown Prince, he had not yet been restored to princely rank.

Now nineteen, Li Ch'ung-jun was not Chung-tsung's oldest son. He had a half-brother named Li Chung-fu, who was two years his senior but had been born to a concubine of lowly rank and so was not first in line to succeed. Although this had hardly mattered when they had been in exile, now that Chung-tsung had been restored to the succession it was a cause of jealousy.

Chung-tsung also had a number of daughters. One of them was Princess Yung T'ai – the name means 'Forever Tranquil'. She was married to Wu Ch'eng-ssu's eldest son, Wu Yen-chi, who would also have been in line to the throne if the Wu claim had succeeded. One day Li Ch'ung-jun, Wu Yen-chi and Princess Yung T'ai were discussing the strange relationship between the Holy and Divine Emperor Wu Chao and the Chang brothers. Li Ch'ung-jun's elder brother Li Ch'ung-fu got to hear about this conversation and sought to use the knowledge to his advantage: he went to Chang I-chih and told him what they had said. Chang I-chih then reported this to Wu Chao, who was furious. By this time Li Ch'ung-jun and Wu Yen-chi had fallen out. Wu Chao did not want the Wus and Lis squabbling and she had had quite enough of people criticizing her relationship with the Chang brothers. So she ordered the three gossiping grandchildren to commit suicide, leaving Chung-tsung without a legitimate heir, and Li Ch'ung-fu exiled. In another account, Li Ch'ung-jun was flogged to death on the third day of the ninth month, Ren-chen, year one Ch'ang An – 8 October 701. In yet another account, it was the Princess Yung T'ai who was flogged to death. According to her epitaph she died the day after her husband and brother, though she was thought to be pregnant at the time. Under T'ang Law a pregnant woman would be given a stay of execution until one hundred days after she had given birth, so it is thought that she miscarried out of grief.

However, according to Li Ch'ung-fu's biography, he was not the elder brother. The conversation between Li Ch'ung-jun, Wu Yen-chi and Princess Yung T'ai had leaked because they fell out, and the story was put about by Wu Chao to give her an excuse to send Li Ch'ung-fu away. In this version the various punishments meted out were left up to Chung-tsung himself. However, there must have been considerable coercion from Wu Chao to make him kill his own children and deprive himself of a legitimate heir.

But the matter did not end there. As Li Ch'ung-fu was thought to be responsible for the death of Lady Wei's only son, he earned her undying hatred. When Chung-tsung came to the throne, Wei used her position as Empress to have Li Ch'ung-fu officially banished and removed from the succession, and Chung-tsung's third son Li Ch'ung-chün became Crown Prince. This only stored up more trouble for the future.

As an elderly woman, Wu Chao could be unpredictable. She had killed three of her grandchildren over a petty slight to the Chang brothers, but when a scholar named Su An-heng wrote a memorandum urging Wu Chao to abdicate she rewarded him. Su An-heng pointed out that she had held the Empire in trust for twenty years. Chung-tsung had now shown himself to be both mature and capable, and it was time the throne was returned to him. Meanwhile the Wu princes should all be reduced in rank to dukes or marquises. She had more than twenty grandsons who could now occupy their princely titles. This would end the anomaly of having two imperial clans and avoid a future clash between them.

Surprisingly, this argument was well received by Wu Chao. She invited Su Ang-heng to an audience and plied him with lavish gifts and gave a banquet in his honour. She did this probably because others privately shared his views and she wished to placate them. However, she did not heed his advice. Instead, in November 701, she returned with the court to Ch'ang-an for the first time in twenty years. She may have got over her fear of cats, but she still avoided the ghosts of the Empress Wang and the Pure Concubine. Instead of staying in the imperial palace inside the city, she remained outside in the Palace of the Nine Perfections, where Kao-tsung had spent the last years of his life.

Some sources say that she made the move back to Ch'ang-an for reasons of health, but her real motives seem to be political and ideological. The return to the T'ang capital was an implicit recognition that the T'ang dynasty would soon be restored. She even changed the reign name to Ch'ang-an. The move was also designed to remind people of the Duke of Chou, Chou-kung, who had consolidated the power of the Chou dynasty in the twelfth century BC by resisting the temptation to seize the throne after the death of his brother Wu-wang, serving instead as regent to Wu-wang's young son Ch'eng-wang. After seven years, during which he put down a rebellion by supporters of the former Shang dynasty and stabilized the political system throughout northern China, Chou-kung stepped down. Perhaps she would do the same. The administrative framework the Duke of Chou established was a model for future Chinese dynasties and Chou-kung was esteemed as a paragon by Confucius. So by making the move to Ch'ang-an, Wu Chao implicitly paid her respects to Confucianism.

In Ch'ang-an, in 702, year two Ch'ang-an, Wu Chao extended the civil service examination system to the military. The new exam for soldiers came in seven parts:

Static target archery – shooting a target at one hundred and five paces, with a bow weighing one hundred and eighty pounds.

Pedestrian archery – shooting a straw mannequin, while walking.

Mounted archery – at a gallop, shooting at a target of two small deer, three inches tall and five inches long.

Mounted lancemanship – at a gallop, knocking two-and-a-half-inch-square plates off four wooden figures, two to the left, two to the right, with a twelve-pound lance an inch and a half in circumference and eighteen feet long.

Discourse – delivering a speech that demonstrated leadership abilities.

Height – preferred candidates should be over six feet tall.

Weightlifting – carrying eight-and-three-quarter bushels of grain twenty paces on your back and raising a bar three-and-a-half inches in diameter and seventeen feet long ten times.

Wu Chao strengthened the administration of the state university and commissioned a new national history. These can all be seen as Confucian acts. Wu San-ssu was put in charge of compiling the national history, which could be seen as a way for Wu Chao to secure her place in the history books before going into retirement – rather than let the Li do it.

On 5 June 702 – the second day of the fifth month, Geng-zi, year two Ch'ang-an – Su An-heng presented a second memorandum again advocating that Wu Chao stand down. It reminded her that her power was derived from the T'ang and that the Crown Prince Chung-tsung – a T'ang – was now forty-six and fully capable of ruling in his own right. Had she forgotten the love a mother was supposed to have for her son? Why, at her great age, did she continue to work night and day? Time was flowing by and her days were short. What would she say to her husband the late Celestial Emperor when she met him in the world of shades? The hearts and minds of the people had again turned to the T'ang dynasty. Although peace had reigned while she sat on the throne, things happened when the time was right. When the cup was full, it overflowed. Again Wu Chao neither heeded these words nor punished their author.

Su An-heng had taken care to avoid the fate of Li Ch'ung-jun, Wu Yen-chi and Princess Yung T'ai and had failed to mention the real reason that the hearts and minds of the people were turning to the T'ang. Several times in her reign she had surrounded herself with some pretty unpleasant characters. But they had all been men of ability and, when the time was right, she had got rid of them. Now she lavished greater favour than ever before on the Chang brothers, who had nothing to recommend them beyond their pretty faces and their musical abilities. And the greed and corruption of their family were causing the people genuine distress.

Wu Chao did not see any of this. She was now old and frail and the Chang brothers danced attendance on her. Basking in her favour, they believed their position was unshakeable. Wu Chao would accept no criticism of her sexual life. As Emperor, was she not allowed such indulgences? And as the Changs played no part in politics, she did not see the political danger.

However, the Chang brothers were building up resentment at the highest level of government. They showed no respect for the protocol of the court and snubbed its officials seemingly with impunity. On one occasion they invited rich merchants from Szechwan to drink and gamble at Wu Chao's table. The Vice President of the Chancellery protested that men of such low rank should not be allowed in the palace and got his servants to throw them out. The other guests were aghast, believing that the Vice President of the Chancellery would soon lose his head. However, Wu Chao praised the man for speaking out. But such occasions were rare.

While the Chang brothers were thoughtless and frivolous, they found themselves pawns in the hands of a skilled player of the political game, Wu Chao's surviving nephew Wu San-ssu. A much cleverer man than his cousin Wu Ch'eng-ssu, Wu San-ssu had not given up hope of becoming Emperor. But he bided his time and laid the foundations for his rise to power. He assiduously cultivated the friendship of the Chang brothers to give him easy access to the Holy and Divine Emperor.

Although he realized that there was no way to stop the Crown Prince succeeding when Wu Chao died, he had no time for Chung-tsung, considering him weak and spineless. Instead he threw in his lot with Lady Wei, who, as Chung-tsung's consort, would be power behind the throne when her husband succeeded.

Wu San-ssu was not the only one to suck up to the Chang brothers. The President of the Secretariat, Yang Tsai-ssu, was also a practised flatterer. One evening he was at a party given for the Changs by another of their brothers, Chang T'ung-hsiu. The host told Yang Tsai-ssu that he looked like a Korean. It was merely a passing remark, but Yang Tsai-ssu turned his purple robe of office inside out so that, with its the white lining showing, it looked like a Korean coat and wound a white cloth around his head to make a Korean turban. Then he performed a Korean dance.

Another guest then tried to ingratiate himself directly to Chang Ch'ang-tsung by saying, 'Sixth Young Master, your face is as beautiful as a lotus.'

The whole company fell over themselves to agree – except for Yang Tsai-ssu.

Asked why he did not think that Chang Ch'ang-tsung's face was as beautiful as a lotus, Yang Tsai-ssu trumped them all by saying, 'No, the lotus is as beautiful as the face of the Sixth Master.'

Even the imperial family kowtowed to the Chang brothers. Even though they were responsible for the deaths of Li Ch'ung-jun, Wu Yen-chi and Princess Yung T'ai, Chung-tsung, Jui-tsung and Princess Tai-ping petitioned the Holy and Divine Emperor to make Chang Ch'ang-tsung a prince. Wu Chao turned down the request, possibly to spite her children. Undeterred, they renewed their petition. Again Wu Chao refused. Instead she made Chang Ch'ang-tsung and Chang I-chih dukes, ostensibly for their work on the *San-chiao chu-ying*. This was bad enough in most people's eyes.

Even though everyone was falling over themselves to toady to the Chang brothers, they did have one very obvious enemy in government. When Wei Yüan-chung had returned from exile after the fall of Lai Chün-ch'en, he had been made district governor of metropolitan Luoyang. It was there that he encountered the corrupt Chang Ch'ang-i who was prefect. Chang Ch'ang-i regularly interfered in the yamen of the governor, although the office was senior to his own. The previous governor had put up with this, but Wei Yüan-chung would not and ordered Chang Ch'ang-i out of his residence. He had also crossed swords with Chang I-chih when one of Chang I-chih's slave girls, presuming on the authority of her master, created a melée in the marketplace. Wei Yüan-chung had her flogged so severely that she died.

Despite the opposition of the Changs, Wei Yüan-chung rose to become President of both the Secretariat and Chancellery. As the most powerful First Minister to the throne, Wei Yüan-chung continued to thwart the Changs. In year three Ch'ang-an – 703 – Wu Chao proposed appointing Chang Ch'ang-ch'i to Wei Yüan-chung's old post as district governor of metropolitan Luoyang. The more obsequious ministers agreed that Chang Ch'ang-ch'i would be an excellent choice. Only Wei Yüan-chung opposed the appointment. When Wu Chao asked him to suggest a better candidate, Wei Yüan-chung said that the man currently holding the office was the best qualified. Wu Chao replied that he had held the post for a long time and, as she wished to make a change, would Chang Ch'ang-i not do? The other ministers again applauded her choice. Again Wei Yüan-chung alone opposed them. Chang Ch'ang-i, he said, was manifestly unsuitable.

When Wu Chao called Wei Yüan-chung to explain his opposition to the appointment, he said that Chang Ch'ang-i was young, irresponsible and wholly lacking the experience necessary to hold the office. He pointed out that the only position of responsibility Chang Ch'ang-i had ever held was a provincial governorship and then people had fled the province rather than submit to his rule. Running a huge city like Luoyang was much more difficult than controlling a sparsely populated province and Chang Ch'ang-i plainly did not have the competence to discharge the duty.

As Wei Yüan-chung had held the office himself, he plainly knew what he was talking about. Wu Chao relented, but she was displeased. The Chang brothers actively began looking for an opportunity to bring down Wei Yüan-chung.

One day, after some government policy had gone wrong, Wei Yüan-chung said that he blamed himself for taking political office under Wu Chao. The last Celestial Emperor Kao-tsung had first shown him favour and he should have been faithful to his patron until death, since the throne was now surrounded by people who were unworthy. Wu Chao knew that he was referring to the Chang brothers. Criticism of her private life was off-limits and she was very annoyed. This gave the Changs the chance they had been looking for.

In the ninth month of year three Ch'ang-an – October 703 – Wu Chao fell seriously ill and it was feared she would not recover. If she died while Wei Yüan-chung was still in office, the Changs knew they were done for. So they had to move against him quickly. For Chang Ch'ang-tsung, organizing the downfall of Wei Yüan-chung presented an opportunity to kill two birds with one stone. His first entrée into palace had been as the Princess Tai-ping's lover. But Tai-ping now had a new lover named Kao-chien and Chang Ch'ang-tsung was jealous. As Chang Ch'ang-tsung was one of the few people who could see Wu Chao when she was ill, he seized the opportunity to tell her that Wei Yüan-chung had been overheard talking privately with Kao-chien.

'The Holy and Divine Empress is ageing,' Wei Yüan-chung had said. 'Now is the time to align yourself with the Crown Prince if you want to benefit in the long run.'

To Wu Chao this was clear evidence that they were plotting to take the throne. She had Wei Yüan-chung and Kao-chien arrested and put Chang Ch'ang-tsung in charge of the investigation.

Such a flimsy story was not enough to topple a man of Wei Yüan-chung's reputation. So the Changs sought to manufacture more evidence against him. They attempted to suborn a witness. Chang Ch'ang-tsung secretly approached Chang Yüeh, who was no relation, but had been a hero of the war against the Turks and was then one of the grand secretaries of the Secretariat. In return for a considerable advancement in his career, he agreed to say that he had overheard Wei Yüeh-chung privately advocate Wu Chao's abdication – in itself treason.

By this time, Wu Chao had recovered a little and called the full court to hear the case against Wei Yüan-chung and Kao-chien. Even the Crown Prince Chung-tsung and Jui-tsung, Prince of Hsiang, were present for what became the most famous trial of the T'ang period. From the beginning, the case went badly for the Changs as the whole court strove to demonstrate Wei Yüan-chung's innocence. But finally, Chang Ch'ang-tsung sprang his surprise witness and asked for Chang Yüeh to be called.

Chang Yüeh was sitting outside the Hall of Audience with the other grand secretaries when Wu Chao's summons came. As mere grand secretaries, they were not of a high enough rank to attend court itself. When Chang Yüeh stood up to go in, one of the other grand secretaries, named Sung Ching, stopped him and urged him not to bring down such a great man as Wei Yüan-chung with lies. If telling the truth got Chang Yüeh into trouble with the Changs, Sung Ching swore to defend him to the death. The other grand secretaries joined in admonishing Chang Yüeh to tell the truth and pledging their support no matter the consequences. Chang Yüeh does not seem to have responded. He remained silent as he entered the Hall of Audience. And when Wu Chao questioned him he continued to hold his tongue.

Wei Yüan-chung found this frustrating.

'Chang Yüeh,' he cried out, 'are you going to join Chang Ch'ang-tsung spinning this web of treachery around me?'

It was clear to Chang Yüeh from what had happened outside the Hall of Audience that everyone in court expected him to lie. That Wei Yüan-chung thought so too clearly nettled him.

'Wei Yüan-chung, you are First Minister,' he replied. 'How can you listen to such low gossip?'

As things were plainly not going his way, Chang Ch'ang-tsung panicked. He was standing beside Chang Yüeh and nudged him, urging him to repeat what he had been told to say. But Chang Yüeh was now in possession of himself. He turned to the Holy and Divine Emperor and said, 'Your Majesty can see with her own eyes that I am being cajoled and harassed even in Your Presence. So Your Majesty may easily imagine how much worse it is outside. But now I face the whole court, I dare not do anything else but speak the truth. I did not hear Wei Yüan-chung advocate your abdication. However, Chang Ch'ang-tsung suborned me into bearing false witness to that effect.'

The two Chang brothers responded by accusing Chang Yüeh of being part of the conspiracy. Wu Chao then asked what evidence there was for this accusation. They replied that Chang Yüeh had been heard comparing Wei Tüan-tsung to the two great sages of history, the Duke of Chou and I Yin of the Shang dynasty, both of whom had acted as regents and had stood aside when the time came.

'If that is not proof of conspiracy, I don't know what is,' said the Changs.

But Chang Yüeh was an educated man and could easily respond to this.

'Chang I-chih and his brother Chang Ch'ang-tsung are ignorant men,' he said. 'Hearing the names the Duke of Chou and I Yin, they do not even know their stories. I spoke these words on the occasion when Wei Yüan-chung had been made First Minister and was first donning the purple robes. All the other court officials had come to congratulate him, but he said, "I have done nothing to deserve this promotion, I am overcome with fear." So I said, 'Excellency, you possess abilities like those of the Duke of Chou and I Yin. Why would you fear the duties of an official of the third grade?' The Duke of Chou and I Yin had been admired from ancient times as faithful ministers. If Your Majesty's ministers are not to model themselves on the Duke of Chou and I Yin, whose example should they follow?'

Chang Yüeh then turned on his accusers.

'Who in China does not know that if you cling on to Chang Ch'ang-tsung you will rise and prosper?' he asked. 'And who does not know that those who follow Wei Yüan-chung risk seeing their families ruined? But I fear the vengeance of Wei Yüan-chung's ghost and I will not slander him.'

Wu Chao had no reasonable answer to Chang Yüeh's question, but to admit that her two favourites were ignorant liars would mean losing face. So she denounced Chang Yüeh as a scoundrel and ordered Chang Ch'ang-tsung to include Chang Yüeh in his investigation of Wei Yüan-chung. The court was then dismissed.

After a few days, Cheng Yüeh was brought before Wu Chao again and questioned. But he stuck to his story – that Wei Yüan-chung had said nothing treasonable in his hearing and that Chang Ch'ang-tsung had asked him to lie in court. The Holy and Divine Emperor was angered by his obstinacy and ordered a new enquiry. This was to be conducted by the First Ministers under the leadership of Wu I-tsung, who had prosecuted the Liu Ssu-li conspirators with such brutal efficiency.

However, this time Wu I-tsung found he had his hands tied by Wei Yüan-chung's fellow First Ministers. They insisted that Wei Yüan-chung was palpably innocent and that Chang Yüeh was speaking nothing but the truth. Su An-heng also submitted a memorandum saying that prosecuting two manifestly innocent men was bringing the regime into disrepute and spreading alarm and despondency among ordinary people. And he went further, saying that the favour Wu Chao was showing two such unworthy creatures as the Chang brothers drove honest men from court. This would weaken her administration and, if it continued, would one day result in a revolution. When that happened, what would she have to say to justify her actions?

When the Chang brothers saw the memorandum, they were furious and planned to have Su An-heng put to death. But he was protected by the General Secretary of the Secretariat, Huan Yen-fan, who had been recommended for the post by Ti Jen-chieh, and managed to escape their wrath.

The Chang brothers' plot had manifestly failed. In the face of the evidence and the protests of the court, there was no way Wu Chao could find Wei Yüan-chung guilty and have him executed. But neither could she condemn her two favourites as perjurers. So on the ninth day of the ninth month, Bing-chen, year three Ch'ang-an – 23 October 703 – Wei Yüan-chung and Chang Yüeh were exiled to provincial posts in the southern province of Ling-nan. Out of respect for all he had done during his long career, Wu Chao granted Wei Yüan-chung one last audience.

'I am old and now I am going to Ling-nan,' he said. 'I have just a one-in-ten chance of surviving. However, of one thing I am certain – one day Your Majesty will have good cause to reflect on this case.'

Wu Chao asked him what he meant.

Wei Yüan-chung turned to the Chang brothers who were standing by her side.

'These two brats will eventually be the cause of a revolution,' he said.

This alarmed the Chang brothers, who thought that they were being accused of plotting a *coup d'état*. They rushed to the steps of the throne and prostrated themselves in front of the Holy and Divine Emperor, protesting their undying loyalty. This demonstration of sycophancy was embarrassing for everyone present and Wei Yüan-chung was asked to leave.

With the banishment of Wei Yüan-chung and Chang Yüeh, the Chang brothers had appeared to triumph. However, it was an empty victory. The rest of the court had considered them amusing fools, but they had brought down Wu Chao's best and most faithful minister. Now no one was safe. A censor came to Wei Yüan-chung's defence, but Wu Chao took no notice and Sung Ching, the Grand Secretary who had urged Chang Yüeh to tell the truth, warned him that it would be better to drop the matter. Wei Yüan-chung and Chang Yüeh had escaped with their lives. Any further protest would put them in mortal danger. Besides, the Chang brothers would get their comeuppance. Despite the pestilential conditions in Ling-nan, Wei Yüan-chung might well outlive Wu Chao. If he did, he would almost certainly return to power, and then all the Changs would be swept away.

The Chang brothers knew this as well as anybody and made one last attempt to take the life of Wei Yüan-chung. It was customary for a high-ranking official sent into exile to be given a farewell party in the suburbs by his colleagues. In this case, there was sure to be a certain amount of talk about the injustice of the sentence which could be interpreted as seditious. The Chang brothers were depending on it.

Chang I-chih suborned another informer to report to the throne that Wei Yüan-chung's farewell party was, in fact, a meeting of conspirators who were plotting the overthrow of the Holy and Divine Emperor. Wu Chao knew that the trial of Wei Yüan-chung had made her very unpopular and feared that such a thing might be true. Even Wei Yüan-chung himself had warned her that a revolution was imminent, so she ordered a censor to investigate.

The censor went about his investigation methodically, but was constantly interrupted by messengers from Wu Chao telling him to hurry up.

'The evidence of conspiracy is plain enough, what is all the delay for?' he was told.

But the censor asked for the informer to be produced so that he could be questioned. Chang Ch'ang-tsung, remembering how badly wrong things had gone with the court appearance of Chang Yüeh, had seen to it that the informer was nowhere to be found. Wu Chao told the censor that the man could not be located, but could he not proceed on the basis of the man's deposition? What need was there to question him?

But the censor was an honourable man and certainly could not give in to Wu Chao's demands when the whole weight of court opinion was against him. He stuck to the rules. Without the witness, he said, there was no case. Wu Chao was beside herself.

'Do you, sir, wish to let these criminals go free?' she asked.

'I would not dare to let criminals go free,' replied the censor. 'But Wei Yüan-chung has been a First Minister. He has now been degraded and is being sent to a provincial post. His friends and relatives are innocently seeing him off, but they have falsely been accused of conspiracy. That is the truth. How would I dare to conceal it?'

The censor then pointed out that she herself had adjudged Wei Yüan-chung's offence as one not meriting death but now she wished to execute those who were seeing him off. If the Holy and Divine Emperor wished to exercise her sovereign rights of life and death, she was perfectly entitled to do so. But she had only ordered him to make a judicial investigation. He had done so and could only report the truth as he had found it.

By this time Wu Chao's temper had cooled.

'So you want me to consider them all innocent?' she asked.

'My understanding of these things is dull and shallow,' he said. 'But I cannot, in truth, find them guilty.'

Wu Chao now understood that she had overstepped the mark with the trial and exile of Wei Yüan-chung. She was not as adept politically as she had been in her middle years. Then she had maintained a balance between those competing in her court. Now, by favouring the Changs, she had turned all her other courtiers against her. A change was needed, so early in the tenth month, Ding-si, year three Ch'ang-an – November 703 – she returned to Luoyang.

CHAPTER TWELVE

THE THRONE
OF BLOOD

BACK IN LUOYANG, Wu Chao developed a new burst of energy, though she was nearly eighty and far from well. She sought to win her way back into the hearts of her people by cashiering a number of corrupt officials and cancelling the construction of an expensive Buddha that would have cost one hundred and seventy thousand strings of cash. The harvest that year was bad and she said that the compassionate Buddha would have wanted the money to be spent on her famine-stricken subjects. She tried to solve the growing problem of vagrancy and, after a protest in Ling-nan, she sent special commissioners to examine provincial administration by the six standards set by the Han dynasty. When provincial administrators were found wanting, she sent twenty capable and experienced administrators from the capital out to the provinces as prefects. This last move did not work well, since relegation to the provinces was traditionally seen as a punishment. However, it did give the appearance, at least, that the Holy and Divine Emperor was, once again, working for the good of the people.

But this did not solve the problem closer to home. Because of the Chang brothers, her own officials had turned against her and no doubt many of them were secretly plotting her downfall. The easiest way to solve the problem would have been to send the Chang brothers away. But she depended on them, so in an attempt to find favour with her officials she allowed all those who had been exiled under previous persecutions to return home. Sadly, that only succeeded in bolstering the ranks of the opposition.

Seeking relief from the pressures of the capital, she spent most of the year in the San Yang Palace in the Shansi mountains, in the country district of Ch'in, one hundred and eighty li, or sixty miles, outside

Luoyang. Her health benefited from the forested mountains and the spacious parks, and she could relax with her favourites far from the rigid protocol of the court.

However, communications were poor and it was difficult for her ministers to visit. There were few rooms for the courtiers to stay in and ministers found themselves sleeping in grass-roofed huts. In 700, before he had fallen from favour, Chang Yüeh had written a memorandum detailing the shortcomings of the place. He concluded that the park lands were better given over to agriculture, and that the lack of a perimeter fence and the surrounding trees left the palace open to the predations of thieves and assassins.

But there was one man in particular who did not want her back in the capital. Wu San-ssu wanted a free hand for his political manoeuvrings. For him, it was much better that his ageing aunt remained closeted with the unpopular Chang brothers out of town. So he set about an expensive refurbishment of the San Yang Palace, despite the hardship such expenditure would cause her hungry people. Early in 704 – year four Ch'ang-an – the palace was rebuilt on a nearby hill called Wan An Shan, or the Mountain of the Thousand Tranquillities, at a cost so great that it drew protests from the censors.

The Chang brothers were not unaware that they were now very unpopular with the palace officials and sought to reverse their opinions. They now fawned on ministers who had previously fawned on them. At their behest, Wu Chao staged a huge banquet that all ministers and officials were invited to. The seating arrangements at these events was all important. Guests had to be seated in order of precedence – courtiers sometimes even came to blows. As Wu Chao's favourites, the Chang brothers were usually seated above even the highest government minister. But when Chang I-chih saw Sung Ching, now the Vice President of the Board of Censors and a formidable opponent, he sought to ingratiate himself. So Chang I-chih moved down the table and said to Sung Ching, 'You were the first one here. How come you are sitting below me?'

Sung Ching replied, 'My talents are inferior to yours and my rank is low. How can the Lord Chang think that I should be first above him?'

The Vice President of the Board of the Civil Service who was sitting nearby overheard this and said to Sung Ching, 'Vice President, why do you address the Fifth Young Master as "Lord"?'

'According to his rank he should be addressed as "Lord",' Sung Ching replied. 'But you, sir, are not a slave of his household. So why do you call him "Young Master"?'

Both men, in their own way, had delivered a withering slight. Such talk was dangerous as long as the Changs had the ear of the Holy and Divine Emperor. On the other hand, palace officials knew Wu Chao always had a genuine fondness for those who were honest and outspoken.

Although Chang I-chih and Chang Ch'ang-tsung were still untouchable, their other brothers were not. On the twelfth day of the seventh month, Bin-yin, year four Ch'ang-an – 16 August 704 – three members of the Chang family – Chang Ch'ang-i, Chang Ch'ang-ch'i and Chang T'ung-hsiu – were charged with corruption. Wu Chao ordered that the case be investigated by two boards of censors – the Left Board and the Right Board. Operating essentially as the prosecution and defence, these would give the proceedings the air of judicial impartiality. Under the rules of investigation Chang I-chih and Chang Ch'ang-tsung should also be interrogated. Wu Chao could have stopped this. Instead, she ordered that they submit themselves to interrogation. No doubt she intended that their detractors would be silenced when they were cleared.

Initially, the prosecutors found Chang Ch'ang-tsung guilty of a minor offence – using his authority to illegally occupy the land of a private individual – and it was recommended that he be fined ten kilos of copper. This small fine would demonstrate that the Chang brothers were not above the law. However, being found guilty of a trivial offence would imply that he was not guilty of a more serious one.

But then things began to go very wrong. It was found that the other brothers, Chang Ch'ang-i, Chang Ch'ang-ch'i and Chang T'ung-hsiu, had amassed vast sums through corruption. Then, in open court, Huan Yen-fan, Su An-heng's protector and now a censor, presented convincing evidence that Chang Ch'ang-tsung, himself, had taken more than four million strings of cash in bribes, and recommend that he be dismissed from government service.

This accusation took the whole court, including Wu Chao, by surprise.

Chang Ch'ang-tsung cried out, 'I have served the state well. I do not deserve to be dismissed for this offence.'

This was a tacit admission. As the charge could not now be refuted, Wu Chao could only try and mitigate the offence and asked the court whether it was not true that Chang Ch'ang-tsung had gained merit in the service of the state. Only one person would stand up for him. This was Yang Tsai-ssu, the President of the Secretariat who had compared the beauty of a lotus to that of Chang Ch'ang-tsung's face. And even he was equivocal.

'Chang Ch'ang-tsung has provided an elixir that proved beneficial to Your Majesty's body,' he said. 'Is this not a great act of merit?'

This was tantamount to saying that Chang Ch'ang-tsung should not be punished because he was Wu Chao's lover. At the time, in China, 'elixirs' were often aphrodisiacs. Indeed the word here could even be construed to mean semen, since this contained the yang energy that sustained Wu Chao in power. Whichever was meant, Wu Chao decided that providing her body with vital elixir did gain him merit and Chang Ch'ang-tsung was, consequently, acquitted.

On the thirtieth day of the seventh month — 3 September 704 — Chang Ch'ang-i, Chang Ch'ang-ch'i and Chang T'ung-hsiun were found guilty of taking brides and were demoted and sent to provincial posts. Charges against Chang I-chih were still under investigation. But before his case came to court the prosecutor was transferred to the provinces. Before he left, he arranged a secret meeting with Chung-tsung.

'The two Chang brothers have been abusing their position,' he told the Crown Prince. 'There will be a revolution and Your Highness must be ready.'

The court proceedings had done little to dampen down the scandal surrounding the Chang brothers as Wu Chao had hoped. Indeed they had probably made things worse. So she now courted popularity by appointing the well-liked and capable Chang Chien-chih a First Minister. He had been recommended by the late Ti Jen-chieh. Now eighty years old, Chang Chien-chih had spent much of his life in the provinces in semi-disgrace. There, he had been plotting the overthrow of Wu Chao for some time. Only his closest associates knew that his plan was now well advanced. Other courtiers had been plotting, but their aim was to bring down the Chang brothers by legal means. Chang Chien-chih realized that the only way to get rid of an old woman's toyboys was to get rid of the old woman herself.

Wu Chao was oblivious to the danger. She was ill and could no longer carry the full burden of government. Chang Chien-chih was an accomplished administrator who could take much of the weight. And, as he was a T'ang loyalist of the old school, she thought his appointment might placate the court. Like Wei Yüan-chung and Ti Jen-chieh before him, Chang Chien-chih could guarantee a clean transfer of power once she died and the T'ang dynasty was restored.

The Holy and Divine Emperor Wu was now so ill that, for two months, she received no visitors from court. Her only attendants, outside her household staff, were the Chang brothers. This caused great disquiet. If Wu Chao died while in seclusion, the Chang brothers could fake decrees purporting to come from her that would rid them of their enemies and allow them to seize power. However, at the end of the eleventh month, Geng-wu, Wu Chao's condition eased and the Vice President of the Secretariat, Ts'ui Yüan-wei, a man Wu Chao herself had selected for office because of his integrity, presented a petition saying that, from then on, the Crown Prince Chung-tsung and Jui-tsung, Prince of Hsiang, should be allowed in to see her when she was ill. In such a dire situation, the petition said, it was not fitting that members of another family were administering her medicines. Wu Chao acknowledged the loyal sentiments in the petition and approved it, but it was never acted upon and, as her condition worsened again, the Chang brothers remained the sole means of communication between the court and the Emperor.

The Chang brothers may have taken some small satisfaction from their position of trust. But they must have known they could not survive her demise. If they had been adept at court politics they would have cultivated the Wu, whose princes still held important commands in the Imperial Army. It was not beyond the bounds of possibility that the Wu would stage a coup in the interregnum before Chung-tsung ascended the throne. But the Chang brothers had already alienated the Wu by recommending that Chung-tsung be named Crown Prince at the prompting of Chi Hsiu. They could at the very least have attempted to play the Wu off against the Li. But they had also alienated the T'ang loyalists by engineering the downfall of Wei Yüan-chung. And their arrogance and corruption had turned everyone against them.

As Wu Chao's life began to ebb, the Changs tried to form a faction of their own. But it was too late. No one outside their own family would dream of supporting them. And their inept manoeuvrings were counter-productive. In the streets, posters appeared accusing Chang I-chih and Chang Ch'ang-tsung of plotting a coup. Wu Chao heard of this but paid it no mind. The Changs were, after all, silly little boys whom she kept for her amusement and pleasure, not serious players on the political stage. It was impossible to imagine that they could usurp the throne, or even control who sat upon it. The accusations against them were, therefore, the work of her enemies who were seeking to discredit her.

However, these very accusations began to find substance. On the twelfth day of the twelfth month, Xin-wei, year four Ch'ang-an – 15 January 705 – Chang Ch'ang-tsung was accused of treason. It was alleged that he had visited a fortune-teller who had said that he had the appear-ance of an Emperor and that, if he built a Buddhist monastery at Ting Chou, the hearts of the people would turn towards him. The charge seemed flimsy, particularly as the fortune-teller seems merely to have been trying to raise money for the monastery at Ting Chou. But in the case of the unpopular Chang brothers it was strong enough for the censors to take seriously.

Ever devious, Wu Chao settled on a stratagem. She picked a three-man commission to investigate. One would be Sung Ching, a well-known opponent of the Changs. The other two she chose were bound to find for the accused. In a majority vote, Chang Ch'ang-tsung would be acquitted. But with Sung Ching on the commission, justice would be seen to have been done.

The facts of the case were beyond dispute. Chang Ch'ang-tsung had been to the fortune-teller and the latter had said the words alleged. Chang Ch'ang-tsung had told Wu Chao so himself. As there had been nothing clandestine about this, he was innocent according to law. However, as expected, Sung Ching took a contrary view. He argued that the Holy and Divine Emperor had lavished every favour on Chang Ch'ang-tsung, so why was he going to a fortune-teller in the first place unless he harboured some further ambition in his heart? Moreover, the fortune-teller had told

Chang Ch'ang-tsung that he had drawn up a horoscope of the Holy and Divine Emperor. This in itself was a treasonable act, since a horoscope would surely predict when Wu Chao would die. Chang Ch'ang-tsung had not reported this treason – which was treason in itself. Sung Ching argued that Chang Ch'ang-tsung and the fortune-teller were plainly co-conspirators. Even though Chang Ch'ang-tsung had reported his visit to the fortune-teller and the soothsayer's words to the Empress, he had not told her the whole truth. This was because he secretly harboured the hopes the fortune-teller's predictions had aroused. He was guilty at the very least of thinking treason – which, again, was treason in itself. Sung Ching demanded that Chang Ch'ang-tsung be executed and his family's property be forfeit according to law.

Although the other two judges found for the accused, Sung Ching's argument could not be overturned. When he delivered his dissenting verdict, Wu Chao remained silent for a long time, unable to make up her mind what to do. Sung Ching urged that the sentence be carried out immediately; otherwise, he feared, allowing Chang Ch'ang-tsung to get away with palapable treason would shake the loyalty of the people. But Wu Chao told him the execution must wait. Such a weighty matter could not be decided without more detailed evidence.

When Sung Ching withdrew, her other ministers urged her to do what Sung Ching recommended, but Wu Chao insisted on having more time to think the matter through. After a few days, though, she could come up with no counter to Sung Ching's argument, so she ordered him to go out to the provinces to investigate charges of corruption that had been brought against local officials. She plainly hoped that with Sung Ching out of the way the matter would be forgotten. The Changs, too, saw this as an opportunity to lay charges against Sung Ching and silence their enemy once and for all.

But Sung Ching simply refused to go to the provinces. It was against regulations, he said. When a prefect or district magistrate was accused, as in this case, the rules said that the matter must be investigated by the censors of the Court of General Affairs or, if the accused were of a low rank, the censors of the Court of Exterior Affairs. A man of Sung Ching's rank from the Court of Palace Affairs was only sent if some military necessity was involved or the matter directly affected the security of the Empire. As this was not the case, he dared not break the regulations by taking up the commission. Again Wu Chao could come up with no counter-argument and Sung Ching remained in the capital.

The censor recommended by Ti Jen-chieh, Huan Yen-fan, then sent a memorandum to Wu Chao saying that Chang Ch'ang-tsung had earned no merit other that that bestowed on him by Her Majesty. And, despite all the titles and wealth she had given him, he still harboured treasonous instincts. He had continued seeing the fortune-teller even after he had been charged with treason. He had only told her about his visit because he thought it would come out anyway and that, if he confessed to her, that would be an end of the matter. These were the actions of a traitor who was trying to cover his tracks. If he was to be acquitted, who would be found guilty? What's more, if he was pardoned, he would think that his ruse had succeeded. He would then be emboldened in his treachery. Thinking that he had immunity, others would join him. As he had escaped death, people would think that he had the mandate of heaven. If treacherous courtiers were not executed, the dynasty would be imperilled.

Wu Chao's own man, the Vice President of the Secretariat Ts'ui Yüan-wei, also urged her to let the law take its course, but she refused. Sung Ching tried to force her hand by demanding the arrest of Chang Ch'ang-tsung, but Wu Chao said that he had already confessed his fault and was, therefore, immune to further prosecution. But Sung Ching would not back down. It was, he said, in her own interests to arrest and execute Chang Ch'ang-tsung. The entire court were united in their opposition to him. The people knew of his treachery from the posters that had been displayed in the streets. He had confessed his crime, but that did not absolve him of it. The sheer gravity of his crime demanded action; otherwise she put her reign in peril.

'If Chang Ch'ang-tsung is not executed,' he said, 'what use are laws in this Empire?'

Sung Ching was angry and grew red in the face. Wu Chao tried to calm him, but he refused to pipe down.

'I know that Chang Ch'ang-tsung has received exceptional favours from Your Majesty,' he said. 'And I know that my words bring me to the brink of destruction. But even if I am to die, I do not regret them. They come from the heart.'

There could be no doubt about the meaning of 'exceptional favours' in this case. The court had long been awash with gossip about the sexual liaison between the Chang brothers and Wu Chao. It was a matter that she was particularly sensitive about. Several people, including three members of the imperial family, had already lost their lives over it.

Fearing for Sung Ching's life, Yang Tsai-ssu, the silver-tongued President of the Secretariat, stepped in. He said that the audience should be brought to a close and that Sung Ching should withdraw. But Sung Ching turned on him.

'The Holy and Divine Emperor is present,' he said. 'It is not for a First Minister to give orders.'

Wu Chao could see that Sung Ching would not be silenced – and she did not dare make an issue out of his conduct for fear of making the situation worse. In her younger days, she would have demanded his blood. When Ch'ü Sui-liang had opposed her being made Empress because he remained loyal to Empress Wang, Wu Chao had called for him to be executed from behind the curtain in the court of Kao-tsung. Now Sung Ching opposed her to her face in far more intemperate language and she did nothing. She was old and ill and frail. Finally, she conceded and issued the warrant for Chang Ch'ang-tsung's arrest. But this was merely a feint. Wu Chao was not to be bested. She still had another trick up her sleeve.

Once in custody Chang Ch'ang-tsung was taken to appear before the Tribunal of Censors. Sung Ching was already on his feet and began his interrogation without any formalities. But after only a few minutes a messenger arrived from the Holy and Divine Emperor bearing a special amnesty for Chang Ch'ang-tsung. The procedures were rapidly brought to a close and Chang Ch'ang-tsung left a free man. Sung Ching was furious.

'Why didn't I beat the young scoundrel's head in straight away?' he was heard to say.

Rejoicing in her triumph, Wu Chao sent Chang Ch'ang-tsung to pay a courtesy call on Sung Ching to thank him for his co-operation. Sung Ching refused to see him and barred the door.

Although Wu Chao thought she had won the day, her judgement had faltered. Up until this point the Changs' opponents had tried legal means to get rid of them. But Wu Chao had simply overridden the law with her special amnesty. Now those who opposed the Changs would have to go outside the law to ensure their downfall.

Until then, the Changs too had been playing by the rules. They had successfully used legal means to silence Wei Yüan-chung and other opponents. But now, thanks to Wu Chao's special favouritism, they found themselves above the law. So they hired an assassin to rid themselves of Sung Ching. During a wedding at Sung Ching's home, the man mingled with the other guests. But Sung Ching had been forewarned and escaped in disguise on a farm wagon.

At the end of year four Ch'ang-an – early February 705 – Wu Chao fell gravely ill once more. It was plain that she could not live much longer. All the Changs' opponents had to do was wait. When the Holy and Divine Emperor died, Chung-tsung would take the throne and deal with them then. But this was not the mood of the court. Ministers feared that the Chang brothers might make a last-minute alliance with Wu San-ssu or the other Wu princes. Or, with the dying Wu Chao in their hands, they might still be able to dispose of all those who opposed them. So now a real conspiracy was hatched – by the leading members of the government. The First Ministers began plotting a palace coup.

Chung-tsung was not consulted. He was not an able or clever man. Nor did he have much backbone. Throughout his life he had been the plaything of his mother. So he was of no earthly use to the conspirators, except as a figurehead.

Sung Ching also played no part in the plot. Though he was an outspoken opponent of the Changs he was a man of faultless integrity – not the type that makes a good conspirator. Besides, his opposition to the Changs was too open, too public. His involvement would have drawn attention to the plot.

The leader was First Minister Chang Chien-chih, who had been planning the putsch for some time. Also in on the plot were the Vice President of the Secretariat Ts'ui Yüan-wei, Vice President of the Department of State Affairs Ching Hui and Huan Yen-fan, the Vice Minister for Justice. The Chief Administrator of the Household of the Prince of Hsiang Yüan Shu-chi was also brought in to lend the authority of Jui-tsung to the conspiracy.

Chang Chien-chih had laid the ground well, appointing sympathizers to key posts. There were supporters among the generals of the now greatly expanded Yü-Li Guard which guarded the palace. One of them was a man Chang Chien-chih had met when he was exiled to the south. In a small boat crossing the Yangtze, they had discussed the restoration of the T'ang. Huan Yen-fan, Chin Hui and Li Chan – the youngest son of Li I-fu, whose petition set Wu Chao on the road to power – were all given positions in the Yü-Li Guard.

The Chang brothers were aware of these changes being made around them and grew uneasy. At last they began to get some political nous of their own and countered Chang Chien-chih's moves by securing the appointment of Wu San-ssu's nephew Wu Yu-i to the Yü-Li Guard. But this was too little, too late. In fact, seeing the Changs courting the Wu only hardened the determination of the T'ang loyalists.

The general in overall command of the guard was Li To-tso, who had served with distinction in wars against the Tibetans and the Turks. A career soldier, Li To-tso had played no part in the political manoeuvrings against the Chang brothers and his opinion of them was not known. Yet he was key to the success of the coup. Chang Chien-chih approached him.

'General, to whom do you owe your rank and wealth?' asked Chang Chien-chih.

'To the late Celestial Emperor,' replied Li To-tso, meaning Kao-tsung.

'You realized that the late Celestial Emperor's two sons are now in mortal danger from young scoundrels?' said Chang Chien-chih. 'Have you thought of repaying his beneficence?'

'If what you propose is for the good of the state, I am yours to command,' said Li To-tso. 'I will not think of myself, my wife or my family.'

Together Chang Chien-chih and Li To-tso swore an oath to heaven and earth and began the detailed planning of the insurrection.

Short of good ministers, Wu Chao recalled the outspoken Yao Yüan-ch'ung, who had once been recommended by Ti Jen-chieh, from his provincial posting. But when he returned to the capital, he was invited to join the conspiracy. Then Huan Yen-fan began to have cold feet, fearing for his family if anything should go wrong. He told his mother about the plot and asked for her approval.

'Go ahead, my son,' she said. 'Loyalty does not have two paths. The state must come first, the family second.'

Now that everything was prepared, Huan Yen-fan and Ching Hui went to Chung-tsung to ask for his endorsement. They entered the Eastern Palace, where he lived, via the northern gate, out of sight of the city. The Crown Prince listened to what they had to say and gave his assent.

Towards nightfall on 24 February 705 – the twenty-second day of the first month, Ren-shen, year one Shen Lung – Huan Yen-fan, Chang Chien-chih and Ts'ui Yüan-wei took five hundred men of the Left and Right Bodyguard and rode to the Hsüan Wu Gate – later known as the Yüan Wu Gate – the vulnerable north gate of the palace. There they waited. Li Chan and Li To-tso were sent to the Eastern Palace to get Chung-tsung, but the Crown Prince's nerve failed him at the last minute and he refused to come with them.

'The late Celestial Emperor bequeathed his throne to Your Highness,' said one of Li To-tso's officers, Chung-tsung's own son-in-law Wang Tung-chiao, husband of Princess Ding An. 'But you have suffered deposition, exile and imprisonment for twenty years. Now heaven has taken pity on your suffering. The north and south garrisons of the palace bodyguard are both on your side. They are ready to slay the evil rogues who oppress you and to restore the Li family to the throne. We want Your Highness to accompany us to the Hsüan Wu Gate to fulfil the hopes of all your people.'

But Chung-tsung vacillated.

'The evil rogues must certainly be destroyed,' he said. 'But the Holy and Divine Emperor is not well. We should not disturb her. I think it would be best to postpone the endeavour.'

But the coup could not be delayed. Five hundred soldiers were waiting at the Hsüan Wu Gate. The conspirators had gone too far to back out now. If they faltered, the Changs would seize the initiative. With Wu Chao and the Wu clan on their side, all those involved in the conspiracy would die. But without the Crown Prince, there could be no coup.

Li Chan then had a bright idea. He turned to Chung-tsung and said, 'With no thought for their families or themselves, the ministers and generals have taken this action to protect the state. They are willing to step into a cauldron of boiling water for your sake. So if Your Highness wants to postpone this endeavour, I ask that Your Highness should ride to the Hsüan Wu Gate himself and tell them to stop.'

Hoodwinked by this deception, Chung-tsung left the Eastern Palace. Wang Tung-chiao helped him mount his horse and, with his escort, Chung-tsung rode to the Hsüan Wu Gate. At the gate, the sight of him was enough. His appearance was the signal for the coup to go ahead. Without the Crown Prince's presence, the guard would not act. Before Chung-tsung had a chance to tell them to stop, the guard broke down the gate and the whole force stormed into the palace. The die had been cast. It was too late for Chung-tsung – or anyone else – to stop the coup going ahead.

Wu Chao and the Changs occupied apartments on the west side of the Palace City in a building known as the Ying Hsien Palace – the 'Palace that Welcomes Immortals'. The conspirators went straight there. The Chang brothers were found in the palace courtyard and, on Chang Chien-chih's orders, they were beheaded on the palace verandah. Wu Chao's eunuchs were seized and tied up. Then the Holy and Divine Emperor herself was woken.

When she came out of her apartment and saw the conspirators, Wu Chao asked simply, 'Who started the revolt?'

She must have realized that her long reign was over.

'Chang I-chih and Chang Ch'ang-tsung were plotting a rebellion,' she was told. 'We, Your ministers, received orders from the Crown Prince to execute them. We could not inform Your Majesty in advance, for the two Changs would have heard of it. However, for the crime of bringing armed men into the palace, we deserve to die a thousand deaths.'

Wu Chao made one last attempt to save the situation. Seeing Chung-tsung in the shadows, she ordered him to return to the Eastern Palace.

'How can the Crown Prince go back to the Eastern Palace?' asked Huan Yen-fan. 'The late Celestial Emperor entrusted his beloved son to Your Majesty. He is no longer young and has lived too long in the Eastern Palace. The will of heaven and the hearts of men have turned towards the Li family. Your officials have not forgotten the virtue of T'ai-tsung and the late Celestial Emperor. So now that the Crown Prince has ordered the execution of the two rogues, we ministers wish Your Majesty to abdicate and hand the throne to the Crown Prince in compliance with the will of heaven and all mankind.'

Finding no answer to this, Wu Chao looked at the faces of those who confronted her. Seeing Li Chan, son of Li I-fu, she said, 'So you too are one of the brave generals who killed Chang I-chih. I was generous to both you and your father; now I live to see this day.'

Li I-fu had no words for her and flushed.

Then she saw Ts'ui Yüan-wei and said, 'These other ministers have all been promoted because of the recommendations of other men, but you were my own choice. Why are you here?'

But Ts'ui Yüan-wei was more skilled in the ways of the court that Li Chan.

'I am here to repay Your Highness's great beneficence,' he said.

Wu Chao then turned and went back into her apartment, where she lay on the bed and said no more about the coup that had swept her from power after fifty years. The Chang brothers were dismembered and their heads were displayed on the Bridge of the Ford of Heaven. When it was discovered that their bodies were as white as pork fat, their flesh was cooked and eaten – in retribution, it was said, for the way they had cooked live animals. However, Wu Chao's secretary Shang-kuan Wan-erh managed to retrieve Chang Ch'ang-tsung's penis and brought it to her.

'This is Loh Long,' sighed Wu Chao.

'Loh Long' was her version of *liu-lang* – 'Sixth Young Master' – and her pet name for Chang Ch'ang-tsung. She put the severed penis in a jade box and left instructions that it was to be buried with her.

Jui-tsung joined the revolt. He and his major-domo Yüan Shu-chi scoured the streets of the capital for any Chang supporters, but found none. The remaining Chang brothers were rounded up and beheaded. There was no opposition in the country to the coup. With the T'angs firmly in power in Luoyang, the Wu stayed their hand and no move was made against them. With Kao-tsung's son now on the throne it would be difficult to convince anyone of the validity of Wu San-ssu's claim and no one saw the point of riding to the rescue of Wu Chao, who was an old woman with no more than a few months left to live.

Chung-tsung took over as regent on 21 February – the nineteenth day of the first month, Ren-shen, year one Shen Lung – and Wu Chao formally abdicated the following day. The day after that, Chung-tsung returned to the throne as Emperor once more. His mother was declared *Tse-tien ta-sheng huang-ti* – 'Follower of Heaven, Great Sage, Emperor'. A general amnesty was declared, except for members of the Chang party. This allowed Wei Yüan-chung to return to court. Jui-tsung was given further honours in acknowledgement of his part in the coup. Princess Tai-ping was also honoured. Although she had always been close to Wu Chao, she had fallen out with the Chang brothers over her lover Kao-chien and had, at the last minute, joined the opposition. Ranks and titles were returned to all living members of the Li family and those who were dead were honoured posthumously. Even Li Hsien, who had died in 684, year one Wen Ming, benefited. He was re-interred in a magnificent tomb decorated with scenes of his favourite pastime, hunting. Also discovered in his tomb was a statue of a horseman carrying an angry cheetah. This confirms what was known from literary sources – that the Chinese hunted with cheetahs. With Chung-tsung, the name of the dynasty was changed back to T'ang. The robes, titles and insignia also reverted and it seemed like the long nightmare was over.

On 24 February, the twenty-second of Ren-shen, Wu Chao was taken under escort from the Palace City to the Shang Yang Palace in the Imperial Park outside the west wall of Luoyang. She was allowed to take with her the tented throne Chang Ch'ang-tsung had given her. Li Chan was to be her guard there. Although she was under house arrest, she was to be treated with dignity, respect and due ceremony as befitted an Emperor. The new Emperor Chung-tsung himself visited her there at the head of the entire court to enquire after her health. These visits, initially, took place every ten days. Later they occurred on the first day and the fifteenth day of each calendar month.

The name Shen-tu – 'Sanctified Capital' – was dropped and Luoyang was redesignated the Eastern Capital. The chief conspirators were rewarded with high office and were ennobled. Even Yan Tsai-ssu, who was despised by most T'ang loyals for his sycophancy towards the Chang brothers, was made viceroy of the Western Capital, Ch'ang-an. Only Yao Yüan-ch'ung was refused preferment. He had been seen crying when Wu Chao was being removed from the palace, and Huan Yen-fan and Chang Chien-chih had remonstrated with him.

'Why are you weeping?' they asked. 'We fear you are bringing shame on yourself.'

'I served the Empress for many years,' Yao Yüan-ch'ung replied, 'and I cannot help feeling sorrow at being parted from her. I followed you gentlemen the other day to slay traitors, which was an act of merit in a subject. Today bidding farewell to a former sovereign is also an act of merit in a subject. If I am to be convicted because of this, I will kiss the rod willingly.'

Even at the time, Wu Chao's short-lived Chou dynasty was not seen as a sharp break from the T'ang. Indeed, in the proclamation restoring the T'ang dynasty in 705, Chung-tsung said,

> The Emperor Tse-tien ta-sheng was brilliant, virtuous and wise. She responded to the needs of the times. She employed the splendid policies of the first beings. Her excellent plan of 16 October 690 [taking the throne] began the great design of the Supreme Unity. Moving the jade seal, she destroyed the greedy and, conferring the golden halberd, she killed the immoderate. She received the stone of the Lo river on which it was written that she must follow the calendar of Fu Hsi. She cared tenderly for those of virtue among the people and together they obtained humanity and long life. Finally she embraced the search for the Tao and fixed her thoughts on the *wu-wei* [art of inaction], enduring a life of toil for the sake of the imperial throne. Then she 'restored it respectfully to an intelligent prince' ... She made ancestral offerings at the temple of Kao-tsu and respected the altars of T'ai-tsung.

The phrase 'restore the throne to the intelligent prince' – *fu-t'ien yü ming-p'i* – was used of dowager Empresses in the Han dynasty who, eventually, stepped down as regent and handed the throne to their sons who had come of age. Chung-tsung went on to say that nothing had really changed under Wu Chao. She had continued the basic policies of the T'ang. She was acting for the Li family when she built schools and temples, encouraged education, commissioned many literary and historical works, appointed officials on the basis of ability alone and restored to grace many victims of evil officials who had temporarily deceived her. This remained the official line until the twentieth century, when Wu Chao came to be seen as a champion of the masses in their struggle against the landlords and aristocrats. Under the Communists, she became a working-class hero.

Although Chung-tsung probably did not write the proclamation himself, by issuing it he recognized that a woman had been an Emperor, in contradiction of the tenets of Confucius, and he legitimized her rule. This made a rod for his own back, since it allowed other ambitious women to seek to usurp him.

One of Chung-tsung's first acts as Emperor was to have the bodies of his son and daughter Li Ch'ung-jun and Princess Yung T'ai re-interred in a magnificent tomb more fitting to their rank as the offspring of an Emperor. The tomb of Princess Yung T'ai was excavated in 1964, but the inscription on her coffin said that she died in childbirth. This differs substantially from the story told in the official history. It seems that the epitaph on the coffin was falsified to conceal her disgrace. The alternative is that the written accounts – that she was forced to commit suicide or was beaten to death on the orders of Wu Chao – were invented to vilify the Empress. However, the official version is very much in keeping with what we know about Wu Chao. Another interesting thing found in Princess Yung T'ai's tomb was a fresco depicting her attendant ladies in the fashion of the period. Their dresses have a plunging décolletage that would have been considered shocking in the times before and after the reign of Wu Chao.

Wu Chao was now an onlooker in a country she had once ruled and soon her worst fears for the succession were realized. It soon became plain that Chung-tsung was no more fit to rule at fifty than he had been at twenty-eight. During his exile in Fang-chou, Chung-tsung had lived in constant fear of death. Any messenger who arrived could be bringing orders for his execution or suicide. One day, when he heard that a messenger was on his way, the terror got too much for him and he decided to kill himself. He was stopped by his wife Lady Wei's comforting words: 'Good and bad fortune do not last for ever. One can only have one death; why go out to meet it?'

From then on Chung-tsung relied on Lady Wei's courage and promised that, if he ever saw the sunrise again he would put no restriction on her. So when he returned to the throne, she had her say in government.

On the fourteenth day of the second month of year one Shen Lung, Lady Wei became Empress once more. This must have amused Wu Chao. Chung-tsung was weak-willed and indecisive like his father Kao-tsung, while Wei was now to play Wu Chao's old role.

The five ministers who had organized the putsch objected to a woman having a hand in government, particularly as Empress Wei favoured men who had been the supporters of the Changs. Aides also urged the five ministers to move against the Wu, but Chang Chien-chih and Ching Hui refused. This was unnecessary, they said, since the enthronement of Chung-tsung had settled the succession once and for all. But they were wrong.

Secretly Wu San-ssu had cultivated contacts within the palace. The most important of these was Shang-kuan Wan-erh, the granddaughter of the statesman Shang-kuan I, who had risen to become Wu Chao's secretary and confidante. She was so influential in court that she re-introduced a fashion from the second century. Around 700, year one Chiu Shih, following her lead, women began using red, yellow and black pigments to paint beauty spots in the shapes of flower, leaves, birds, coins, and crescent moons on their faces. These were sometimes used to hide blemishes and sometimes as pure decoration. In Shang-kuan Wan-erh's case this was of vital importance. Her relationship with Wu Chao was sometimes stormy. According to Shang-kuan Wan-erh's biography, she once offended Wu Chao seriously. But, as her talents were so useful to the administration, instead of having her killed, Wu Chao merely had Shang-kuan Wan-erh's face branded. On another occasion, according to legend, Wu Chao once caught Shang-kuan Wan-erh flirting with Chung-tsung, or even rising from the same bed as him, and threw a dagger at her which left a scar on her forehead. Hence the face decoration.

Despite this display of jealousy, the two women remained close. This was remarkable, since Wu Chao was responsible for the death of Shang-kuan's grandfather, the great court poet and Vice President of the Secretariat Shang-kuan I, and the downfall of her family. It has been suggested that Wu Chao befriended Shang-kuan Wan-erh because she felt guilty about the death of Shang-kuan I, though this would have been uncharacteristic. Perhaps it was a case of 'keep your friends close, but your enemies even closer'. The Chinese call this keeping a 'dagger at your side'.

As it was, the two women had a lot in common. Like Wu Chao, Shang-kuan I was just fourteen when she entered court and she had been an insider during numerous palace intrigues. Although Shang-kuan Wan-erh had no official titles, she drafted important edicts, was allowed to express her opinion during discussions of state affairs and may even have helped bring up Wu Chao's children. It has even been suggested that Wu Chao had urged Chung-tsung to take Shang-kuan Wan-erh as a concubine so that she would have an official position in court after Wu Chao's death and could continue her valuable role as political advisor from his bedchamber.

When Chung-tsung came to the throne, Shang-kuan Wan-erh became an indispensable aide to the inexperienced Emperor and the devious Empress Wei and was promoted to the rank of Concubine Third Class. Later, she performed her tasks so well she was promoted to Concubine Second Class with the title Accomplished One. This was not an inapt title, since Shang-kuan Wan-erh was certainly accomplished. She was a concubine like no other. When she had come to Chung-tsung's harem she was no virgin as Wu Chao had been. According to *The Secret Chronicles of the Kung Ho Chien*, her lover the Minister of the Army Tsui Shih extolled her cinnabar grotto for its 'pure, clustered flower pistil'. He told Shang-kuan Wan-erh that the qualities of the female genitals vary as much as the male organ. As his penis entered her, he said, 'I felt the tip of my jade stalk pressing against your tender parts, as if being drenched in molten lard, and I felt even my hair melting. Sometimes I put my fingers on your rear opening and felt it contracting and leaping, telling me that you would soon rejoice. Then I paused until your rosebud stopped leaping, so that I might renew and redouble your pleasure.' He then contrasted their own erotic connoisseurship with the clumsiness of sexually illiterate men and women who, 'like beggars, having consumed three buckets of lard, pride themselves on achieving the height of sensuality'.

But this was a bonus; Shang-kuan Wan-erh was required for her contacts rather than her body. Under Wu Chao she had been the centre of a web of sexual intrigue. Her lover Tsui Shih – one of many – had also been Wu Chao's bedmate. Tsui Shih later had an affair with Wu Chao's daughter Princess Tai-ping. Another lover, a duke, grew jealous and threatened to tell the powerful Shang-kuan Wan-erh, unless Tsui Shih let him spend the night with him and his beautiful wife. To continue his affair with Princess Tai-ping, Tsui Shih let the duke have his wife, who spread the word. Other noblemen then threatened to expose Tsui Shih and he had to buy them off with both his wife and his two stepdaughters. But then Tsui Shih also offered his wife to Chung-tsung's nephew Li Lung-chi, the future Emperor Hsüan-tsung.

Finding herself in Chung-tsung's bedchamber as a favoured concubine, Shang-kuan Wan-erh may well have cherished the thought that she could follow the road to power that Wu Chao had trod fifty years before. However, Wu Chao had only become lascivious in her later years. With Kao-tsung she had been chaste and faithful, never risking letting power slip from her hands by indulging her passions. Shang-kuan Wan-erh was altogether more hot-blooded. She began a clandestine affair with Wu San-ssu. Together with Princess Tai-ping's second husband Wu Yu-chi, Prince of Ting, they devised a plan to take the throne for the Wu. To cover their intentions, both Wu San-ssu and Wu Yu-chi resigned their government posts and retired into private life. Shang-kuan Wan-erh then used her influence with the Empress Wei to persuade Chung-tsung to marry his favourite daughter, the twenty-one-year-old Princess An Lo, to Wu San-ssu's son Wu Cheng-hsün.

Princess An Lo was no ordinary imperial princess. She had been born on the road to exile in 684, year one Wen Ming, and Chung-tsung had torn up his own robe to wrap the newborn infant. This gave her the nickname *Guo-er* – 'the Wrapper'. She was Chung-tsung's youngest daughter and the most beautiful. He lavished all his affection on her and, as she had been deprived of all the trappings and status of royalty as a child, he indulged her ceaselessly when he came to power. Not only was she the Emperor's favourite daughter she was also the daughter of the ambitious Empress Wei, who had no son, since Li Ch'ung-jun had been forced to commit suicide after his careless remarks about the Chang brothers. Chung-tsung's other three sons were by concubines of low rank. The eldest was Li Ch'ung-fu, but the Empress Wei insisted that he remain in exile for his part in the plot to bring down Li Ch'ung-jun. So Chung-tsung's third son Li Ch'ung-chün became Crown Prince. His fourth son Li Ch'ung-mao was just fifteen. But the Empress Wei did not want any successor who was not of her own blood. As Wu Chao had ruled during the reign of Kao-tsung and Wei was ruling during the reign of Chung-tsung, she wanted An Lo to rule after her. Consequently the Empress Wei was a natural ally of Wu San-ssu's as he sought to put his son on the throne. If Wu Ch'eng-hsün became Emperor his wife An Lo would be Empress beside him. To secure the alliance Wu San-ssu became the lover of the Empress Wei. This was easily arranged by his mistress Shang-kuan Wan-erh.

This powerful coalition of Wu San-ssu, the Empress Wei, Wu Ch'eng-hsün, Wu Yu-chi, Shang-kuan Wan-erh and Princess An Lo went to work on a scheme to put Wu Ch'eng-hsün on the throne, effectively restoring Wu Chao's Chou dynasty. First they had to get rid of the five ministers. This was easily done. The Empress Wei persuaded Chung-tsung to give the five ministers the imperial title of prince and bestow great wealth on them, but at the same time to strip them of all positions of power. This was accomplished on the sixteenth day of the fifth month of the first year of Shen Lung – 11 June 705 – just three months after Wu Chao had been deposed. Once they were powerless, they could be disposed of permanently. By the end of the year, Chang Chien-chih, Huan Yen-fan, Ching Hui, Ts'ui Yüan-wei and Yüan Shu-chi had all been arrested and executed – no doubt to the great satisfaction of Wu Chao.

All those involved in the putsch of 20 February were stripped of office and Wu loyalists were installed instead. The Emperor Chung-tsung did nothing to oppose this, even though, as a Li, his life was plainly endangered by the ascendancy of the Wu. And behind it all was the Machiavellian figure of Wu San-ssu, who summed up the spirit of the times when he said, 'I do not know what people mean when they talk of good and bad men. For me, men are good when they do me good, and they are bad when they do me bad turns.'

On 16 December 705 – the twenty-second day of the eleventh month, Ren-wu, year one Shen Lung, Wu Chao died in the Shang Yang Palace. In her will, she forsook the title of Holy and Divine Emperor, which she had usurped, and contented herself with the status of Dowager Empress. She also forgave her victims – the Empress Wang and the Pure Concubine Hsiao; Ch'ü Sui-liang, who had sought to block her way to the throne; the stalwart of Empress Wang, Han Yüan; the Empress

Wang's uncle Liu Shih and the various members of her own family she had killed. But there was no posthumous pardon for Kao-tsung's uncle Chang-sun Wu-chi.

In the imperial palace her legacy could clearly be seen. Women were in charge once more and, again, the Wu were ousting the weak-willed Li. The Empress Wei insisted that Chung-tsung establish offices and staffs for his sisters and daughters, a privilege previously reserved for the sons of Emperors. The ascent of women was reflected in fashion. They began to wear male clothing and boots. The fashions of the barbarian Uighur, particularly their hairstyles, were adopted. Women went out with their faces uncovered and some did not don hats, even when riding. But there was no single figure with the dominating personality and political skill of a Wu Chao to mould events.

Sixty-seven years before, when Wu Chao had first entered the imperial palace as Junior Concubine Fifth Grade, the T'ang dynasty was still in its first generation. Since the fall of the Han dynasty four hundred years earlier, few dynasties had lasted more that two or three generations. Usually, the weak son of the founder of the dynasty lost power in a damaging civil war. In her fifty years in power Wu Chao had taken the T'ang dynasty through that critical phase. There can be little doubt that, without her, lacklustre Kao-tsung would have lost power to an ambitious general or minister. At the end of her reign China was united and prosperous and the T'ang dynasty would go on to rule for another two hundred years.

Wu Chao herself has kept a grip on the imagination of the Chinese. There have been numerous novels and plays about her. In some fantasies about her, she occupies the place of the legendary Hsi-wang Mu, 'the Queen Mother of the West'.

After death, the medieval Chinese believed, the spirit separates into *po* and *hun* – the yin and yang components. These could continue to have sex on earth until their energy was exhausted. They could also take a bloody revenge on those who had wronged them. As if Wu Chao had not spilt enough blood in her lifetime, her spirit now haunted succeeding generations, bathing them in blood, for the Chinese saw the spirits of the dead everywhere.

CHAPTER THIRTEEN

THE CHILDREN OF HEAVEN

As THE LOVER OF THE TWO WOMEN who ran China and father of a likely heir, Wu San-ssu was the most powerful man in the country, easily overtaking the Emperor Chung-tsung whom he was doubly cuckolding. His only rival was the twenty-two-year-old Princess An Lo, who now petitioned to have herself named Crown Princess. No one had ever heard of such a title before, since it was an impossibility under the tenets of Confucianism. But Wu Chao had single-handedly changed the political and philosophical landscape. After Wu Chao there seemed nothing that a woman could not do.

Having seen Wu Chao reign for most of her lifetime, Princess An Lo thought it only natural that she too should rule and lobbied tirelessly to have her brother the Crown Prince Li Ch'ung-chün stripped of his title. No doubt Li Ch'ung-chün would have been eager to rid himself of the post, given the life expectancy of its holder. However, Wei Yüan-chung, now the most respected elder statesman in the court, opposed the move, on the good Confucian grounds that women could not rule.

'Wei Yüan-chung is an old wooden block from Shangtung,' said Princess An Lo. 'He is unfit to discuss the affairs of state.'

When Chung-tsung was writing a decree, Princess An Lo replaced it with her own draft. It is said that she 'pulled his front' until he agreed to sign. Though no one is sure what 'pulled his front' means, it seem to have made him laugh. It was clear to everyone in court that Li Ch'ung-chün was not going to hold on to his title much longer.

Being a soldier rather than a government minister, Li To-tso had escaped the fate of the conspirators who had brought down Wu Chao. He saw that, less than a year after its restoration, the T'ang dynasty was imperilled again. He persuaded the Crown Prince to join with him in a conspiracy to wipe out the Wu and Wei clans and free the Emperor from their grasp. Then, perhaps, Chung-tsung could be persuaded to abdicate in favour of his son who, by then, would have proved himself capable of running the country. The precedent had been set by T'ai-tsung, who had deposed his father Kao-tsu, and T'ai-tsung's own sons had tried it, unsuccessfully.

They struck quickly. The Crown Prince led troops into the Wu mansion in the middle of the night and killed everyone they found, including Wu San-ssu and his son Wu Ch'eng-hsün. Li Ch'ung-chün and Li To-tso then rode on the imperial palace to deal with Princess An Lo, the Empress Wei and Shang-kuan Wan-erh, who, as centre of the conspiracy, he hated most of all. They arrived at the Hsüan Wu Gate with about a hundred men and tried to force entry. But, forewarned, loyal ministers had rallied the palace bodyguard and barred their way. Hearing that the Crown Prince was calling for her head, Shang-kuan Wan-erh said to Chung-tsung and the Empress Wei, 'Now he asks for me, but when I am killed he will ask for the Empress. Your Majesty will be next.'

Then the Empress Wei, along with An Lo and Shang-kuan Wan-erh, dragged Chung-tsung to the Hsüan Wu Gate. From the tower above it, the Emperor leant over the balcony rail and called down to the soldiers below, 'You who should be my claws and teeth, why are you rebelling?'

The rebel soldiers were taken aback by this. They had been told that they were moving against the Wu and the Wei, in support of the Emperor. Now it appeared that they were rebelling against the Emperor himself. Chung-tsung gave them a chance to redeem themselves.

'Return to your allegiance,' he said. 'Cut off the heads of Li To-tso and those with him and I will reward you with honours and wealth.'

The soldiers immediately turned on their leaders and beheaded Li To-tso and his associates. Only Li Ch'ung-chün escaped. He fled and headed for the Turkish border. But now that he had lost his position, he was friendless. The following night, he was hiding in a forest when his attendants turned on him and killed him. To cash in on the Emperor's offer, they returned to the capital with his head. Princess An Lo took charge of it as a souvenir and displayed it as a sacrifice before the coffins of her husband, Wu Yu-chi and Wu San-ssu.

Princess An Lo was not the sort of woman who would let a little thing like the death of her husband stand in her way. She simply found herself another Wu, the dead Wu Ch'eng-hsün's cousin. As the dynastic history puts it, 'After the death of Wu Ch'eng-hsün, the Princess sought out Wu Yen-hsiu and promptly incestuously married him.' This was done with unprecedented splendour as if the heir to the throne were being wed. Even though marrying the cousin of a dead husband was technically incestuous, no one sought to object.

In fact, Wu Yen-hsiu was a better catch, since he was the son of Wu Ch'eng-ssu, the older cousin of Wu San-ssu who had himself once been a serious contender for the throne. Unfortunately he had been the prisoner of the Khan, since he had been sent to marry Mo-ch'o's daughter, and he had only been returned after the death of Wu Chao. In fact, Prince An Lo and Wu Yen-hsiu may have been lovers before Wu Ch'en-hsün's death. One authority explicitly states this. During his captivity Wu Yen-hsiu had learned Turkish songs and the 'whirling dances of the Turks'. These accomplishments entranced Princess An Lo and she was fascinated by his wild appearance and his barbaric behaviour. Certainly Wu Yen-hsiu was the more glamorous of the two cousins and Princess An Lo was not in a milieu where the bonds of marriage were rigidly observed. Nor was she the sort of woman who would have been bound by them.

As well as upgrading her husband, Princess An Lo had benefitted in another way from the coup. It had rid her of the Crown Prince. And no one immediately thought of conveying that albatross of a title to his younger brother Li Ch'ung-mao. Meanwhile the Empress Wei got Chung-tsung to grant women the right to bequeath hereditary privileges to their sons, which was previously only a male prerogative.

Princess An Lo set about enriching herself by selling ordination certificates and official posts. It was said that for three thousand cash, anyone of social rank could be ordained into the Buddhist clergy and, for ten times that amount, could get a position on the staff of one of the princesses. It was discovered in 712, year two Ching Yun – 'View of a Cloud' – that over twelve thousand monks and priests had been fraudulently ordained this way. The demand for these positions was great because they excused the holder from corvée labour and taxes, providing landlords and wealthy merchants a chance for advancement. However,

Princess An Lo and her sisters made themselves unpopular by seizing land around the capital to build luxurious mansions and selling the children of the poor into slavery. And gold, jade and priceless pieces of calligraphy were stolen from the imperial treasury. Princess An Lo became so rich that she had the imperial workshops make two skirts for her, each containing the feathers of a hundred birds. The skirts were iridescent and looked one colour from the front, another from the side; one colour in the sun, another in the shade. The feathers were woven into patterns that depicted the birds themselves. These feather skirts became so popular that much of the colourful wildfowl of the Yangtze river valley became extinct.

Commoners' land to the west of Ch'ang-an was expropriated by Princess An Lo to build a pleasure park. A lake fifty li, or sixteen miles, in circumference was dug and a river was diverted into the shape of the Milky Way, disrupting agriculture for miles about. Labourers piled rocks to create a mountain that resembled Mount Hua, a sacred peak to the east of the capital. The pavilions and covered walkways there were with inlaid with jade, pearl, silver, and gold.

But An Lo was not the only one to behave so badly. All her sisters lived life to the full. Princess Chang Ning competed with An Lo in building fancy houses and gardens. When Princess I Cheng discovered that her husband had a mistress, she cut off the woman's nose and ears and shaved her husband's head. When Chung-tsung heard about this, he banished the husband and degraded Princess I Cheng, though she was returned to royal status when her brother took the throne.

Shang-kuan Wan-erh also joined this corrupt coterie. She became the first woman to preside over the selection of examination candidates, which brought her substantial amounts in bribes. The civil service was expanding at an extraordinary rate. Official sources say that 'tens of thousands' of new men were taken on. One minister was ostracized after he sacked fourteen hundred men who had been given superfluous posts. Shang-kuan Wan-erh also sponsored literary soirées where silk and gold were awarded as prizes. Money was lavished on new Buddhist temples while, one minister complained, the granaries were empty.

The Empress Wei seemed to shed few tears over the death of her lover Wu San-ssu. The abortive coup had strengthened her position at court. She sold the higher government posts as they fell vacant and regularly consoled herself with other lovers. Although several ministers found the courage to tell Chung-tsung of her infidelity, he did nothing about it. After all, with the hundreds of concubines he had to get through each month, he had his hands full. Besides he was self-obsessed and inordinately fond of his own appearance. He a had huge burnished-bronze mirror made with a frame that looked like a Chinese cinnamon tree with silver leaves and gold blossom. It was ten foot square so, when he mounted his horse, he could see the reflection of both the horse and its rider.

Eventually, though, at Princess Tai-ping's prompting, Chung-tsung did begin to express disquiet about his wife's behaviour. So the Empress Wei and the Princess An Lo poisoned him with a lethal dose in his favourite cakes on the twenty-eighth day of the fifth month, Bing-zi, year four Ching Lung, 'View of a Dragon' – 3 July 710. The Emperor's death was concealed for two days while the Empress Wei appointed her own relatives to key military posts. Then on the fourth day of the sixth month, Ding-chou – 8 July – fifteen-year-old Li Ch'ung-mao was put on the throne. It seems that the two women did not dare to put Princess An Lo on the throne while a son of Chung-tsung's remained alive, though it is clear that they intended to dispose of him in due course.

Although everything seemed to be going Princess An Lo and the Empress Wei's way, there was one other skilled player of the dangerous political game on the field. This was Wu Chao's daughter, the redoubtable Princess Tai-ping. She was forty-six years old and had sharpened her political skills in her mother's palace intrigues. Wu Chao had entrusted her with important tasks, such as the disposal of her former favourite, the lascivious monk Hsüeh Huai-i. She was also well connected, numbering numerous ministers, courtiers and noblemen among her lovers. And she found a powerful ally in Li Lung-chi, the third son of her brother Jui-tsung. He had been born the son of a concubine in 685 – like Wu Chao in the year of the cock – and was now twenty-five. Made the Prince of Ch'u in 687, he became the Prince of Lin-tz'u in 693 after Wu Chao had usurped the throne in her own name in 690. He had spent much of his childhood imprisoned in the palace with his father, but under Chung-tsung had been given some minor posts, rising to become Vice President of the Court of Imperial Insignia – a ceremonial job without prospects. Recently he had been dismissed, so he could spend his full time plotting in the capital.

On the twentieth day of Ding-chou – 24 July – the conspirators struck. That night, Li Lung-chi with a handful of men went to the barracks of the palace guards, won them over and beheaded their Wei commanders. Then they stormed the Hsüan Wu Gate and took the palace. It seems unlikely that a man like Li Lung-chi – who was relatively powerless, held no official position or military post and was well down the pecking order of the imperial family – could have organized such a coup unaided. However, Princess Tai-ping was a wealthy woman who was in a good position to distribute bribes. She had influence in the palace and was more than capable of corrupting the palace guards, so it seems clear that the plot was her doing. She had even encouraged her son Hsüeh Tsung-chien to join the conspiracy. No doubt, following the example of Wu Chao, Wei and An Lo, Princess Tai-ping saw no reason why women should not rule. But there was one thing that not even the most adept woman could aspire to at that time – and that was to command troops. Li Lung-chi was needed for that, but he was of no consequence and could easily be pushed aside afterwards.

The Empress Wei fled, but ran into some of the rebel palace guard and was executed. Her severed head was presented to Li Lung-chi. Princess An Lo was caught applying her make-up. At the time the fashion was for ladies to pluck their eyebrows and paint more exaggerated ones on. Princess An Lo was in the middle of this delicate process when the palace guard arrived and she was beheaded in front of her mirror. Her skirts made of the feathers of a hundred birds were burned by Li Lung-chi in front of the palace and her pleasure park was seized by the government and turned into a public park.

Shang-kuan Wan-erh was happy to throw her hand in with anyone who seemed to be winning the struggle for power. According to the *Comprehensive Mirror*, Shang-kuan Wan-erh, candle in hand, led a procession of her handmaidens to welcome the victors. She protested that she was not an ally of the Empress Wei and Princess An Lo and presented to one of the conspirators, Liu Yu-chiu, her draft of a decree proclaiming Li Chung-mao Emperor, showing that she backed the legitimate succession. Deftly it also proclaimed Li Lung-chi's father Jui-tsung regent. Liu

Yu-chiu was swayed, but Li Lung-chi was unimpressed. He lopped off her head under the rebel standard.

The Wei and Wu clans were rounded up. Li Ch'ung-mao remained on the throne two more days. During that time, he proclaimed a general amnesty for all those except the Wei and Wu. Then Princess Tai-ping entered the Hall of Audience and pulled Li Ch'ung-mao off the throne, saying, 'This is not the seat for a child. The Empire must now be returned to the Prince of Hsiang [Jui-tsung].' The boy was stripped of the imperial robes and ornaments, which were sent to her brother.

It was not without a certain reluctance that Jui-tsung returned to the throne. After all, his previous occupancy of it had cost him his wife and his favourite concubine. And, as before, his title would only be nominal. For the first thirty-six of his forty-eight years he had been a prisoner of his mother. More recently he had been permitted a residence of his own, but he had played no part in the affairs of state and under Chung-tsung he had been ignored. He had had no part in the plot that led to his restoration. Once again he was merely the pawn of a powerful woman. The last time he had occupied the throne his mother ruled in his name. This time it would be his sister Princess Tai-ping who would be in control. After all, he had no experience of power politics himself, except as its victim. However, as Emperor, there was one thing he could do. He conferred the title of Empress consort on Lady Liu and Lady Tou, his murdered wife and concubine, and, as their bodies had never been discovered, held a ritual called the 'Calling Back of the Spirits for Burial' in Luoyang.

Although Jui-tsung occupied the throne, Princess Tai-ping made all the decisions, hired and fired officials and handled the administration. All key posts were occupied by her followers and the female rule established by Wu Chao under Kai-tsung was re-imposed. As one source puts it, 'Whatever she wished, the Emperor granted. From the Chief Ministers down, appointment and dismissal hung on one word from her ... The most powerful people in the land flooded to her doorway as if it were a marketplace.'

The only problem remaining was that of the succession. Li Lung-chi was not the oldest son of Jui-tsung. Nor was he the son of the late Empress Liu, whom Wu Chao had had killed seventeen years earlier. Jui-tsung's eldest son Li Ch'eng-chi was the son of Empress Liu and was, thus, eligible to become Crown Prince. Jui-tsung had four other sons by senior concubines, one of whom, Li Hui, was older that Li Lung-chi. Previously, under the T'ang, this matter would have been resolved by bloodshed. However, Li Ch'eng-chi stepped aside on the grounds that his brother Li Lung-chi had saved the T'ang dynasty. Li Hui took a similar view and Li Lung-chi became Crown Prince, later succeeding as Emperor Hsüan Tsung. With no rivalry for the throne the three brothers remained lifelong friends.

This line of succession did not suit Princess Tai-ping at all. According to one source, 'She considered the Crown Prince too young and envied his courage and military capacity. She wished to remove him and pick a Crown Prince who was a weakling, so that she could perpetuate her own authority.'

Like her mother before her, Princess Tai-ping had spies throughout the palace and, in year one Ching Yun – 711 – she began a slander campaign against Li Lung-chi. Fearing the outcome, Li Lung-chi offered to stand down as Crown Prince but Jui-tsung would not allow this. He told his son that he must 'take the throne before my coffin', otherwise tragedy was sure to ensue for the family. Li Lung-chi then sought political means to defend himself and secured two important commands for his brothers. This infuriated Princess Tai-ping, who summoned the First Ministers and demanded the Li Lung-chi be deposed. However, among them were Yao Yüan-chih and Sung Ching, who had had the courage to oppose Wu Chao's favourites, the Chang brothers. They refused to countenance this and urged the Emperor to get rid of Princess Tai-ping. She was stripped of her staff and sent to P'u Chou, in southern Shansi – a not too distant place of exile.

Although a hothead in his youth, Li Lung-chi soon developed the craft of statesmanship. He realized that the last thing he needed was the resentful Princess Tai-ping as an enemy and sought to pacify her by having Yao Yüan-chih and Sung Ching sent away. Now short of experienced advisors, Jui-tsung sought to abdicate, but was dissuaded from doing so by the court. After just four months of banishment, Li Lung-chi asked for the Princess Tai-ping to be recalled to help his father. It was, perhaps, also easier to keep an eye on her intrigues if she was in the capital. Nevertheless, soon after, Jui-tsung insisted on abdicating in favour of his son. Taking the title of Supreme Emperor, Jui-tsung remained nom-inally in charge, while Li Lung-chi handled the day-to-day administra-tion as Emperor Hsüan-tsung. He was of noble lineage. His mother, the murdered Lady Tou, was a descendent of the cousin of the Empress Tou, wife of the first T'ang Emperor, Kao-tsu. Again the elevation of Hsüan-tsung did nothing to dampen Princess Tai-ping's ambition for the throne. Indeed, he seemed to encourage it when he formally received Wu Chao's official records, along with those of Chung-tsung and Jiu-tsung, to be used as the basis for the *Kuo-shih* – or 'National History'. Doing this, he implic-itly recognized Wu Chao as Emperor, even though she had renounced the title on her deathbed. If she had been Emperor, why not Tai-ping?

But deposing a sitting Emperor was much harder than pushing aside a Crown Prince and, with the young and decisive Hsüan-tsung on the throne, Princess Tai-ping's influence was considerably diminished. So she made one last bid for power. She still had a considerable following in the palace, including two senior generals of the bodyguard and five of the seven First Ministers. With their patron now sidelined, their own posi-tion was precarious. They could hardly expect to survive long if they were known to oppose Hsüan-tsung. Princess Tai-ping urged them to poison Hsüan-tsung. But he was too well guarded and the opportunity did not present itself.

Time was running out for Princess Tai-ping. Her own plot to rid her-self of the Empress Wei and Princess An Lo had given Hsüan-tsung the authority to rule. With the succession decided and a young Emperor on the throne, people looked forward to a period of stability and the politi-cal forces began to realign themselves. Even Hsüeh Tsung-chien, Princess Tai-ping's own son, who could expect to benefit if she toppled Hsüan-tsung, begged her to stop her machinations. She would not listen and had him flogged.

Princess Tai-ping's last bid for power was to follow the now well-established template. Her commanders were to take the palace body-guard, storm the Hsüan Wu Gate, seize the palace and kill Hsüan-tsung. However, it was clear that the Princess Tai-ping was going to try some-thing along those lines and Hsüan-tsung was ready. A popular and palpa-bly able Emperor, he found out when the coup attempt was to be. Without telling Jui-tsung, who might have counselled against such precipitous action, he rode to the bodyguard's barracks the day before the supposed coup and beheaded Princess Tai-ping's two generals. Their heads were displayed on the north gate of the palace while the rest of the conspirators were rounded up. They were beheaded in front of the Hall of Audience.

Hearing the commotion, Jui-tsung took refuge in the tower of one of the palace gates. Hsüan-tsung sought him out and told him what had happened. Then the Supreme Emperor declared a general amnesty for all those except for Princess Tai-ping's followers and their families. Princess Tai-ping herself fled and sought asylum in a Buddhist temple on nearby Tsung-nan mountain outside Ch'ang-an. But there was no hope of escape. After three days she returned to her own mansion, where she was allowed to take her own life. Of her family, her son Hsüeh Tsung-chien alone escaped death, since he had tried to dissuade his mother from her plotting. He took the imperial surname Li, which he was entitled to as a grandson of Kao-tsung. Her property was forfeit to the state and when the bailiffs arrived at her palace they were astonished at the great number of sex toys they found.

Jui-tsung soon gave up all exercise of power and died in 716. Hsüan-tsung went on to serve as Emperor for forty-four years, during which the T'ang dynasty reached the height of its prosperity and power. This earned Hsüan-tsung the posthumous name Ming Huang – which means 'Brilliant Emperor'. His reign has been immortalized by poets and painters.

His reign began with a wholesale reform of the civil service. He fired thousands of civil servants of ministerial rank who had achieved their posts by patronage or bribery – though many of the ministers who had served under Wu Chao were kept on – and he reduced by eighty per cent those passing the civil service entrance exam. Thirty thousand spurious monks were defrocked and thereby returned to the lay life and the tax rolls. He moved the capital back to Ch'ang-an and restored the canal system which Wu Chao had allowed to fall into disrepair while she lived in Luoyang. He improved the food transport system, whose limitations had previously forced the court to commute between Luoyang and Ch'ang-an to avoid famine, and introduced a series of sweeping economic reforms. Coinage was improved and the population was re-registered.

Households that had fled the Turkish and Khitan invasions of Wu Chao's reign, famine, military service, and other hardships had occupied unregistered lands and were not being taxed, families were offered six years' exemption from taxation and compulsory labour in return for fifteen hundred coppers, if they registered voluntarily. More than eight hundred thousand families signed up this way, producing more than a billion cash by 724. This gave Hsüan-tsung the revenue to abandon conscription and build a professional army of more than six hundred thousand men by the end of his reign. He launched successful campaigns against the Turks, Khitan and Tibetans, and set up as series of permanent garrisons to guard China's northern boarder.

On the home front, he abolished the death penalty and throughout the Empire made the poorest ten — later thirty — families in every village exempt from tax. He raised the age when men became eligible for compulsory labour and taxation from nineteen to twenty-two, ordered that the undergrowth ten paces either side of the roads be cut down to prevent people being bitten by snakes and banned the Maitreya sect, which had ushered in Wu Chao's reign. Hsüan-tsung was also an accomplished musician, poet, calligrapher, and even a dancer. In 690, at the age of five, he had performed the dance 'The Long-Lived Lady' in front of Wu Chao. This was unusual as most dances performed by the princes of the blood were more martial. At the same banquet, another young prince danced 'The Prince of Lanling Breaks through the Battle Formation', celebrating the victory of a northern general in the sixth century, and a perennial favourite was 'The Prince of Qin Smashes Battle Formations', commemorating T'ai-tsung's defeat of a rebel army in 622, when he was still the Prince of Qin. His men had composed the air, but T'ai-tsung also committed the choreography to paper in a diagram.

Hsüan-tsung and his brothers patronized the arts and Hsüan-tsung himself composed the poem for his *feng-shan* sacrifices. This is now known as the 'Stele Engraved on Rock', since it can still be seen carved into the face of T'ai-shan mountain where the *feng-shan* sacrifices were performed. He also rehabilitated the memory of Shang-kuan Wan-erh. He commissioned the publication of her poems and other writings and asked his minister Chang Yeuh to write an introduction to them. As a result Shang-kuan Wan-erh was remembered as one of the most talented people of the dynasty and her work was celebrated by later T'ang poets. One even wrote a poem about discovering a book that had once been in her collection in a market in Ch'ang-an. On the domestic front, Hsüan-tsung increased his imperial harem to forty thousand women, who tossed gold coins to see which of them would favour the Emperor that night. Traditionally, there was one eunuch for every ten concubines, so he had to commandeer all eunuchs from private households to guard his harem. And Hsüan-tsung's most trusted eunuch slept in a curtained area at the side of his bedchamber.

But Wu Chao was not forgotten. Years after she was dead, Li Shou-li, the son of former Crown Prince Li Hsien, was living in the court of his cousin the Emperor Hsüan-tsung. Li Shou-li was known as a *bon viveur* and an amusing dinner guest. One day during a drought, Li Shou-li told the young princes that it would rain the following day. The princes told Hsüan-tsung this, claiming Li Shou-li had magical powers. The next day it did rain and Li Shou-li was called upon to explain himself. He told the Emperor, 'Back in the time of Empress Wu, after my father had been judged guilty of some crime, I was imprisoned in the palace for years and often beaten severely. Now, when it is going to rain, the old weals begin to ache.' Hsüen-tsung, who had shared his imprisonment, must have sympathized.

Only one branch of the Wu clan survived the overthrow of the Empress Wei and Princess An Lo. The nephew of Wu Chao, Wu Yu-chih, a man of great literary tastes who studiously avoided politics, was spared, owing to the esteem in which he was held. His daughter Wu Hui-fei, whose mother was of the Yang clan, became the favoured concubine of Hsüan-tsung and bore him three daughters and four sons.

In 722, relations between the Emperor and his wife, Empress Wang, became strained. Hsüan-tsung discussed removing her because she was childless. A favourite at court named Chiang Chiao leaked details of the conservation. He was flogged and banished, dying on the road into exile. Realizing the precariousness of her position, Empress Wang obtained an amulet to ensure that she had a child, and her brother Wang Shou-i arranged for a monk to perform magic ceremonies. When this was discovered in the seventh month of 724, Wang Shou-i was forcibly divorced from his royal wife, exiled and ordered to commit suicide. The

Empress Wang was demoted to the rank of commoner, but not punished otherwise. She was allowed to live in separate quarters in the palace, where she died three months later. She was well liked and Hsüan-tsung later repented of degrading her and regretted the punishment of Chiang Chiao.

The Lady Wu was promoted to *hui-fei* – 'Favoured Consort of the First Rank'. This position was all the more important because, in his restructuring of the imperial harem, Hsüan-tsung slimmed the Four Ladies of the First Grade down to three and, as Favoured Consort, she was second in rank only to Empress. Then in 726 Hsüan-tsung made Lady Wu his third Empress. This drew protests because the Wu were, by now, the traditional enemy of the T'ang and people remembered what had happened last time a Wu became Empress.

Another difficulty with making Lady Wu Empress was the problems it would cause for the succession. Lady Wu had three daughters and four sons, though only those raised outside the palace survived infancy. Among them was her only son Li Mao, the Prince of Shou. The heir apparent at that time was Li Ying, whose mother was not Li Lung-chi's wife the Empress Wang but his concubine Lady Chao. She was a provincial courtesan and when Li Lung-chi came to the throne he had made her First Lady of the First Grade with the title *li-fei*, or 'Beautiful Consort'. But, as she and others lost the royal favour to Lady Wu, Li Ying's position as the Crown Prince became precarious because Lady Wu planned to supplant him with her own son Li Mao. Via her two daughters Princesses Hsien-i and Tai-hua and their husbands, and the First Minister Li Lin-pu, she began a slander campaign against Li Ying and his half-brothers who supported him. One day in 737 the three princes were told that some rebels had got into the palace and their father was in danger. Without realizing that this was a trap set up by Lady Wu, they rushed to his defence. When they appeared armed in the Emperor's presence, Lady Wu immediately accused them of treason. The three princes were summarily condemned and perished in prison. Although she successfully removed the obstacles to her son's advancement, Lady Wu died of some mysterious disease later that year before she could make him Crown Prince. Palace rumour-mongers said that she had died because she was haunted by the ghosts of the three princes. Hsüan-tsung gave Lady Wu the posthumous title of Empress but then fell into a long period of melancholy. For years Lady Wu had been almost a wife to him and he found it difficult to find someone else to take her place. Without his mother, Li Mao lost support in court. When it came to making a decision about the succession Hsüan-tsung took the advice of his chief eunuch Kao Li-shih, who had been made a general for his part in overthrowing Empress Wei and controlled the Imperial Guard. Kao Li-shih told Hsüan-tsung that nobody would dare criticize him if he made his oldest surviving son Li Heng heir and Li Mao was pushed out of the running.

But there was no shortage of powerful women waiting to bring the T'ang down. One of them was the white-skinned beauty Yang Yu-huan – *yu-huan* means 'jade ring'. The daughter of a high official named Yang Hsüan-yan, she was one of the few fat women in Chinese history to be considered beautiful, but that was the fashion then. She may have been overweight because of her love of the lychee that she had shipped hundreds of miles from her home in Szechwan. To compensate, she took an inordinate amount of effort over her appearance, calling out the names of six gods of female fashion as she went about her toilette. They were the god of ointments and pomades, the god of eyebrow tinctures, the god of face powders, the god of lip glosses, the god of jewellery and the god of gowns. She was also well known for her wigs.

She was originally the concubine of Hsüan-tsung's son Li Mao, but the Emperor, who was thirty-four years her senior, fell for her when the imperial family was wintering in Hot Spring Palace on Li mountain in Shensi province. He forced his son to give her up – though Li Mao may have relinquished her voluntarily in the hope that it might improve his chances of becoming Crown Prince. However, some tricks needed to be played to make their incestuous relationship lawful. A decree was issued announcing that Lady Yang had volunteered to become a Taoist priestess to pray for the afterlife of the Emperor's mother Lady Tou, who had been murdered by Wu Chao in 693. This finesse aped Wu Chao's brief sojourn in the convent when she was incestuously conveyed from T'ai-tsung to his son Kao-tsung. The plan seems to have been facilitated by Kao Li-shih's sister Princess Yu Chen, who was a Taoist priestess. Lady Yang moved into a Taoist temple inside the palace, taking the religious name *Tai-chen* – or 'Utmost Truth' – effectively divorcing her husband. Hsüan-tsung then took her and her two sisters into the imperial harem.

Lady Yang became the Empress in all but name and soon all the servants called her 'my lady'. This suited Lady Yang who was given a budget of one million cash for cosmetics alone. She wore silkworms and cicadas moulded from camphor woven into her robes, and the great poet Li Po, who was then in court, wrote poems in praise of her beauty. However, it was not until 745 that Li Lung-chi officially made her his concubine, giving her the long abolished title *kui-fei*, or 'Noble Consort', with a status high above all the women in the royal household. Hsüan-tsung loved admiring her naked body as she bathed so he rebuilt the Hot Spring Palace, renaming it the *Hua-ch'ing* – or 'Glorious Purity Palace' – which they visited every year. There in the Lotus Blossom Spa he built a bathhouse that was so big that he and Lady Yang could sail in a lacquered boat across the pool, which was surrounded by sixteen smaller baths for the imperial concubines.

According to her biography, Lady Yang committed some minor offences in 746 and 750 and was banished from court, though on both occasions the Emperor soon asked her to return. She was not a political person although many of her relatives were gradually brought into the court and government. Her cousin Yang Kuo-chung, whose mother was Chang I-chih's sister, was a gambler and an opportunist. He became First Minister Li Lin-pu's protégé and eventually took Li's place after his death. Lady Yang's other male cousins married into the imperial family and three female cousins were made the Duchesses of Han, Kuo and Chin. The most beautiful was the Duchess of Kuo. A T'ang poem describes how she rode into the palace gate to greet the Emperor without any make-up on – which was unusual for the time – because she feared the cosmetics would diminish her natural beauty. A painting titled *The Spring Outing of the Duchess of Kuo* still survives depicting her riding in the middle of her female retinue in a man's attire. A wealthy widow, she was also said to have an incestuous liaison with her own cousin, First Minister Yang Kuo-chung.

Another story was told of the high-handed attitude of the Duchess of Kuo. Supposedly she turned up at the house of a former high-ranking minister named Wei, who had just died, in a palaquin. Dressed in a tunic and skirt of yellow gauze, she entered the house with twenty of her maid-servants. When she found Wei's sons, she said, 'I've heard your mansion is up for sale. How much do you want for it?

They replied, 'This was the home of our ancestor, so we cannot bear to part with it.'

But before they had finished speaking, several hundred workmen arrived and began dismantling the house. The Wei brothers and their servants only had time to rescue their books and zithers, and were compensated for the seizure of their hall with just two acres of wasteland. The Duchess was much more generous with the workmen. When they finished building the main hall of her new mansion, which had been fashioned from the material of the Wei house, she paid them two million coppers.

The golden era of Hsüan-tsung's reign then came to a abrupt end with the An Lu-shan rebellion of 755, caused largely by the manoeuvrings of Lady Yang. A young general of Sogdian-Turkish origin, An Rokan, or An Lu-shan as he is known in Chinese, rose to prominence thanks to Lady Yang, who adopted him as her son in Sogdiana, Central Asia, as a diplomatic gesture to the non-Chinese military governor. It is said they became lovers. They were certainly dance partners, learning the Western Spinning Dance together. With the help of Lady Yang, An Lu-shan came to command an army of two hundred thousand. This threw him into a power struggle with Yang Kuo-chung, whom Lady Yang had also helped to power. The rivalry between her lover and her cousin eventually forced An Lu-shan to rebel against Hsüan-tsung. Capturing Luoyang in 755, An Lu-shan proclaimed himself Emperor of the Great Yen dynasty. Then, when Ch'ang-an fell the following year, the Emperor and his court had to flee to Szechwan, home of the Yang clan. When they reached the relay station at Ma-wei, First Minister Yang Kuo-chung was seen tending to the Tibetan ambassadors who were travelling with them, and the soldiers shouted that he was a traitor. Urged on by Crown Prince Li Heng, the soldiers killed Yang Kuo-chung, together with his son and the Duchesses of Han and Chin.

When Hsüan-tsung heard of this he sent Kao Li-shih to talk to the soldiers, saying that now the 'traitors' were dead the journey should continue. But the soldiers refused to obey, saying that the root of the treason was still in the ground – meaning Lady Yang. They feared that if she were allowed to live she would take her revenge once they reached her home province of Szechwan. At first Li Lung-chi refused to accede to their demands. But Kao Li-shih and other courtiers pointed out that he was powerless in the face of the Imperial Guard, and he bid farewell to his beloved Lady Yang. Kao Li-shih led her into a Buddhist chapel in the back of the relay station and strangled her. She was thirty-eight. The imperial party then moved on, leaving a small group of attendants to take care of the Lady Yang's body.

During the insurrection at Ma-wei relay station, Yang Kuo-chung's mistress, the Duchess of Kuo, escaped on horseback along with his wife and children. But they were soon pursued by the local governor, probably a supporter of the Crown Prince, into a bamboo grove. There, at the request of Yang Kuo-chung's wife, the Duchess of Kuo killed the wife and the children, before trying to slit her own throat. However, she was still breathing when the pursuers caught up with her and she was thrown into prison.

'Are you loyalists or rebels?' she asked her gaoler.

'A bit of both,' he replied. Then she died.

Soon afterwards Crown Prince Li Heng decided to split from his father to remain in the north at Ling-wu to organize resistance. On the ninth day of the seventh month of Tian Bao, 756, he announced that his father had retired and he usurped the throne, becoming Emperor Su-tsung. His mother, another Lady Yang, was the great-granddaughter of Yang Shih-ta, a minister under the Sui, who was also the father of Wu Chao's mother. So the Emperor Su-tsung inherited his usurping Wu genes from both sides of the family.

It was over a month later that Hsüan-tsung learnt that his son had deposed him. The Emperor's retinue was down to just thirteen hundred. He was old, ill and racked with remorse over the death of Lady Yang. He acquiesced in his abdication without demur and sent his imperial regalia and Chief Ministers to Su-tsung's headquarters. The longest and most brilliant reign of the T'ang dynasty was over.

The following year, An Lu-shan was murdered by a eunuch slave with the connivance of his eldest son, though rebellion rumbled on until 763 when it was put down by General Guo Ziyi. After the two capitals had been recaptured from the rebels, Su-tsung summoned Hsüen-tsung back to Ch'ang-an, where he was received with great honours, though their relationship was, of course, damaged.

On his way to Ch'ang-an, Hsüan-tsung sent servants to Ma-wei to exhume the body of Lady Yang for a proper burial, but they found nothing in her supposed grave. This led to the legend had Lady Yang had escaped death at Ma-wei and had fled to Japan with her attendants. There are a number of places in Japan that are said to be Lady Yang's final resting place, though none has strong evidence to back its claim. However, in the 1960s a girl appeared on Japanese TV claiming to be a descendant of Lady Yang and presented some family heirlooms in an attempt to substantiate her claim.

Hsüan-tsung intended to live out his retirement in Xingqing Palace, which was situated at the city centre and was built out of his former residence when he was a prince. By that time only his sister Princess Yu Chen, Kao Li-shih and an old concubine remained in his household. From time to time he appeared at his balcony to greet the people and give out wine to the aged. But Su-tsung's wife Empress Chang and his trusted eunuch Li Fu-kuo thought that even these rare appearances by the former Emperor posed a potential political threat. So Kao Li-shih was banished. The three hundred procession horses belonging to Hsüan-tsung were confiscated and the old man was moved into the inner palace where he could be kept out of the public eye.

One day when Su-tsung was supposed to have a private meeting with a Taoist high priest, he turned up with his baby daughter in his arms.

'Please don't be offended by this,' he said as he asked for the priest's pardon. 'I would miss her so much that I cannot be parted with her for a moment.'

'I guessed the retired Emperor is probably feeling the same,' the priest replied. These words brought tears to Su-tsung's eyes.

Hsüan-tsung died at the age of seventy-seven in 762. Kao Li-shih had already been pardoned and was on his way back to Ch'ang-an when he heard of Hsüan-tsung's death. On hearing the news, it is said that he spurted blood and died. After hearing of his father's death, Su-tsung, who was already seriously ill, also passed away a few days later.

His body had barely turned cold, when a palace coup was staged once more by a strong woman in the mould of Wu Chao. Empress Chang was planning to depose the Crown Prince and seize power. Learning this, Crown Prince Li Yu joined forces with the eunuch Li Fu-kuo and murdered his stepmother. A few months later, Li Fu-kuo was assassinated on Li Yu's orders. Wu Chao would have been proud and the T'ang dynasty, who were now her descendants, stayed in power until 907.

Wu Chao was buried in a massive domed mausoleum with her husband Kao-tsung outside Xian in Shensi, one hundred and eighty li, sixty miles, from the pits housing the famous terracotta army. It is as yet undisturbed, but can be visited to this day at the end of an avenue lined with huge stone guards. She was given the posthumous name Wu Hou, which means simply 'Empress Wu'. However, she is usually known to posterity as Wu Tse-tien. This comes from the title given to her after she was deposed, *Tse-tien ta-sheng huang-ti*, and means 'Wu, Emulator of Heaven'. However, the name might also have come from the Tse-tsien Gate where Wu Chao proclaimed herself Emperor in 690. The mausoleum was completed in the eighth century and Kao-tsung has a stone tablet with an inscription written by Wu Chao herself extolling his virtues and accomplishments. But Wu Chao's own tablet is blank. It was said that, in her will, Wu Chao asked for it to be left bare so that the world could assess her some time in the future. Perhaps that time is now.

DRAMATIS PERSONAE

An Lo, Princess – Daughter of Emperor Chung-tsung and Empress Wei.

An Lu-shan – Chinese general who led a rebellion against Hsüan-tsung and proclaimed himself Emperor in 755.

Chang Ch'ang-tsung – One of the notorious Chang brothers and favourite of Wu Chao.

Chang Chien-chih – Popular official who rose to be First Minister and one of the five ministers who deposed Wu Chao.

Chang I-chih – One of the notorious Chang brothers and favourite of Wu Chao.

Chang-sun Wu-chi – Elder statesman and uncle of the Emperor Kao-tsung who opposed the elevation of Wu Chao.

Chang Yüeh – Grand secretary who refused to testify against Wei Yüan-chung.

Chi Hsiu – Influential courtier.

Ching Hui – One of the five ministers who deposed Wu Chao.

Chou Hsing – Police chief and torturer.

Ch'ü Sui-liang – Elder statesman and famous calligrapher.

Chung-tsung – Emperor, son of Wu Chao and Kao-tsung, posthumous name of Li Che.

Han Yüan – President of the Chancellery and opponent of Wu Chao.

Hei-Ch'ih Ch'ang-chih – Korean general and T'ang loyalist.

Ho-Lan, Lady – Wu Chao's older sister.

Ho-Lan Kuo-ch'u – Daughter of Lady Ho-Lan, Wu Chao's niece and rival for the affections of Emperor Kao-tsung.

Ho-Lan Min-chih – Son of Lady Ho-Lan and Wu Chao's nephew.

Hsiao, Lady – Pure Consort, favourite concubine of Emperor Kao-tsung.

Hsü Ching-tsung – Supporter of Wu Chao who rose to become First Minister.

Hsü Yu-kung – Respected advocate, assistant to the Supreme Court of Justice and later censor.

Hsüeh Huai-i – Lover of Wu Chao and Buddhist monk.

Hsëuh Shao – Wu Chao's son-in-law, first husband of Princess Tai-ping.

Huan Yen-fan – One of the five ministers who deposed Wu Chao.

Jui-tsung – Emperor, son of Wu Chao and Kao-tsung, posthumous name of Li Tan.

Kao-tsung – Emperor, husband of Wu Chao, posthumous name of Li Chih.

Lai Chih – President of the Secretariat and opponent of Wu Chao.

Lai Chün-ch'en – Wu Chao's chief torturer and persecutor of the T'ang loyalists.

Li Chao-te – Trusted minister and T'ang loyalist.

Li Chan – Son of Li I-fu and conspirator against Wu Chao.

Li Chen – Prince Yüeh and leader of the princes' revolt.

Li Chi – Statesman and conqueror of Korea.

Li Ching-yeh – Grandson of Li Chi, leader of rebellion against Wu Chao.

Li Ch'ung – Son of Li Chen, rebel.

Li Ch'ung-jun – Son of Chung-tsung and the Empress Wei, one-time heir apparent.

Li Hsiao-i – Duke of Liang, general and Wu loyalist.

Li Hsien – Prince of Yung, probably son of Emperor Kao-tsung and Lady Ho-Lan passed off as Wu Chao's, one-time Crown Prince.

Li Hung – Son of Emperor Kao-tsung and Wu Chao, Crown Prince who died in mysterious circumstances.

Li I-fu – Corrupt minister key to the advancement of Wu Chao.

Li Lung-chi – Wu Chao's grandson, son of Emperor Jui-tsung, and future Emperor Hsüan-tsung.

Li Shang-chin – Son of Emperor Kao-tsung by a low-ranking concubine.

Li Su-chieh – Son of Emperor Kao-tsung by the Pure Concubine Hsiao Liang-ti.

Li To-tso – General and commander of the palace guard.

Liu Jen-kuei – Trusted general and Wu Chao's viceroy in Ch'ang-an.

Liu Wei-chih – Scholar of the Northern Gate and Vice President of the Secretatiat.

Lo Pin-wang – Rebel and leading anti-Wu Chao polemicist.

Mo-Ch'o – Khan of the Turks who fought against Wu Chao.

P'ei Yen – Minister who conspired against Wu Chao.

Shang-Kuan I – Poet and elder statesman who opposed Wu Chao.

Shang-Kuan Wan-erh – Granddaughter of Shang-Kuan I who became favourite of Wu Chao, concubine of Emperor Chung-tsung.

Sung Ching – Grand secretary and later censor who opposed the Chang brothers.

Tai-ping, Princess – Daughter of Kao-tsung and Wu Chao.

T'ai-tsung – Emperor, father of Kao-tsung and early consort of Wu Chao.

Ti Jen-chieh – Trusted minister.

Ts'ui Yüan-wei – One of the five ministers who deposed Wu Chao.

Wang, Empress – First wife of Emperor Kao-tsung.

Wei, Empress – Wife of Emperor Chung-tsung.

Wu Chao – Empress, Dowager Empress and then Emperor of China; posthumous name Wu Hou, aka Wu Tse-tien.

Wu Ch'eng-ssu – Wu Chao's nephew who aspired to succeed her.

Wu San-ssu – Wu Chao's nephew who also aspired to the throne.

Wu Shih-huo – Wu Chao's father.

Wu I-tsung – Wu Chao's cousin, Prince of Ho Nei.

Wu Yu-chi – Wu Chao's cousin, second husband of Princess Tai-ping.

Yang, Lady – Wu Chao's mother.

Yao Yüan-ch'ung – Minister.

Yüan Shu-chi – One of the five ministers who deposed Wu Chao.

SELECTED
BIBLIOGRAPHY

Adshead, S. A. M., *T'ang China – The Rise of the East in World History*, Palgrave Macmillan, New York, 2004

Barrett, T. H., *Taoism under the T'ang*, Wellsweep, London, 1996

Benn, Charles, *China's Golden Age – Everyday Life in the Tang Dynasty*, Oxford University Press, Oxford, 2002

Byron, John, *Portrait of a Chinese Paradise: Erotica and Sexual Customs of the Late Qing Period*, Quartet, London, 1987

Capon, Edmund, and Werner Forman, *Tang China – Vision and Splendour of a Golden Age*, Macdonald Orbis, London, 1989

Chu, Valentin, *The Yin-Yang Butterfly*, Simon & Schuster, London, 1994

Couling, Samuel, *The Encyclopedia Sinica*, Oxford University Press, Oxford, 1983

Der Ling, Princess, *Son of Heaven: A Life of the Emperor Kuang Hsü*, Appleton-Century, New York, 1935

Dora Shu-fang Dien, *Empress Wu Zetian in Fiction and in History – Female Defiance in Confucian China*, Nova Science Publishers, New York, 2003

Edwards, E. D., *Chinese Prose Literature of the T'ang Period,* AD 618–906, Arthur Probsthain, London, 1937

Fang Fu Ruan, *Sex in China – Studies in Sexology in Chinese Culture*, Plenum Press, New York, 1991

Fitzgerald, C. P., *Son of Heaven – A Biography of Li Shih-Min, Founder of the T'ang Dynasty*, Cambridge University Press, Cambridge, England, 1933

Fitzgerald, C. P., *The Empress Wu*, Cresset Press, London, 1968

Goldin, Paul Rakita, *The Culture of Sex in Ancient China*, University of Hawai'i Press, Honolulu, 2002

Guisso, R. W. L., *Wu Tse-T'ien and the Politics of Legitimation in T'ang China*, Western Washington University Press, Bellingham, WA, 1978

Guisso, R. W. L., and Stanley Johannesen (eds), *Women in China*, Philo Press, Amsterdam, 1981

Heng Chye Kiang, *Cities of Aristocrats and Bureaucrats – The Development of Medieval Chinese Cityscapes*, University of Hawai'i Press, Honolulu, 1999

Hinsch, Bret, *Women in Early Imperial China*, Rowman & Littlefield, Oxford, 2002

Jolan Chang, *The Tao of Love and Sex*, Wildwood House, London, 1977

Kang-I Sun Chang and Haun Saussy, *Women Writers of Traditional China: An Anthology of Poetry and Criticism*, Stanford University Press, Stanford, CA, 1999

Lin Yü-t'ang, *Lady Wu – A True Story*, William Heinemann, London, 1957

Millan, Betty, *Monstrous Regiment: Women Rulers in Men's Worlds*, Windsor, England, Kensal Press, 1982

O'Hara, Albert R., *The Position of Women in Early China*, Orient, Hong Kong, 1956

Schafer, Edward H., *The Divine Woman: Dragon Ladies and Rain Maidens in T'ang Literature*, University of California, Berkeley, 1973

Twitchett, Denis, *The Writing of Official History under the T'ang*, Cambridge University Press, Cambridge, England, 1992

Twitchett, Denis, and John K. Fairbank (eds), *The Cambridge History of China*, Cambridge University Press, Cambridge, England, 1979

Van Gulik, R. H., *Sexual Life in Ancient China – A Preliminary Survey of Chinese Sex and Society from ca. 1500 BC till 1644 AD*, E. J. Brill, Leiden, The Netherlands, 1974

Wechsler, Howard J., *Mirror to the Son of Heaven – Wei Cheng at the Court of T'ang T'ai-tsung*, Yale University Press, New Haven, 1974

Wright, Arthur F., and Denis Twitchett (eds), *Perspectives on the T'ang*, Yale University Press, New Haven, 1973

Xiong, Victor Cunrui, *Sui-Tang Chang'an – A Study in the Urban History of Medieval China*, Centre for Chinese Studies, University of Michigan, Ann Arbor, 2000

INDEX